GRANDAD, THERE'S A HEAD ON THE BEACH

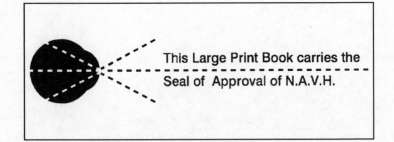

This Large Print Book carries the
Seal of Approval of N.A.V.H.

GRANDAD, THERE'S A HEAD ON THE BEACH

COLIN COTTERILL

THORNDIKE PRESS

A part of Gale, Cengage Learning

Detroit • New York • San Francisco • New Haven, Conn • Waterville, Maine • London

GALE
CENGAGE Learning®

LIBRARY OF CONGRESS CATALOGING-IN-PUBLICATION DATA

Cotterill, Colin.
    Grandad, there's a head on the beach / by Colin Cotterill.
        pages ; cm. — (Thorndike Press large print reviewers'
    choice) (A Jimm Juree mystery)
    ISBN 978-1-4104-5184-2 (hardcover) — ISBN 1-4104-5184-4 (hardcover)
    1. Women journalists—Thailand—Fiction. 2.
    Murder—Investigation—Fiction. 3. Large type books. I. Title.
    PR6053.O778G73 2012b
    823'.914—dc23   2012023544

Published in 2012 by arrangement with St. Martin's Press, LLC.

Printed in the United States of America
1 2 3 4 5 6 7 16 15 14 13 12

ACKNOWLEDGMENTS

With thanks to Tony, Quentin, Hans, Apple, Nok, Lizzie, Kay, Kye, Janet, David, Shona, C.G. Moore, Dad, Andrew, Rachel, Hannusia (and the faculty of Georgetown), and Bouy.

But this book is dedicated to the lounge singers, cover bands, and karaoke exponents of Thailand who bravely attack English songs phonetically without suffering the inconvenience of meaning. It is from them that over the past twenty years I have assembled my catalog of mangled English lyrics, some of which I use in this tome with gratitude. If, like me, you are of a certain age and like to keep a check on the speedy advance of your dementia, I've put the correct lyrics for the chapter headings at the end of the book so you can test yourself.

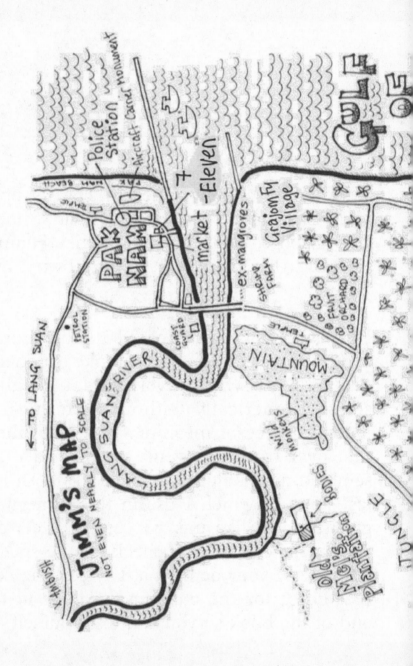

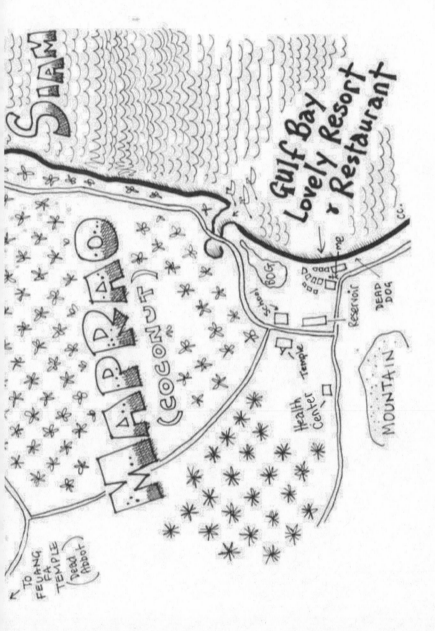

1.
SLIPPING ON THE DOG

(from "Raindrops Keep Falling on My
Head" — BURT BACHARACH)

"Grandad?"

He didn't so much as look up. He had a
lot of problems, did Grandad. Deafness
wasn't one of them. Ignorance was. He
feigned the former to achieve the latter.

"Grandad?"

He knew I was there, but I admit I'd
chosen a bad time to get through to him. It
was the morning rush hour in downtown
Maprao and he had traffic to examine. As
the fishermen traveled to or from their
boats, a lot of them stopped off at Jiep's
rice porridge stall across the street. Six
thirty was as busy as it would ever get. He
sat beside the road in his white undervest
and his Fred Flintstone shorts and he
tsssked and *tutted* at the passing vehicles.
Like an ex-matador might sit on a farm

9

fence glaring at a bull, pondering how, in his prime he would have demeaned and disfigured the beast, so Grandad gave the evil eye to every passing truck and motorcycle sidecar. There weren't that many, but every one of them flouted the highway code in one way or another. Grandad knew every regulation. He'd been a traffic policeman for forty years, and then for fourteen more years he'd subscribed to the *Royal Thai Police Force Road Users' Gazette* to keep up with amendments. He was a living compendium of petty legislation: probably the most knowledgeable man on the subject in Chumphon province, if not the whole country. We'd often urged him to send in an application to Channel Five's *Genuine Fan,* where people who'd spent their entire lives focused on something utterly useless — combative stag beetles, designer handbags, English Premiership football results and the like — had a chance to answer questions on their chosen specialty and win a refrigerator. Grandad Jah would have had a fleet of Toshiba freezers by now.

I glared at him, still hoping for a response. It was like waiting for Cro-Magnon man to evolve. I wondered what use we might have found for him if he'd invested his vast memory on nuclear physics rather than traffic regulations.

In rural Thailand it's unlikely anyone would know the first thing about the rules of the road, especially not the police. If you were too poor to front up to the Motor Car License division with a generous bottle of whiskey and a wink (in which case your license would be expedited), you'd be asked to fill out a multiple choice quiz whose correct answers were well indented on the pad from the previous twenty applicants. You'd then drive your vehicle to a tree, beneath which the examiner sat. He or she would ask you to park. If you managed to do so without knocking over the tree or hitting the examiner, you had a license. The few people who knew the rules were at a disadvantage down here. The north–south highway, Route 41, passes through Chumphon, and it's the most dangerous stretch of road in the country. All those righteous smart-alecs from Bangkok who learned when to signal politely and how to adjust their hands at the ten-to-two position on the steering wheel were invariably sideswiped by unlit coconut-carrying pickups coming at them at full speed in the wrong direction. Arrogance is punished in Chumphon.

So, anyway, there I was trying to get Grandad's attention for a matter I considered to be infinitely more urgent than traffic.

"Grandad," I called in an irritating screechy voice. "There's a head on the beach."

If that didn't grab him, nothing would. He'd been glaring at a truck with conflicting plates. The one on the back was handwritten on cardboard. The number at the front was different. It was a traffic policeman's nirvana, but I got a dab of eye contact before his attention returned to the truck.

"A head of what?" he asked quietly.

"What?"

"Head of fish?"

He always spoke slowly and enunciated like a teacher at a special school. Despite the fact that I was a moderately sane thirty-four-year-old Thai woman, he often talked to me as if I was a mentally challenged youth.

"Head of dog?" he continued. "Head of cabbage?"

"Head of man," I said, as calmly as I could under the very annoying circumstances. It's always a bother to decide who to tell when you find a head on the beach. I mean, there is no protocol. And when I say "always" here, I may be exaggerating somewhat because I can't say I've stumbled over too many heads on my morning dog walks. I'd seen body parts in morgues, of course, and accident scenes, but that Wednesday was my first detached head. It upset me that it hadn't upset me enough.

My inner alarm clock had woken me up at six, as was its habit. It doesn't have an inner snooze button, so I got up. This was not a habit born out of a desire to watch the sunrise or to frolic gaily along the sand with my doggy friends. It was a habit begat by the fact that there was absolutely nothing to do at night in the mulch pit we'd arrived in a year earlier. "Maprao" means coconut, and that pretty much sums the place up: thick skinned, dull as dirt, and containing nothing of substance. I'm spending too much time here on sidetracks and making a mess of what should be a tense and exciting opening to my story, so I'll save all the gripes and family intrigues for later.

Back to the beach. We had two dogs. Or perhaps I should say the two dogs had us because there were no walls to keep them in. They arrived at mealtimes from whatever mischief they'd embroiled themselves in, and would deign to sleep at our modest seaside resort — or not. Unfortunately, whenever I opened my cabin door of a morning, there they would be; wagging. Gogo, bitch in every sense of the word, was one of my mother's roadside rescues. No manners. No gratitude. No intestines. She ate like a horse and defecated like a cow. Our vet, Dr. Somboon, who was fortunately a livestock specialist, told us that Gogo was physically unable to digest. So we gave her a mountain of food every day in the expectation that a small hillock of it might find its way to her muscles. That had not yet happened.

Dog two: Sticky Rice, white, one enormous black eye, had been a temple pup. He was a thief. Not yet seven months of age, but no excuse. Were he a human teenager, he would be under lock and key at a juvenile correctional facility. No shoe was safe in front of the guest rooms. No bottom-shelf instant noodle pack, no drying squid, no garden vegetable. He had them all. And, cunning beast, he left no evidence because he ate everything: leaves, packets, laces. He gave a new definition to the word "consumable." If you've never seen a dog chew through a breeze block and not spit out the crumbs, you've not met Sticky.

All right. I'm lost again. So, there we were, on the beach. The wind *du jour* was just starting to roll the polystyrene blocks like

14

tumbleweeds. Plastic bags were being thrown up by the tide. There was nothing pleasurable about our amble, but my mother, Mair, insisted I walk the dogs twice a day — as if they didn't have legs and minds of their own. It was November, so you could barely make out any sand under all the garbage. Urban dwellers who have a river passing behind their houses see it as a sort of free, convenient, garbage-disposal system. Toss a plastic bag full of diapers into it and *voilà,* it's gone. Nature is truly a wonder. All that disgusting junk gets spewed out of the Lang Suan River estuary and obligingly sent to our bay via the incoming monsoon tides. The dogs love garbage days because there are obviously so many more nutrients in putrid fish and half-drunk cartons of congealed chocolate milk than there are in the extortionately expensive Pedigree Chum that Mair feeds them.

The hounds were forty meters ahead and they'd found something among the debris. They were excited. When Gogo comes across something that confuses her, she whimpers and does a sort of canine native-American war dance. When Sticky comes across the unexpected, he eats it. But it was obviously too big to eat because he was doing the forward-backward tango and bark-

15

ing the hell out of it. As I got closer, I thought a rubber mask had been washed up on the tide. A face stared at me with one of those frightening Hallowe'en expressions. I decided it would be a lot of fun to take it back to the resort and scare the daylights out of my little brother. I even got close enough to reach down to pick it up. And then I realized.

My "sister" and I have it in mind to one day become wealthy by writing screenplays for movies. A couple of months earlier I'd sent off treatments to our hero Clint Eastwood in Carmel, California. He has a movie company called Malpaso Productions. They unequivocally *do not* accept movie treatments by e-mail. This is to be expected as not only do they not have an e-mail address, they also don't even have a Web site. How much more secure does a man have to be in his own omnipotence than to spurn the Internet? How can you not love such a man? No harassment from annoying amateurs taking up his valuable time. No groupies. Clint is an unapproachable guy unless you happen to have a former brother who's an Internet criminal. Sissi handles the Web like a .44 magnum. Through some basic hacking exercises that I'm told any third-grader can do, Sissi found the top-secret e-mail address of Clint's personal assistant, Liced. I've only ever seen that written down, so I have no idea how you'd pronounce it. I'm leaning toward Liced as in "full of lice." But anyway, Sissi began a line of communication with Liced that initially entailed my sister saying how lucky Liced was to be working with Clint, and Liced telling her to get off her personal e-mail or she'd file a harassment suit. But as often happens in these stalking relationships, animosity turned to friendship. Their relationship was cemented when Sissi sent a kilogram of cat's whisker herbal capsules when she learned from the lady's private medical file that she had kidney stones. It was a birthday present. Liced was overwhelmed, and it was through this back passageway that we submitted our treatments and you're probably wondering what the hell all this has to do with a head on the beach. Right? Well, you'd be perfectly within your rights to be irritated. Here it is.

My first reaction on seeing a decapitated head on the beach should have been "Oh, my God. [Scream optional as there was nobody around to hear it.] How awful," etc. Whereas, in fact, the opening scene of a movie flashed into my mind.

EXT-COCONUT BEACH —

EARLY MORNING

A beautiful Asian girl is jogging along a pristine white sand beach with Tin Tin her golden retriever at her side. The sweat causes her flimsy T-shirt to cling to her pert breasts offering a suggestion of nipples. Not so obvious as to alienate the censor early on, but enough to pull in half a million horny teenage boys once they've seen the trailer. She stumbles over a severed head on the sand . . .

It needed work. I mean she'd have to be blind not to notice a head on a pristine beach. Perhaps I could make Tin Tin a guide dog. But the point was . . . the head had set off my imagination long before it occurred to me I should have been repulsed by it. I hoped with all my tiny little heart that this was a psychological defense mechanism. That my subconscious was blanking out the horror of my discovery and replacing it with a screenplay. All being well, I'd burst into tears and be inconsolable later.

I studied him. Head. Male. Thirties. Maybe younger without the wave-buffeting and salt water puckering. Two earrings on his left ear. Long hair wrapped around him like seaweed. A "No! For God's sake, don't do it" expression on his waxy face. Propped against a shoe. It's astounding, but our beach is a single-shoe repository. A lot of one-legged people come to Maprao to supplement their shoe supplies. Our head leaned against a pale green platform clog at such an angle as to suggest a possibility — a vague and distant possibility — that the rest of the body was buried at attention beneath it like a Chinese terracotta warrior. Given the number of years it had taken to inter a terracotta warrior, I rather doubted it, but a good investigative journalist didn't leave anything to chance. I poked it with a stick.

It was a mistake on a number of levels because the head spun around to stare glassily straight into my face. The mouth dropped a fraction, as if to begin a speech, and a crab walked out. My heart took refuge behind my sternum for a brief moment. Sensing my distress, Sticky jumped in to protect me. He grabbed our head by the nose and started to shake it. It was very brave of him, and I'd like to believe he was acting as my bodyguard rather than merely starting breakfast early. But when Grandad Jah accompanied me to the beach twenty minutes later, that was the reason our head was covered with a plastic laundry basket

19

with a rock on top of it. I called it the preservation of evidence. I removed the basket and took photographs of the head from several angles with my cell phone while Grandad sat cross-legged on the beach.

"You think he was attacked by a shark?" I asked.

I often plied Grandad with theories I already knew the answers to. It made him feel superior and got his creative juices flowing. It might seem odd that I should consult a traffic cop on matters related to head severance, but deep down Grandad had been a real policeman in the Western sense. He would probably have been a great detective if only he'd allowed himself to accept the odd bribe every now and then. Corruption was a necessary stepping stone along the pathway to promotion in the Thai police force. How could anybody have faith in an honest policeman? None of his colleagues could trust him. There's probably some whistle-blower joke I could put in here, but I really have to keep track of the story. All I need to say is that after forty years in the force, he had reached the humble rank of corporal and, without those odd baksheesh bonuses, pretty much survived from the proceeds from our family shop in Chiang

Mai. If only he'd dived into the slush I know he could have been somebody. He had a marvelous policeman's instinct.

"No," he said.

On the negative side, getting words out of him was like waiting for a whale to give birth.

"No what?"

"Unless the shark was carrying a saber" — he took time out to sigh at my ignorance — "this had nothing to do with sea creatures."

I admit the neck wound was very neat, but I knew first impressions could be deceptive. I suppose I still had in mind the foreigner a few months earlier who'd put a plastic bag over his head, tied a rope around his neck, and jumped off a bridge. The noose had snared and the body had snapped clean off and continued down into the river. All that remained was a head in a plastic bag at the end of a rope. For weeks the police believed it was a Mafia revenge killing. But the pathologist confirmed it was all due to gravity. Heads are obviously not as well connected as we'd like to believe.

"Why's that?" I asked.

He gave me the look.

"Think, Jimm, think. First, in spite of what the Thai cinema would have us believe, there aren't really that many creatures in the sea that rip people apart for the hell of it. Sharks are the most feared deep-sea psychopaths, but they are actually a rather maligned creature. In fact, they would prefer to hoover up plankton rather than go to the trouble of chewing on human gristle. If we don't bother them, they don't eat us. Simple as that. There's more likelihood of being hit on the head by a bullet fired into the air during a celebration than there is of being attacked by a shark. Second, the tissue and vertebrae of the neck is especially tough. A sea creature would have to shake and gnaw to get through it. There is no bruising here. This was a clean single cut performed by a skilled swordsman."

"So how do you think our friend here wound up on the beach without his body?" I asked.

Grandad shimmied across the sand and, to my amazement, picked up the head and turned it over, like an antique dealer looking for a manufacture date.

"Sharp knife?" he said. "Machete? Sword? Don't know. I wasn't a forensic scientist. I directed traffic."

I switched my cell phone to CALL mode and started to search for a number.

"Who are you calling?" he asked.

22

"Police."

He always assumed this lemony expression whenever I mentioned the police.

"Just go and tell Headman Beung," he said.

It turned out there was a protocol after all, and who better to deal with heads than the head man? I learned later that bodies and parts thereof washed up on the beach was not an unusual phenomenon. There were regulations about it posted on the club house wall at the trawlermen's recreation facility. A surprising number of fishermen couldn't swim, and an even higher number imbibed stimulants of various kinds to stay awake through the night. A quart of Red Bull might just convince a man he was a dolphin. On the Gulf here, you'd need to get those images of eight-meter waves washing over the deck of pirate ships out of your mind. Three meters was our perfect storm, and you could roll over that in a rubber inner tube quite safely. We aren't ever going to see a tidal wave on the east coast. But every now and then a man might step over the side and be lost in the shadows of the squid spotlights.

On the occasion of encountering a dead body on the beach, the discoverer shall inform the village headman.

(Regulation 11b)

In our case, this was *Pooyai* Beung. *Pooyai* literally translates as "big person." So I sarcastically call him Bigman, in English, 'cause he's not. I've never had cause to put Beung on a scale, but if I ever did, I doubt he'd weigh much more than a haddock. He's in his sixties but remarkably upright. He dyes his sticky-up hair light brown, so he reminds me of a paintbrush. He has one wife here at home in Maprao, another lesser wife in Grajom Fy near the crematorium, and a girlfriend in Lang Suan. I doubt he has the stamina to trouble any of them between the sheets, but I don't suppose that was the point of his assembling his harem. Beung is all about show. He has a closet full of uniforms he wears at the slightest excuse: volunteer highway patrol, village security unit, coastal alert force, scout leader, village headman's association, and many more. I'd even seen him in camouflaged army fatigues putting manure around his palm trees. I hadn't spotted him at first. I doubt he's ever seen military service, but it seems anyone down here can dress up any way they like. On top of his uniform fetish and his odd looks, Bigman Beung is a sleazeball. So, it was with great reluctance that I rode Mair's shopping bicycle around the bay to his house.

"Aha! My favorite little starlet," he said. "Just in time. I was starting to feel a bit stiff. How's your massage skills?"

He was lounging on a wooden recliner on the balcony in front of his house. He was wearing a military cadet jacket and unrelated shorts. He had a can of Leo beer at his elbow. It was seven A.M. His major wife was a few meters away from him, plucking chickens. A woman built like an industrial washing machine. I'd never heard her speak.

"*Pooyai* Beung, there's a head on the beach," I said.

"Just here," he continued, pulling up one leg of his shorts to reveal a cadaverous thigh. "Real knotted it is. Must of pulled a muscle. Few minutes of massage should loosen it up . . . if it doesn't have the opposite effect. Hee hee."

I doubted very much he had any muscles, and I was starting to wonder whether he had ears. Hadn't I just told him there was a head on the beach? I tried again.

"Beung, listen. There's a human head just down from our resort. Washed up on the beach." I described it.

He smiled and his upper denture dropped like a guillotine. He used his tongue to push it back up.

"Got legs, has it?" he asked.

"What?"

"This head of yours. Has it got legs?"

"It's a head. If it had legs, it'd be a body and I would have said, 'Beung, there's a body on the beach.' What we have is a head. Understand?"

I suppose I should have shown more respect to our headman. There were people in our village who treated him with deference — only dared make fun of him behind his back. But there are thirteen villages in Maprao — population five thousand — and Bigman Beung was the grand overlord of village thirteen. At the most, fifty houses. Not exactly the mayor of New York City. And have I mentioned he's a sleazeball?

"If it's got no legs," he said, "it isn't going anywhere, is it? Won't be running off, will it? Still be there after the savings cooperative meeting. Not urgent, so no reason to call around to all the co-op members to cancel. Am I right?"

"Not urgent?" I was getting agitated. "It's somebody's head. It used to be attached to that somebody's body. He probably has family concerned about him. He could have been the victim of a murder. The perpetrator's walking around this very minute look-

26

ing for victim number two. And all because nobody's reported a death. Doesn't that worry you?"

"*Nong* Jimm," he said. *"Nong"* — little sister — inevitably the launch pad for a condescending flight. I knew what was coming.

"*Nong, nong* Jimm," he repeated. He sipped at his breakfast beer and smiled with his tongue holding up his teeth to be sure they wouldn't snap shut again. "What worries me is that such a sexy child as you is so hung up on bad things. Murder and evildoers. Crime. Rape. The little breasts of teenaged girls being fondled. If you don't mind me saying so, you're well away from that world. It's good for you to be here in our peaceful community so you can see how much love and kindness there is on the planet. We have loving for you, Jimm Juree. Right here." His hand dropped absently to his crotch. "Cool that hot heart of yours."

That world he was referring to was the world of crime reporting. I'd been one small kidney failure away from becoming the senior crime reporter at the *Chiang Mai Mail*. Over a year had passed since my cruel wrenching from the job, so I imagined the old head of crime was already at that big AA meeting in the sky. They'd have given the post to annoying Arkom — great speller, lousy journalist — and it should have been mine. Jimm Juree, Thailand's second female senior crime reporter. That sounded so right. Respected. Admired. Interviewed in *Time Asia:* "Thai Woman Achieves Greatness." And where do I end up? Cook and dishwasher at the Gulf Bay Lovely Resort and Restaurant. Nearest town, Lang Suan: a place you'd only come to if the train broke down.

"So, you aren't going to inform the police?" I said.

"Of course I will. Of course," he said. "It's a terrible thing. Head on the beach. Terrible. After our nine o'clock meeting I'll hurry down there with a representative of the Coastal Alert Force to verify that it's actually a head."

"You think I don't know what a head looks like?"

"*Nong.* Calm down. Of course you know what a head looks like. But you are merely stage one of the protocol, an unofficial eye witness. Regulation fifteen states that all claims have to be substantiated by an incumbent official."

"So despite the fact it's only five minutes' motorcycle drive from your house and you have two hours to kill before your meeting, you're just going to leave the head sitting there till . . . what time's the meeting over?"

"Ooh, could be about eleven."

"That's four . . . ?"

I got it. Of course. I was being a bit slow that day. Paperwork. It was November, a month of high tides. By eleven there would be no beach. The head would have been washed away along the bay in the monsoon musical chairs that pushed all the garbage south and brought us a different batch. Every day you got a chance to experience new flotsam. The head would be somebody else's problem by lunchtime. In my country a period of inactivity can solve almost every problem. I looked at my cell phone.

"Can you confirm that it's seven fifteen?" I said.

He raised his splendid diver's watch and said, "Yes."

"Thank you," I said and snapped his photo.

"For what?"

"For completing the interview," I said.

"What interview?"

"Yours."

I held up the cell phone for him to see his photograph.

"You weren't . . . ?"

"Recorded every word," I said. "Sorry. I'd

29

already reported the head to *Thai Rat* newspaper. They wanted me to go through the
official channels to see how the system
worked. I'll just have to tell —"

"Wait!" he said, glaring at my phone as if
it was loaded and pointed at his head. "You
mean a human head?"

I had to laugh. I heard a cluck. As the
chickens were dead, I assumed it had come
from Beung's wife.

"Don't bother, Beung," I said. "I'm not
recording anymore."

Beung looked concerned, but I've learned
from experience that sleazeballs don't get
violent. They slime their way out of trouble.

"My sweet little *Nong* Jimm," he said.
"How long have we been friends?"

I was about to say "Never," but he didn't
give me the chance.

"This is clearly a misunderstanding
brought about by our different cultures," he
said. "North meets south. Language dif-
ficulties. Only to be expected."

I was certain we'd been speaking central
Thai together. He winked at me and reached
for his cell-phone-on-a-string hidden among
the amulets dangling from his neck. He
speed-dialed and I could hear John Denver's
"Take Me Home" as he waited in a queue.

Once he was connected, he said just two words,

"Code M."

But then again I suppose *M* isn't a word. I rode Mair's bicycle back along the beach road and smiled to myself. Clever me. I knew there were cell phones with recording functions, but I didn't have one of those.

We were having breakfast when the head-collection service began. We hadn't told Mair about it. It might have meant nothing to her, but she was in a delicate state. A few years earlier she'd started to be overwhelmed by numbers and names and sequences of events. There were times when details of our family fluttered back and forth like candle-charred moths. She'd call me Sissi and start talking about the operation that had turned me from male to female. She'd see our long departed, virtually unknown father in the face of Grandad Jah and begin embarrassing anecdotes we had to nip in the bud. She regularly put on odd shoes and told us it was a fashion statement, and she was convinced those little packets of preservatives they put in food were condiments. She'd eaten so many she'd likely live to 150. The fact that these lapses were rare and that for long periods she would be the normal, caring person we loved, only served to make her condition all the more frustrating. We'd forget that this other person lived inside her. We were sure it wasn't the actual Mair that had sold our family home in Chiang Mai and relocated us to this embarrassing five-cabin bungalow. Five banana-leaf gazebo tables. One half-empty shop. Dirty beach. Warm, jellyfish-infested water. We'd left real lives, careers, dreams to come with her because we knew she'd perish by herself. I left the newspaper. Brother Arny deserted his ambition to be the bodybuilding god of Thailand. Grandad Jah . . . well, he didn't leave anything, but he was just as peeved as the rest of us because peeved was his natural state. Only Sissi had overcome filial responsibility and remained behind.

November blew in annoying winds from the northeast. They kicked up sand and whipped the salt off the surf. So my little brother Arny had made walls of green plastic gauze on three sides of the restaurant gazebo. We lost our view of the ocean and the bay, of course, but the novelty of living on the coast had long since worn off. We did, however, have a splendid view of the car park while we ate.

"We have generals," said Mair.

I looked up to see a truck parking in front

32

of our shop and two men in military uniforms stepping out. The growl of the surf had blotted out their arrival.

"That's Bigman Beung, Mair," I said. "The village headman. And Pot from the bicycle repair shop."

"But they have medals."

"Ribbons, Mair. You buy them with the uniform. They're stitched on. Means nothing."

"They look so elegant." She smiled. "I do love a man in uniform. Have I ever told you about my fling with the fighter pilot?"

"Yes," we all said.

"He had such a peculiarly shaped —"

"YES," we said again.

"Why are they here, do you suppose?" she asked.

"Beach inspection," I told her. "Looking for evidence to nail the households that throw their garbage in the river. Utilities bills. Photographs. Identifiable body waste for DNA testing."

My lie was backed up by the arrival of a dirty cream and brown truck from which stepped a police officer I'd never seen before. He was overweight and wore a toupee so obvious that it could have just been blown onto his head by the gales. It had been two months since my last official dealings with the Pak Nam police, and I knew that during that time a dozen officers would have come and gone. It was like a TV sitcom. You had your regulars who couldn't leave: Major Mana because he had a thriving Amway direct-sales dealership here; Sergeant Phoom and constables Ma Yai and Ma Lek because they were born and grew up and raised families here and refused to leave; and my own darling Lieutenant Chompu because nobody else wanted him. But all the other actors were on their way to and from elsewhere: transfers, probationary placements, demotions, punishment. Pak Nam was one of those places to which they sent disreputable officers officially "transferred to inactive posts." Pak Nam was the perfect location in which to be inactive. In fact, there were long periods, months even, when it was unavoidable.

A third vehicle pulled up beside the police truck and filled our car park. It was a huge black SUV with a roll bar garnished with a stack of lights. On its doors was a familiar sticker: the rear view of a heroic man in overalls with a voluptuous but unconscious woman draped in his arms. Whenever I saw that logo, I had an urge to throw up. This was the symbol of the national rescue foundations — in our case those bold men of the SRM, the Southern Rescue Mission Foundation. Supposedly a charitable organization whose duty it was to facilitate the journey of the soul to a better place. First at the scene of accidents, murders, and suicides. There are those of us who see the men of the SRM as bloodsucking, money-grubbing, cold-hearted vultures. Charity is good business in Thailand. The missions often receive large sums of money in donations, find themselves bequeathed entire estates in wills. So being the first at the scene, getting there before any other foundation is, in my mind, a financial rather than a spiritual necessity. I'd been at accidents where two foundations were going at each other with tire irons while the victims bled to death on the road. I've seen foundation workers checking a pulse over and over at the scene of a drug overdose. A dead body, you see, is worth more bonus points than delivering victims to a hospital. Heaven forbid they should survive. Yet so vital have these goons become to the industry of death, the police no longer find it necessary to get their hands bloody. The collection and dispatch of bodies is left entirely to the foundations.

The two dark-skinned men who climbed

down from the SUV looked like Socrates and Ben, the rats from the movie *Willard.* They were dark and gristly. They joked with the policeman and nodded at our Coastal Alert Force. I'd told Beung that the head was to be found beneath the leaning palm, so they didn't ask me to accompany them as they walked down to the sand together. They began picking their way through the garbage, then became a blur as they passed behind our gauze.

"They're very diligent," said Mair.

"Pollution, what can I say?" I told her. "Brings people together."

No more than ten minutes later, the entourage was back at the car park. I'd rather expected them to put the head in a polystyrene box. At the very least they could have carried it in the laundry basket I'd left covering it. I hadn't in my wildest imagination expected Socrates, the taller of the rats, to be swinging the head like a censer at the end of its long hair. He wore one large yellow rubber glove. I was further astounded to see them produce a camera and take it in turns to pose with the head, beside their truck. I felt sick. They all knew we were sitting not twenty meters away, but they didn't care. Beung and the policeman drove off. The SRM boys put the head in the back of their truck and washed their hands at our free tap. I turned to Mair. She was sitting there nursing her *Titanic* smile, the meaningless grin she wore whenever everything around her was sinking beneath the icy water of the Atlantic.

"Poor man," she said, and I knew she was referring to the head.

I was outraged. I shot to my feet and pushed my little chest ahead of me as I marched across to their big shiny hearse. My brother Arny is built like the Terminator, but he's gentle and pathetic in the nicest sense. I knew he dreaded the thought of a confrontation, but he was my sibling and I sensed his presence just behind me when I poked the skinny Ben rat in the chest.

"What do you think you're doing?" I asked.

Skinny looked at me, then at Arny.

"Washing."

"You know what I mean," I said. "That head."

He was eyeing me up and down. I hate that. It was one of those times I really needed Arny to be as tough as he looked. I wanted him to say, "You look at my sister like that, and I'll crush your head like a tin can," or something equally gratuitous. But Arny was a jumbo jet with the disposition of a pigeon.

"You a relative?" Socrates asked. I presumed he meant of the head.

"No," I said.

"Well then, I suggest you mind your own business," he said.

"But I found it."

"Ain't you clever, sweetheart."

"And on his behalf I demand some respect."

They laughed.

"You know what you can do with your respect?" He smiled. "You can stick it up your boyfriend's back passage."

Arny surprised me by taking a step forward, but Ben rat was suddenly holding a flick knife, thumb against his chest, blade forward. I had no idea how he got it in his hand so fast, but he had a look on his face that said he'd used it before. He glared at Arny, who'd frozen to the gravel.

"Come on, Twinkie," he said. "Let's see how much skin you lose before you get to me."

He smiled. All his left side teeth were missing. His lips were sucked into the void when he spoke.

"I'm a reporter for the *Chiang Mai Mail*," I said, unable to keep the tremor out of my voice.

"Ooh, that's scary." Socrates laughed again, and suddenly he had a knife too. What was it with these people?

"Write without fingers, can you?" he asked.

"You can't frighten me," I said, although by then it was quite obvious from the lack of blood in my face that he could. He stepped right up to me and leaned down so my face was bathed in his wormy breath. I was determined not to step back. I glared, half-heartedly.

"Just in case you forget," he said, "you didn't find anything on the beach this morning. OK?"

I've learned that there are very few situations where smart-arse responses don't do wonders for the atmosphere. This was one of them.

"OK," I said.

He looked at Arny, who was as white as Finland.

"OK?" he asked.

"OK," said Arny in a remarkably high-pitched voice.

Before that morning, *menace* had always been a concept I'd had trouble defining. Here were two losers, skinny hombres, nerds with switchblades. See them shopping at the market and you'd think yourself lucky

39

you hadn't been reincarnated as one of them. But even then, as you passed them by, you'd feel the loose connection. Smell the burning wires. There'd be something about them that would make your skin crawl. And you'd look in their eyes, and you knew they weren't playing. They were the real thing. They'd kill you as soon as let you have the last pumpkin (I'm still with the market analogy here). Menace, that was them. They walked a slow lap around us, prodding with the tips of their knives. I was half expecting them to piss up against our legs. They owned us.

The side window of their SUV shattered into a billion atoms of glass, accompanied by the sound of a clap of thunder. We all looked around to see what had happened. The rats saw him first. Grandad Jah was standing in front of the kitchen with this big black handgun. I have no idea where he'd got it from.

"I'm old," he shouted, "and I only have two months to live, so I have nothing to lose. Next bullet goes into the potted hibiscus there in front of you as a marker. After that will be the tall ugly freak, followed by one to the head of the short ugly freak. Or maybe I'll start with Shorty. Nothing wrong with my eyesight or my aim. Just my

40

mind's a bit out of whack. Know what I mean? It's the medication."

It was a monologue worthy of Clint.

He closed one eye, let the handgun swing as if he couldn't handle the weight, then let fly. The hibiscus was blown to kingdom come. I'd just bought it the weekend before. Little shards of pot rained down on us. The rats didn't run in panic like the villains do in the movies. They looked at each other, smiled, and walked to their vehicle with a touch of arrogance. They even paused to wipe the shattered glass off the seats before getting in and pulling away. They drove out in slow motion, both of them glaring at Grandad and nodding. Socrates rat pointed two fingers and fired them in Grandad's direction. I got the feeling we'd just made the very worst kind of enemy.

2.

Because a Fisher Softly Creeping, Left Disease While I Was Sleeping

(from "The Sounds of Silence" —
PAUL SIMON)

"How are the drugs? You feeling any effects?"

"No."

"That's impossible."

"Not really. I haven't taken them out of the package yet."

"Jimm, you promised."

"I know. It's just . . . being a guinea pig for untested pharmaceuticals seems a bit risky to me."

"They're perfectly safe. Trust me. I know the chemist. And the company pays a lot of money. And it's all legal. As long as you and Mair refuse to accept 'dirty money' from me, I have to find you an income elsewhere. And tell me you can't use a lot of money right now."

"No, we could use it. But what if there

are side effects they haven't thought about? What if my breasts swell up grotesquely?"

"Then you'd have two fewer reasons to be depressed. They're antidepressants, not hormone replacements. Take the damned pills. Fill in the damned questionnaire and take the damned money. You're an unemployed journalist in an unoccupied motel, who's rapidly approaching middle age with little hope of finding a man. You need income."

I had so much I could have come back at her with, but there was no point in both of us feeling sorry for ourselves.

"So what makes you think I'm depressed?" I asked.

"Right, and what makes you think I haven't met a sweet girl and proposed marriage?"

My phone conversations with Sissi, née Somkiet, were a lifeline from the constant sinking feeling of living in a coconut. She was plugged into the unreal world through the Internet. She played high-stakes poker in LA. Was a celebrity judge on YouTube Cover Dance, where desperate teenagers mimicked popular dance routines. Her alter egos dated the alter egos of losers from Brazil to Birmingham and had online sex. And she committed numerous felonies. For the previous eight years, since the mysterious disappearance of her German husband and benefactor, she'd been stealing money willy-nilly. She preferred to restrict her victims to pornographers, the wealthy-but-senseless, and celebrities. She was probably obscenely rich in some offshore bank where money is just a column of numbers on a screen. Money you'd never have to lick your fingers to count. But as she only lived inside her computer, that seemed appropriate in some way.

Her off-line self, once the most stunning Miss Tiffany Transvestite World in the history of the competition, was now podgy and unkempt and lived in a dark condominium in the northern capital. Apart from the occasional walk on the roof, she hadn't been outside for a year. Her food was delivered. A PA did all her real life business, and she hadn't felt the touch of a lover for at least six years. It was starting to concern me that I was the most normal person in my family. Just to let her know the actual world still had something to offer, I told her about my beach head and Grandad Jah shooting up the SUV.

"And I thought life would be dull down there," she said.

"See? So why don't you come down? Mair

would really like to see you. And you can protect us from the rat brothers."

"Hmm. You do make it sound tempting. And you know I'd love to, but I've started this exfoliation course."

"So come in a few days when you're finished."

"It's a four-week course."

"You're exfoliating for four weeks? I can't seem to picture you without any skin."

"I have to look my best for Seoul."

"That's soul, the essence of a person or living thing?"

"No, that's Seoul, the capital of South Korea."

"The Cyber Idol thing?"

"They're having a ball. I'm the guest of honor."

Sissi had been offering her pro-bono make-up and personal grooming tips to a massive Web site in Korea called Cyber Idol, where ugly people underwent Photoshop makeovers and submitted their airbrushed avatars for online beauty competitions. No subterfuge barred. Sissi, or at least press photos of herself ten years earlier, had become their guru. She was the fairy godmother of misinterpretation.

"So why buy product?" I asked. "Why not just Photoshop yourself exfoliated? I seem to recall there's a function. *Peel away layers,* or something?"

"Because . . ."

The pause was so pregnant I expected to hear water burst.

". . . it isn't online."

"What? They're having a ball. A gathering of fakes who made themselves look attractive only on their Web sites. How can it not be online?"

"It's called a coming-out party."

"Coming out of what?"

"Of the Internet. There's no pretense. We've seen all the before and after photographs. The winners are the ones who do the most remarkable job of changing from duck to swan. This is a ball for the befores. Ugly pride."

"But that would mean . . ."

"I'm going to Korea."

"But, Sissi, that would entail leaving the condominium. Going to a crowded airport. Sitting beside a complete stranger on a plane."

"First class, of course. I wouldn't be mixing with commoners."

"You'd be seen in public . . . as you are."

"I've booked the tickets."

I screeched down the phone, and birds all around me fled for the sky. The dogs barked.

Mair called out the name of a dog we didn't own and told it to be quiet. I was so excited I did a little dance and tripped over Gogo, who growled at me.

"Oh, Sissi. That's great. I'm so excited."

"Really?"

"Of course. This is massive. It's like you're coming out too . . . out of your shell."

"I'm frightened, Jimm."

"You'll be the belle of the ball. They'll love you."

"You think so?"

"I know they will."

I'd been so excited by Sissi's news that I'd completely forgotten to tell her about our guests. The very fact that our end-of-the-planet resort had guests at all was news. We relied on a modest short-time-half-bottle-of-Mekhong-whiskey-two-condom-two-hour-max-midday-and-late-night trade. It concerned me that we were encouraging promiscuity and turning a blind eye to adultery, but we had bills to pay. Morality is a luxury for the wealthy. You could count the number of legitimate holidaymakers who'd stayed with us on one fist with a couple of fingers left over. We were no threat to Novotel. Double bed with lumpy mattress, fan, TV (local crap, no satellite), drinking water, hot shower if you were quick, and windows that didn't open. If you wanted to hear the surf, you'd have to leave the door ajar and have gales blow you out of bed. We didn't design the place, just took it over from a couple who knew nothing about tourism. We had no budget to fix it up.

We were always amazed when people stopped off on their journey south on our obscure back road and asked about our place. Once they'd seen the rooms, they'd invariably keep going, even if it was late at night and they were running on caffeine. We'd had a birdwatcher for a few weeks, who spent her days up to her knees in the bog next door. We once had a small flock of Taiwanese evangelists working their way south, spreading the word. I would have given anything to be a lizard on the wall when they hit the extremist Muslim south. Oh, then there was the Channel Five news team that took us over for two nights. They were doing a feature on the demise of the Gulf. I didn't see the finished program, but I was told we featured extensively.

And that was it. Our longest stayers of the past year. Was it any wonder we were still living off the savings? But the money we'd made from selling our beautiful little house and shop with attached Laundromat — our livelihood, our birthright, our family culture — was almost gone. The bank had phoned and asked if we were planning to make any deposits into our account. They said, if not, the province would provide loans if we could prove we were in strife as a result of the monsoons. In fact, we were in strife as a result of not having the vaguest idea of how to run a resort. But we weren't too proud to accept government handouts. We took photographs of our place and filled in the grant application. Grants like these were on a waiting list of up to six months. We'd be high and dry by the time it came through. I doubt we'd send it back though. The monsoons had already disintegrated our beach-front ornamental garden, and the high tides were edging closer to the huts. Every morning we awoke expecting to see the guest chalets bobbing off toward the horizon.

Given the season and the state we were in, we should have been grateful for any paying guests we could dredge up. But there was something odd about the couple we had staying in hut three. They'd arrived in a silver Honda City with tinted windows not an hour after we'd finished cleaning up the glass and pot shards from our morning gunfight in the car park. Me and Mair were sitting at the concrete bench/table combo in front of the shop. The car drove past, then stopped about twenty meters ahead. We assumed they'd mistaken our shop for a 7-Eleven since it was coincidentally painted in the same colors. That was as far as the similarity went. We had so little stock we had to space it out on the shelves like museum exhibits. We could offer cold drinks and snacks but nothing else a weary traveler might require. The car reversed slowly and pulled up alongside me and Mair. We found ourselves staring at our own reflections in the window. I mussed up my short hair, which was looking uncharacteristically neat. A faint buzz accompanied the lowering of the window, and we were left with a view of identical smiles on the faces of two angels a generation apart. The younger was so naturally beautiful I wished I could start again and make a better job of myself. The driver was obviously her mother.

I looked at Mair and asked, "Why don't we look like that?"

"Ours is a beauty that takes patience to discover," she said.

"Excuse me," said the young lovely. Her palms were together, her index fingers caressing her lips in a sweet *wai* we were obliged to reply to. "Good day. Do you have rooms available?"

I laughed deep in my throat. Even when all the stables in Bethlehem were jam-packed, we'd still have rooms free.

"I'll check the register," I said, getting to my feet.

"Of course we do," said Mair. "We're completely empty."

I sat down again. For all the training I'd invested in my mother on the subject of business management, she still had that annoying habit of telling the truth. The driver leaned across her daughter. She had shoulder-length hair, but it somehow retained its perfect shape, like early computer animation. She could have stood on her head and her hair wouldn't have budged.

"Here's the problem," she said. "We stupidly left home without our ID cards. My husband has FedExed them to Songkla. So, just tonight we don't . . ."

Mair laughed.

"We're so desperate we'd let Andrew Hitler stay here without checking his ID," she said, and winked. "No questions asked at the Gulf Bay Lovely Resort."

To their credit, the lovelies laughed. They must have known who Andrew Hitler was because they handed over a deposit big enough to rebuild our ornamental garden a hundredfold. I was sure we'd have to return most of it the next morning when they fled in horror, but it was nice to have serious money in my hand for once. Arny walked in front of the Honda, as he herded them to their room like a muscle-bound mahout guiding an elephant. I could see mother and daughter gaze out toward the murky gray sea and the garbage-strewn beach, and I knew they wouldn't be unpacking. But as the car slowly followed Arny, the question that entered my mind was "Why does it have no number plates?"

Arny — born Arnon but edited in admiration of Arnold Schwarzenegger — was in the same boat as me. Once our mother sold up, against everyone's will, and moved to Nevernowayland, we'd had a filial obligation to follow her. She was only fifty-seven then, but we sensed she'd need us. Despite, or perhaps because of, her eccentricities, she had become a popular member of the Maprao women's association. Together they'd formed an animal protection group and a local-produce cooperative. They'd ignored Bigman Beung and taken control of a biodiesel still donated by some Japanese Lions Club. They had oil-waste buckets in all their houses and had arranged weekly pick-ups. They'd already produced enough rough fuel to run all the Weedwackers in the district. All the professional grass cutters now queued up at the still, delighted to be paying half the cost of diesel at the pumps. The women planned to expand and convince truck drivers to drive on waste. As none of these incentives existed before we arrived, I have to assume Mair was the catalyst. Either way, she had a lot more friends than me and Arny. What she didn't have was a man in her life, so what happened the day after our run-in with the rats really caught us all by surprise.

Our family compound is set back from the beach, which gives us a fifty-fifty chance of not being swept out to sea. My hut is a few meters from Mair's. I was woken at two A.M. by a heavy grunting sound competing with the crash of the surf. The grunt was winning. At first, I thought it was Sticky eating my flip-flops again, and I was preparing to go back to sleep when a horrendous scream rent the air. I rushed out of my hut to find Grandad Jah rushing out of his. We were both carrying our fake Movada LD flashlights. The sound had most certainly come from Mair's hut, so we hurried onto the balcony and hammered on the door.

"Mair! Mair! You all right?" I called.

There was no reply. I turned the handle,

but the door was locked.

"Mair?"

Grandad went to the side window, but that too was shut.

"Mair!"

I grabbed the smallest flowerpot and was about to smash the porch window when I heard the click of the lock. The door opened a crack. Mair somehow oozed herself out through the gap and quickly closed the door behind her. I shone my light on her face. She was flushed. Sweating. The wind whipped up her hair. Her ugly Chinese pajamas were disheveled. In fact, the top was inside out. Mair did the *Titanic* smile.

"You all right, child?" Grandad asked.

"Fine," she said. "Why wouldn't I be?"

"There was a scream," I told her.

She looked up at the big black racing clouds as if trying to remember the lyrics to a song.

"Mair?"

"Yes," she said at last, "it was a nightmare. I remember it clearly. In my sleep I must have kicked the TV on and . . . and there was a horror movie. Yes. A scream. Simple as that."

She nodded at the end, as if the explanation might have been in some way credible. From behind her, the sound of a glass falling onto the floor but not breaking. We have sturdy glassware.

"I should turn off the TV," she said. "Go back to bed, both of you."

She turned and squeezed back into the dark room. In the brief second my flashlight beam was allowed inside, I swear I saw movement on the bed.

"You girls never learn from your mistakes," said Grandad gruffly as he turned away and headed back to his hut. The Gulf wind shoved against his skinny carcass, and I feared he might be carried off by it. My mother was on her way to sixty. A girl only in the eyes of a father. I flicked off my light and made heavy footfalls down the wooden steps. And there I waited.

Twenty seconds later Mair giggled and said, presumably to her TV, "They're none the wiser. Go to sleep."

I tried to ignore all the clues, but they were there, flapping around in the wind like dirty laundry. I went back to bed that night wrapped in incredulity and not a little envy. It had been almost eighteen months since my last . . . since I last had a nightmare and kicked the TV. Before attempting to sleep, I reached for the trial drugs now open on my bedside table and took two, washed down with the last of my Romanian red. The room was so black I felt like I'd been painted out of the scene. I didn't know whether to laugh or suffocate myself with my pillow. Instead, I found myself in a dream.

It was disconcertingly erotic. I was locked in a steamy embrace with Ed the grass man in the unfinished hull of his new squid boat. We were on a mattress of curly wood shavings. Ed, I may not have mentioned, was the gangly young man who came every month to cut our grass with his impressive Weedwacker. He'd once begged me to go out with him. Well, perhaps he didn't beg exactly. In fact, he didn't quite get around to asking, but I knew he was about to.

He wasn't bad-looking, as grass cutters went. He had those dark chocolate eyes, not Vosges exactly, more Tesco Lotus plain. But despite that and his knotty muscular stomach, I wasn't about to let him have his way with me. And I was most annoyed to find him there in my erotic dream. Who did he think he was, clunking away there on top of me, his knees banging against the wooden planks? And to make matters worse, I awoke to the realization that the sound of our lovemaking was in fact that of a headboard banging against the wooden wall of the neighboring cabin. My mother's cabin. I looked at the alarm clock. It was six fifteen.

Did she have no shame? I took two more antidepressants and wrote on the questionnaire beside DAY ONE, "No effect whatsoever."

3.
IT'S AMAZING HOW YOU CAN SPIT RICE THROUGH MY HEART

(from "When You Say Nothing At All" —
PAUL OVERSTREET, DON SCHLITZ)

One of my chores at the Gulf Bay Lovely Resort was to prepare meals for the family and, on rare occasions, the guests. Sooner than listen to Mair's headboard, I went to the kitchen early to fix something for our two paying visitors. I was sure they wouldn't have had a moment's sleep in that mildewy, lizard-happy, wind-rattling room and would be on the road early. So, as I wanted them to have at least one positive memory to take from us, I bought some of Jiep's excellent rice porridge in plastic bags and stewed my own *o-liang* orange tea, thick with sugar, as a going-away present. I needed to waylay them long enough to ask about the missing number plates. That was one of the three mysteries I'd decided to solve that day. The second was to follow my anonymous head and find out who he was and how he'd come to be on our beach. Although I'd lied to Bigman Beung about writing an article, further thought had told me it might not have been such a bad idea.

The *Chumphon News*, a weekly, was the nearest thing we had to a local paper. It was based in Chumphon town, eighty kilometers north along the highway. (Chumphon's claim to fame was that it boasted a Tesco, a Carrefour, and a Macro all within a kilometer of each other. In Thailand, our superstores liked to huddle.) I'd done a couple of human interest features for the *News* and the odd petty crime report. My last exposé had been on the smuggling of carrots from China. They paid less than for a table clearer at Kentucky Fried Chicken, but news was in my blood. It's what I did. I needed the buzz of seeing my name in print. And that and my antidepressant trial constituted my total income at the time. I decided I would do a piece on head retrieval and visit the foundation whose job it was to trace the families of the dead. And if, in the process, I could get Ben and Socrates fired, all the better.

My third mystery, and I'd moved my food preparation table to the window so I could observe our cabins, was to discover who had been so active in Mair's bed, night and morning. So far I'd seen nothing. I gutted the lunch mackerel and went through a list of suspects in my mind. Since we lived in a village, I doubted she'd be silly enough to mate with a married man. The smorgasbord of single men in a ten-year radius of her age group was not particularly delectable. Mair was still a good-looking woman, and I hoped she'd demonstrate a little good taste in her choice. This side of the Lang Suan river we had Dr. Prem at the health center, who turned pale at the sight of bodily waste; long-haired Nute, who taught PE at the middle school but was a foot shorter than most of the students; Grit, the good-for-nothing elder brother of Meng, our local private detective and plastic awning installer; Kow, the squidboat captain who was devoid of front teeth and smelled of fish-balls; and Daeng, the dog killer, whom she wouldn't have touched with a three-meter coconut hook. It was a depressing line-up. All I could hope was that Mair had imported someone eligible from another district, but I'd seen no strange vehicles parked round about.

If all else failed, I'd give Mair a sip of wine, stand back, and wait for the blab gates to open. I have a remarkable tolerance for alcohol, but she can't drink to save her life. She spews out embarrassing stories that would make a hooker blush. Nothing is taboo to Mair with a drink in her. Nothing, of course, apart from the whereabouts of our missing father, who fled the scene when I was a toddler, Arny was still in nappies, and Sissi was only five and still a boy. On the subject of absent fathers, Mair had taken a vow of silence that withstood the test of booze.

We were eating our rice porridge — me, Mair, Arny, and Grandad — at one of our resort tables squashed inside the kitchen. We had the shutters closed. The wind from the northeast had obviously had a bad night and was spitting mad. The coconut trees were bent like parentheses, their fronds pointing desperately to Malaysia and more temperate climes. Every now and then, a coconut would break free from the bunch and head off at a forty-five-degree angle to smash a window or fracture a water pipe. The beach was clogged with bamboo roots torn from the streams in the flash floods. They were tangled with discarded nylon nets and garnished with polystyrene. Everything smelled of effluent and old engine oil.

Perhaps you can see why I love this place so.

The mother-daughter matching set from room three poked their heads in the kitchen door. Their hairstyles had been vandalized by the wind. They were not carrying suitcases.

"Good morning," said the mother. "I was wondering whether there might be a chance of a bite to —"

"Oh, my word," said Mair. "Come in and shut that door. Of course we have food for you. Father, give them your seat."

Grandad Jah didn't budge. He was having his breakfast. Arny grabbed two folding chairs from against the wall and placed them at the table for the guests.

"Sorry about the ambience," I said, quite unnecessarily. I'd become a serial apologizer since we moved south.

"No. Not at all. This is very cozy," lied the mother.

I looked at her. Even her casual summer wear was designer. She probably had a kitchen twice this size back home just for her maids to eat in.

"Where are you from?" I asked, dishing up the rice porridge.

"Oh, we move around a lot," she said.

It was a "mind-your-own-friggingbusiness" answer. I'd heard a lot in my career. But she delivered the line with grace and a nice smile. The daughter hadn't yet spoken. She cast nervous glances in the direction of Arny, who sat with his shirt off. We were used to it, but he could be a little overwhelming to outsiders. He was built like a stack of tractor tires. He gushed testosterone. Yet despite his physique and his movie-star good looks — both of which make me think I must have been adopted — he was apparently unaware of the effect he had on others. Some feared him the way you'd be nervous of a killer whale heading down your driveway. Some, both men and women, desired his body, caring not whether he had a mind or a personality. Some felt that animal urge to challenge him. The daughter didn't know what to make of him at all. She was a mid-twenties jaw-dropper, and I'd wager she had saliva trails following her wherever she went. She was used to seduction and had come to expect it. So when naked-torso hunk said "Good morning" and returned to his breakfast without even a cursory glance at her breasts, she was plainly dumfounded.

There was no other woman for Arny. He had met his true love, Gaew, right here in Maprao. She too was a weightlifter. She too had toured the body glamour circuit and won prizes. She too had fallen into that same pit of passion that had claimed my brother. She had taken both his heart and, so we believed at the time, his virginity, in the space of a week. There was only one buckle in this wheel of passion and that was her age. Arny was thirty-two. His "fiancée," Gaew, was fifty-eight. She was the same age as our mother. She and Mair had idolized the same rock singers in high school and learned Hula-Hoop at approximately the same time. In fact, they were becoming good friends. We all liked her. But that just made her relationship with Arny . . . weird. Icky even. She'd won her first award when Arny was still learning to use the potty. So, that's why Arny didn't notice there was a babe in the kitchen.

The guests tucked into their food with gusto. If they had problems with eating with commoners, they didn't show it. I was heating up the gooey orange tea and planning another subterfuge for extracting conversation.

"Sorry about your room," I said.

"The room's wonderful," said the mother.

"Really?"

I couldn't think of one thing that was wonderful about cabin three apart from the fact that it wasn't cabin two. Cabin two had a mouse tap-dance studio in the ceiling.

"We appreciate the simplicity here," she said. "One can get too dependent on luxury items in the city. I'm a firm believer that one needs to stop and experience frugality once in a while."

And here she'd landed slap in the capital of frugality. What luck.

"We were expecting you to be back on the road at first light," I told her.

"We had planned to but it's so lovely here I think we might stay a day or two."

That's when I knew she was lying. Lovely? You'd have to be blind drunk or just plain blind to see anything lovely in Maprao in the monsoon season . . . especially at the Not So Lovely Resort. These two were up to something. I was planning to creep around the block and sneak up on them from the rear with my next question, but Grandad Jah went at them full throttle.

"You got no registration plates on your car," he told them. "That's illegal."

The guests looked at each other and giggled nervously.

"We were coming over the bridge in Lang Suan, the one on the highway," said the mother mechanically. "The road there is riddled with potholes. And of course we hit

65

one of them and the license plate at the front just dropped off. So we st—"

"How did you know?" asked Grandad.

"Know what, uncle?"

"How did you know the plate dropped off. You got an A/C car, so you didn't hear it. It's under the bumper, so you didn't see it. And it's flat, so you sure as hell didn't feel it. So . . . ?"

I could see a desperation in the woman's eyes as she searched for another lie. Her daughter came to the rescue.

"The car behind us beeped," she said. "We stopped and the driver told us we'd lost our registration plate back on the road. We retrieved it and took it to the garage at the main intersection, and they said the housing unit was rusted almost completely away. Same with the one at the back. So the owner is welding us new . . . new housing units to . . . to attach the plates."

She didn't look at us, just sighed and ran her spoon around the inside of her bowl. I glared at Grandad, but I could tell he was already satisfied these two were up to no good. We both knew a two-year-old Honda wasn't going to rust away to nothing. We both knew that the only way anyone would beep you on Highway 41 would be to pull you over and mug you at gunpoint. And why not take a hotel room in town? Why drive all the way to the coast without plates? But an interrogation would only frighten these two away, and like Grandad, I wanted them to stick around. I wanted the chance to use my investigative skills. I only have a small nose, barely a squirrel snout. But it can sniff. Oh yes can it sniff. And my nose sensed a story. A big one.

I'm not sure what it was Mair sensed, but she said, "You'll have to excuse my father. He's a little senile." Grandad's eyebrows almost took off. "Sometimes he thinks he's a detective. Like on the television. He can be impolite at times."

"Yeah. Right," said Grandad. He stood and took his bowl to the sink. "Can I wear my SWAT jacket today?"

"Maybe later," said Mair.

Arny watched Grandad push against the door with all his might and thrust himself into the wind. My brother had no idea what was going on. Sometimes the world was too subtle for him.

"Any more in the pot?" he asked.

The Southern Rescue Mission Foundation had a large car park in front and several sheds around the perimeter with spotlessly clean SUVs and trucks and towing vehicles parked facing forward awaiting the next emergency. While the child-care agencies struggled to pay staff and feed the hungry, the lords of the dead played cards in air-conditioned waiting rooms, ate healthy meals in their canteen, and emptied themselves in state-of-the-art, flushing, American Standard lavatories with free tissue paper you didn't have to dispose of in a pedal bin. I inadvertently parked our Toyota Mighty X in a position that might have prevented the rapid deployment of two, perhaps three shiny black SUVs not unlike the one the rats had driven. Petty? I know. But energizing.

The building marked RECEPTION was in fact a house, the design of which was lifted from the type of Home of Your Dreams catalog my ex-husband used to take into the toilet and drool over. It was a pink mansion squashed into a twenty-five-square-meter plot. I walked in through the front door, where I was assaulted simultaneously by an Alaskan air drift from four ceiling-mounted conditioners and a receptionist in a mini skirt, tights and a turtleneck sweater. She was fiftyish in make-up she probably thought made her look younger. She *wai*'d me violently.

"Welcome to SRM," she said in a shrill,

somewhat frightening voice. "How can I help you?"

My nipples felt larger than my breasts.

"You couldn't turn down the A/C, I suppose?" I replied.

I hadn't seriously been expecting a result from my sarcasm but she immediately went for the remote.

"Chilly, isn't it," she said and chirruped down the chill factor. She came around and pulled the chair out for me. She was very accommodating. I got the feeling I could have asked her to bake me something and she'd have run off to the oven.

"I'm here to inquire about the whereabouts of someone I . . . of a loved one," I told her.

The features on her face suddenly drooped like a facelift's expiration date. She reached for her heart.

"I'm so sorry," she said. "This must be a terrible time for you. I sincerely hope that we at SRM will be able in some small way to relieve the burden on you and your family. Although we are a not-for-profit organization relying entirely on small donations from the general public, we do everything possible to make our accident victims comfortable before their next journey."

It was memorized and cheesy.

"I'm so pleased," I said.

"When did your . . . ?"

I assumed she wanted me to fill in the gap.

"Uncle?" I said.

"Ah, uncles. So, so important to the harmony of a happy family. When did your uncle pass away?"

I hadn't seen her reach for the Tiger balm so I had to assume her tears for my uncle were natural. Impressive. I already had an urge to write her a check for twenty thousand *baht* to further the charitable work of the SRM.

"Two days ago," I said.

"So sudden. So tragic."

My loss sat so heavily on her shoulders she dropped onto her chair and sighed, then flipped open a plastic folder.

"And what was the name?" she asked.

"Mine?"

"Your uncle's."

I hadn't thought that far ahead. I wondered then why I'd opted for this untruth. Why couldn't I simply have said, "I found a head on the beach. Don't know who he was, but I was wondering how he's doing?" Why not? Because I wouldn't have made it past the sympathetic gatekeeper to the beyond, that's why. Not that I was doing that great with the lie.

"Somyuth," I said. "We heard one of your teams came to collect his . . . body from the beach."

"The beach? My word. What were the circumstances?"

"Fisherman. Ehm . . . fell overboard. Snagged in the trawler ropes. Drowned . . . Very sad."

"I feel for you, honestly I do. One of our cats was caught in the snake netting behind our house. Trapped, he was, for a week. Got so desperate he chewed off his own leg to get out. Limped home covered in blood, riddled with insects. He collapsed in front of us with his intestines all hanging out."

I had a feeling there'd be a punchline.

"If only he'd had an organization like ours to clean him up and make him look present-able before" — she gasped — "before that horrible moment when my little daughter came running in to see her beloved Nunu dead and disgusting."

She was good. Really she was. There was no way this woman was a mere receptionist. I bet she was the daughter or granddaughter of the venerable Chinese gentleman whose portrait hung behind her. I bet she'd drained millions from gullible relatives with this routine.

"I'm not that fond of cats," I said.

71

"Of course. Some people aren't."

"I just want to find Uncle . . ." Damn. I'd forgotten his name. "My uncle. Take him home to the family. Loved ones. You know? Uncles. So important. Where is he?"

After I'd given her a bunch of made-up names and addresses and convinced her my national ID card was in the car, she led me out of the rear door. We found ourselves in two meters of clammy open air. In front of us was another door, this in the wall of a long windowless concrete building. We entered. She flicked a switch inside, but the door closed behind us, leaving us in a black hole. Total darkness often makes me want to wet myself. Don't know why. Something deep in my subconscious that needs analysis. I was about to evacuate when a bank of fluorescent lights above us popped into life one at a time. I don't astound that easily, but I was most certainly flabbergasted by what I saw in that building. It was exactly like being in the frozen produce section at Macro. There were open refrigerated units along both walls with a narrow aisle down the center. All it lacked was the trolleys. And laid out in the units were bodies shrouded in green plastic. Only the heads were exposed, some in the throes of an agonizing death, others so at peace they might have just fancied a quick lie down. But the thing I found remarkable was that every head had its hair combed. SRM obviously had a stylist on staff.

I walked along the aisle with the gatekeeper behind me. Some of the green plastic shrouds hinted that the bodies beneath the groomed heads were not all symmetrical or complete. There were a few ways to die in Lang Suan — old age and boredom came to mind immediately — but such horrible deaths as these could only be attributed to the carnage of Highway 41. Our roads were single-handedly culling the population. There were twenty bodies all told, but not one of them was Uncle . . . my uncle.

"I don't see him," I said.

"Did you look carefully? Sometimes the facial features can change after a terrible death."

"I think I know what Uncle looks like."

"Of course you do. Oh, well. Then, if it was the beach . . ."

"Yes?"

"Well, there might have been a mistake. He might have been put in with . . . them."

"Them?"

I was put in mind of the *Alien* movies, tentacles and drool.

"It's almost as comfortable for them," she said and led me to a door at the end of the building. "And, of course, it's refrigerated."

"Oh, good."

"But it's a little . . . congested."

It seemed unfair that all these bodies should be laid out with room to turn over, if they so desired, but that Uncle What's-his-name had to share a room. She opened the door, and I stepped up to take a look inside. It was like a skinny third-class train compartment. Two by four meters. Bodies were crammed in there on bunk shelves like pigs on their way to market. They were dressed in their own clothes, some bloody, others with no telltale sign of how they died. My uncle's head was looking down at me from an overhead luggage rack. He had a ticket attached to his left ear. I heard a voice from behind me.

"Do you . . . ?"

I turned around. Felt quite drained of blood. The gatekeeper grabbed my arm to steady me.

"No, he's not there," I said.

"And you're certain it was one of our trucks that collected the body?"

"Black SUV. Registration number Gorgai 2544."

She looked at me as if I was the first

woman to ever memorize a number plate.

"I wrote it down because the men you sent out were extremely rude," I told her. "Men like that can only give an organization a bad name and make the general public think twice about donating money."

I couldn't mention the knives because then we'd have to involve the police. Apart from the fact that most officers here moonlighted as criminals and fell somewhere between jellyfish and tree stumps on an IQ chart, there was the matter of Grandad Jah's gun and the shattered window.

"I'll look into it," she said without enthusiasm, hurrying me back along the aisle. "That is certainly one of our vehicles. Perhaps they took your uncle to the hospital. Are you sure he was dead?"

No heartbeat, respiration, nerve reaction or physiology beneath the neck.

"Pretty much," I said.

"Then all I can think is that somebody else claimed the body. Another relative?"

"You know? I was just thinking the same thing. He did have a number of minor wives dotted around. It's very likely one of them wanted his body all to themselves for the first time. Yes, that's probably it."

"Well, there you are."

And with that her interest in me vanished

75

completely. I held my ground.

"So, if there's nothing else?" she said.

"I was just wondering . . ."

"Yes?"

"That little room at the end?"

"What about it?"

"I couldn't help notice there's a lot of empty space in the units. Why weren't those bodies laid out here with the others?"

"The freezers are for viewing. Nobody's going to claim the bodies from the end room."

"How do you know?"

"We just know."

She'd been hustling me out of the morgue and into the reception area. I stopped and turned around. I didn't like being nudged.

"I'm asking you a polite question," I said, and I did the glare thing. This time it worked.

"They won't be claimed because they probably don't have relatives here. And if they did, the relatives wouldn't be brave enough to come to collect them. By law we have to hold the bodies for ten days. Then we cremate them. We have a monk at the center. They get a decent sending off. Better than they deserve, most of them."

"But who are they?" I pushed.

"They're Burmese."

76

" 'They're Burmese,' she said. Like they were windscreen debris in fire-ant season. Then she kicked me out 'cause she knew she wouldn't be getting any money out of me. Nasty little bitch."

Lieutenant Chompu sat opposite me, smoking a joint. He was wearing a white silk ankle-length dressing gown and probably nothing else. I didn't ask. He was elegant rather than handsome. There was something early Duke of Edinburgh about his looks. But he was unashamedly effeminate. Gay men seemed to flock to me. Chompu had his official police barrack room near the Pak Nam station and this, a single bedroom bungalow with a nice view of Pitak Island. Here he lived his other life. Family money had prodded him as far as lieutenant in the Royal Thai police force, but that was where his career had stalled. His refusal to act like a good, manly cop — just pretend a little — had seen him dumped here at the end of nowhere. We were both refugees from real life, and we were friends of a sort.

"It's their fault," he said in one of those high-pitched   don't-try-to-speak-while-you're-inhaling-ganja voices.

"Whose?"

"The Burmese."

"For what?"

"All those years when they were totally nasty to us. All those rude invasions and mass murders. It all comes back to haunt you in the end."

"Oh, right. Like we didn't rape and pillage the neighbors too. It was a primeval hobby. They didn't have football in those days. And I think there's a statute of limitations on exacting revenge. Chom, they're just trying to make a living wage."

"They can't have everything, dear. If they want to be spared abuse, nobody's forcing them to come here."

He lay back on his cushion-strewn chaise longue, posing for some unseen photo shoot. The gusts whipped beetle-nut fronds against the glass of his picture window.

"Oh, good," I said, and sipped my lemon juice. "That's a relief. There I was thinking you had no faults."

"And I do?"

"You're a racist pig."

"It has nothing to do with racism. Are they here to help develop our country? Noooo. Do they try to learn our language and assimilate? Noooo. They come solely because

78

on this side of the border they can make three times what they could in Burma."

"And three times what they could earn in Burma still doesn't equal our minimum wage. They're slave labor, and they're doing all the jobs we refuse to take on. If it weren't for the Burmese, there'd be no fishing industry in Thailand, no palm oil or rubber, a greatly reduced tourism . . ."

"Oh, Jimm. You know how my eyes puff up when I cry. It's my day off. Can't we talk about boy bands? . . . Making soufflé? . . . Anything but Burmese."

"I'm angry."

"I know you are, darling. But don't forget, just four days ago you couldn't give a titty about the state of our slave laborers, just like the rest of us."

"I . . . I didn't know four days ago."

"Know what?"

"That we were exploiting them."

"Of course you did."

"Did not. I just looked it up at the Internet café yesterday. Exploitation — Burmese — Thailand. Forty-six thousand sites."

He took a deep toke and blew a little cloud of heaven out of each nostril. I had no problem with ganja, but there were times when I needed to be mellow and times when I wanted to lead with my animosity.

79

"Jimm," he said. "When you lived in Chiang Mai, how many of your neighbors had Burmese nannies or maids?"

"Well, a lot, but . . ."

"And didn't you think it was interesting that they started making breakfast at six and were still there washing the dishes at midnight? What? Did you think they were just showing their love for the kind family that hired them for 120 *baht* a day? And I doubt they got a day off. They knew if they complained there were plenty more menials available in the refugee camps. Sadly lacking a trade union, those people, don't you think?"

"Well, I'm going to do something."

"Fine. There were two million of them working in Thailand last count. I think you should call them in for a meeting."

"No, we'll do it one at a time — or fractions thereof. Let's begin with the head."

"Oh, my word. I've told you."

"I want it investigated."

"It's been investigated."

"Some fat cop with a lump of dead grass on his head walks down the beach, looks at the victim, and hands him over to the body-snatching rat brothers. They shake hands and he drives off. Fifteen minutes all told. I'd hardly call that an investigation."

"He filed a report."

"Oh, good. Now we're getting somewhere. Show it to me."

"Hmm. All right."

"Really?"

"No. Not really. Are you insane? I'm hardly going to risk what little I have left of a career by leaking confidential documents to the press."

"You've done worse."

"Not in public."

I sighed and looked him over. And I have to confess that was a peculiar moment. I knew Chompu would sooner mount a faulty electric junction box during a rainstorm than have carnal knowledge of a woman, but there was something really . . . erotic about him lying there in his silk gown, his tanned muscular legs exposed to the mid-thigh. His hair wet from the shower. I was embarrassed by the emotions dribbling through me.

"I'd let you have sex with me," I said.

He coughed and dropped his joint down among the cushions. He burrowed franti-cally after it before the entire scatter empire went up in flames. You got to see all his neat little teeth when he laughed, and he did laugh long and hard.

"What on earth for?" he asked at last with

81

his rescued joint between his fingers.

"A reward?" I said.

"You're hilarious, really you are. I'd sooner . . ."

"I know."

Gay or not, that kind of reaction didn't do a lot for a girl's self-esteem. I don't know what had come over me. I'd never found him even vaguely sexual before. I put it down to the trauma of discovering my mother in flagrante. But, well, if my body didn't tempt him, I suppose all I was left with was blackmail.

"This is such a nice little house," I said. "Hidden from the road by a long winding driveway through the trees."

"I was waiting for this."

"A stash of marijuana and a stack of special magazines. Unauthorized use of handcuffs. Quite a little love nest."

"You wouldn't."

"An anonymous phone call to the major. A late-night raid."

I sat on my balcony with Gogo and Sticky on either side of me, as full of vim and vigor as roadkill. I was attempting to read the photocopy of Lieutenant Egalat (Egg) Wirawot's report on the discovery of a John Doe on Maprao beach. It wasn't *War and Peace*.

Two and a half sheets, all told. It was getting harder to read as the light drained away. If there had been a sun, it would have been setting behind me, but we were in what they call a lull, a word I'd become very familiar with of late. The wind had died completely and the dark clouds were all low and gathering to drench us for the standard twenty minutes. Mair and Arny were running around closing all the windows. You can't say the monsoon season didn't have a sense of humor. I should have been helping the family batten down the hatches, but I'd only just been sent the report and I wanted to know what it said. If fiction awards were presented in the category of police reports, I had the winner right there on my lap.

FOUND THE HEAD — NO DISTINGUISHING MARKS — LONG HAIR, EARRINGS, DARK SKIN — PROBABLY BURMESE — MARKED OFF A PERIMETER AND SCOURED THE BEACH FOR EVIDENCE — INTERVIEWED AND CONSOLED DISTRAUGHT VILLAGERS — BEGAN SYSTEMATIC INVESTIGATION AT THE DOCKS — NO COOPERATION FROM THE BURMESE FISHERMEN — CONCLUDED THAT THIS WAS ONE MORE INTERNAL

DISPUTE WITHIN THEIR COMMU-NITY SETTLED THE WAY THEY DO.

It began.

There were vegetables, but that was the meat of it. The people behind our resort have three cows. Even on a good day when they get bamboo root treats, those cows couldn't produce half the manure I read there in that report. And his nonexistent, in-depth systematic investigation hadn't turned up so much as a name.

The sky all around me grumbled like a troubled stomach, and the cloud — and I swear I'm not making this up — squatted down on our resort like a huge Malay black bear's bottom. Plonked itself right down on top of us. It was so dark I could no longer make out words on the paper. The dogs, a species renowned for its innate sense of predicting extreme weather conditions, snored through it. Only when the rain tossed itself down in zinc bathtubs and the wind rose to smash it sideways against our little huts did they wake up, stretch, and amble off in search of a drier spot. I was halfway inside my room when I noticed Grandad Jah jogging toward me through the deluge. I'd seen video footage of a horse being picked up by a tornado. A horse weighs a thousand times more than my grandad, and I swear his feet weren't touching the ground.

"Grab something solid," I shouted, but my words were whisked away on the wind. It could only be the weight of the rain soaking through his clothes that stopped him flying off like Mary Poppins. He clambered up the steps and pushed past me into the cabin. He had a smile on his face. It didn't suit him. When the door was shut, he started to undress.

"Grandad, don't."

"Pneumonia," he said. "That's what gets us. Lungs full of rain. Sudden chill. Two days and you're on the pyre. Can't be too careful."

"It's not appropriate to . . ."

But I was too late. His thick soggy shirt was already on the floor, and he was working on the tie string of his fisherman's trousers. Grandad undressing was like a skeleton shedding its ectoplasm. I hurried to the cupboard for a spare blanket and wrapped it around him before I had to witness any more of him.

"What do you want, Grandad?"

"I've got it," he said, his daringly small underpants falling to the floor beneath the blanket.

"I'm sure you have. What is it?"

"The number."

"What num— The engine?"

He grinned.

"But how? It wasn't there last night," I reminded him.

Me and Grandad had crept out under the cover of the crashing surf the previous night and broken into the Honda. We'd left no traces. Grandad Jah was the Ali Baba of grand theft auto. But our clandestine operation beneath the bonnet had only succeeded in confirming that the couple had gone to great lengths not to be traced. The engine number had been filed away to nothing.

"There are ways," he said.

"To read a number that's not there?"

"To read the ghost of that number, young Jimm. When a number is punched onto metal, the metal below it is hardened. Even when the surface is filed level, that hard metal retains the number. By cleaning off the grease with petrol and applying heat from a blowtorch, then by grinding down the area with emery paper and working up a fine shine, with a strong side light you can pick out the relief of the original numbers."

The rain was beating so hard on the concrete tile roof that Grandad had been forced to shout the end of his explanation.

Then, within a minute, the storm was gone, and the rays of the setting sun found a loophole in the convoluted clouds and formed a halo around him. He looked like the starving Buddha. He was, without question, an arrogant, ignorant, genius.

"How are the preparations going?"
"I'm getting wigs made."
"What for?"
"For my head."
"I know where they go," I said. "I'm asking you why you need them. Did you accidently exfoliate all your hair off?"
Sissi was trying to be cool, but I'd known her long enough to sense the girlish excitement in her voice. This gala would be the best thing to happen to post-depression Sissi.
"There'll be three days of mingling," she said. "Participants set up stands with blown-up photos of themselves pre- and post-work. The judges — me being a distinguished foreign judge responsible for grooming and make-up — go around and talk with the contestants. They're gorgeously challenged, and here they are naked without their Photoshop tools. There's no time to rush out for plastic surgery, so all they have are grooming and makeovers to be the

belles and beaux they aspire to be. And nobody's allowed to be their finished Web Idol until the ball. That's when everyone goes glam. Cinderellas and Charmings all. And I have to be especially gorgeous, as I'm such an icon."

"Hence the wigs."

"I'll leave it till the last moment to decide which Sissi I shall be."

It was perverted but so much better than self-imposed imprisonment in a luxury condominium.

"I want to see all the photos," I said.

"There's just the one problem," she said.

"What's that, Siss?"

"I have to pass through Bangkok."

"Wear a mask."

"No, I mean the demonstrations."

A pause here to explain what was going down in our nation's capital. For a month, an army of yuppies with undisguised connections to the aristocracy and the military had been occupying our government house. Had they been merely motorcycle taxi drivers and papaya salad vendors, they would, and some would argue, should, have been mowed down in a barrage of police gunfire. These quiche-eating misérables were making a mockery of our political system. A system, I may add, that had no problem making a mockery of itself. But what these yellow shirts represented made them bulletproof. A baton to the head of any one of them would have left a dent in the kingdom's heritage. So those arrogant yuppies strolled through police lines and set up a holiday resort at that Italo-gothic mansion in Dusit.

Meanwhile, the rightful residents sneaked out the back gate. Led by the brother-in-law of the ex-PM-telecommunications tsar who'd threatened to make us Thailand Inc., the government jumped on the bus and skedaddled out to our old airport at Don Muang. There they were currently conducting the business of running the country in a room behind left luggage. It was all so humiliating I wanted to apply for Lao citizenship. At least the Lao had a nice oligarchy where everyone knew where the lines were drawn.

But that was why my sister Sissi was wary of passing through our hotbed of anarchy and anti-anarchy.

"Come on, Siss." I laughed. "You fly domestic to our brand-new airport at Suvarnabhumi. You travel along the moving walkways to your transit gate, and you flash your first-class documents at the smiling Thai Airways official who whisks you off to the first-class lounge. There you drink complimentary champagne until you're led onto the aircraft. You don't even have to leave the airport. You'll be oblivious to all that violent Ping-Pong and popcorn-making that's going on in Dusit. And, I mean, I doubt very much whether those coffee shop entrepreneurs and middle-aged ladies with expensive perms will be marching out to the airport to throw themselves down in front of your jumbo. You really do worry too much."

"You're right."

"I usually am. Now, to business."

"Why do you never phone me just to say hello?"

"Sorry. Hello! Now, Grandad and I were wondering whether you'd be kind enough to trace a car engine number. It's a Honda B15B9009554."

"I stopped doing that."

"Doing what?"

"Engaging in illegal activities on the Internet."

"No you didn't."

"I did."

"When?"

"A week ago. I have a loving public now. I'm adored. I don't want to endanger my standing. I want my awesome power to be used for good instead of evil."

"You can't be serious."

"I am."

I was devastated. Sissi of all people going straight.

"Well, then. This isn't technically illegal," I tried. "It's just accessing public information."

"It's hacking into the databank of an international company and stealing."

"All right, it's a little bit illegal. But no more illegal than pretending to be the Disney Corporation and having agencies send you baksheesh so their clients get first crack at a new script."

"I don't do that anymore."

"And what are you living on?"

"Savings."

"All ill-gotten."

"When it runs out, I'll get an honest job."

"And what could be more honest than crime fighting? Your awesome power already put one murderer out of business. You're the Sherlock Holmes of cyberspace. Legless Elena your alter ego is the heroine of the Police Beat law enforcers' social network."

"It's a dating site for ex-cops and old hookers."

"Ex-cops with a hundred lifetimes of policing experience. You have a world of detection at your fingertips. There's no end to what you and the old doughnut guys can achieve. Forget make-up tips for teenyboppers. Join me in the fight for justice and fair play."

"No."

Waste of a speech.

"Please."

"What did he do?"

"Who?"

"The car owner."

I told Sissi about our mystery guests in hut three. When I'd finished, there was a pause, during which I knew she was nodding her head. I could hear her seashell earrings jangling. She could no sooner pass up a mystery than I could.

4.

I'M GONNA SHOOT YOU RIGHT DOWN, RIDE OFF WITH YOUR FEET

(from "Boom Boom" — JOHN LEE HOOKER)

We were sitting at dinner that evening when the hand grenade went off. It was just after Mair had asked everyone if they fancied a bowl of mixed-friends ice cream. Hut three spent so much time eating with us it was almost inevitable they'd sprout names. We doubted the names were real. They certainly lacked imagination. They insisted we call them Noy, the mother, high-tone, and Noy, the daughter, low tone. Thai is a wonderful language that leaves many a foreigner ripping out chunks of hair. It has the ability to change a dog into a horse, a skein of silk into a bush fire, an entire town into an irrigation ditch. And all at the mere drop of a tone. For a Thai, when speaking, Noy and Noy were two completely different words. But as I had to write this down I anticipated problems. So I decided to call them Noy and Mamanoy to make everything easier. They had taken to spending every meal time with us in the cluttered kitchen. There were restaurants of a sort a mere ten-minute drive away in Pak Nam, our nearest town, but they never went anywhere. Their car was already caked in salt and had taken a coconut hit on the back bumper. Between meals they hardly left their room.

Our mealtime conversations were all of the tell-us-about-life-on-the-Gulf variety. They were so focused on asking questions and pretending to be fascinated by our answers that they left no gaps for us to talk about them. The few comments they made about themselves were so obviously untrue that only Arny believed them. Noy, having learned that Arny was attached to another woman, became at ease in his company. His fiancée, Gaew, was off in Hong Kong on the seniors bodybuilding tour. She was in good shape for a fifty-eight-year-old, but I wouldn't ever want to see her in a bikini. Muscles on old people started to look like oil-saturated barnacles. Noy's questions to Arny — training, competition, steroids, fan adoration — all seemed sincere. I wondered whether she might have been developing a crush on him. He was a sweet man. Couldn't blame her. And she was closer to my brother's age. A more natural match. I quite liked her, despite the fact that she was a lying little calf. I liked the cow too. The fact that they were on the run made them even more fascinating to me.

"You poor thing," said Mair to Mamanoy. "You must be missing sex terribly."

Mamanoy's spoon clunked onto her plate.

"What?" she said.

"Sex," Mair repeated loudly, as if it was the volume at fault rather than appropriateness.

I looked at Arny. His eyes were closed. We knew Mair was about to launch into one of her bawdy tales from the annals of her long, fascinating life. Sometimes we'd shut her up. Other times we'd ride it out. On this evening I decided a story from Mair would help convince our guests we were all mad and therefore posed no threat.

"I don't —" Mamanoy began.

"You don't have to tell me," said Mair. "When you're away from your man, that's all you think of. Sex, sex, sex."

Grandad Jah looked up and attempted a half-hearted chastisement.

"Girl," he said. "Don't."

But he didn't put a lot of menace into it because he knew our mother wouldn't take any notice of him. Unfettered, Mair burst into her story.

"My husband had been away on a business trip," she said. "At least that's what he called it."

OK. Good. A rare anecdote about our father. We knew so little about him she was guaranteed the undivided attention of her children. To us, our father was a fictional character we only got to meet in stories.

"I was desperate for him," she said. "Two weeks without his strong arms around me. Two weeks without the taste of his tongue. Two weeks without —"

"Mair!" Arny shouted and pointed his fork and his eyebrows toward Noy. I personally doubted the girl was a stranger to strong arms and tasty tongues and the rest. Mair forged ahead with barely a pause. She was there in the past, seeing it all.

"We'd been married for two years," she said. "But I'd never let him believe I was just there for the taking. The only way to fire a man's passion is to make him understand you aren't the house bicycle. He couldn't just climb on and go for a ride around the block whenever the mood took him. There had to be a flat tire now and then. Sometimes the saddle would come loose and you wouldn't have the right size spanner to straighten it. A twig might get stuck in the gears."

I forgot to mention our Mair had a habit of getting tangled up in her own metaphors.

"Men need motivation to perform," she said. "And there's nothing like rejection to make a man try his best. If you beg, he hands out loving like alms to a tired old monk who needs a shave. But if you show no interest, ho ho, his pride pushes him onward and upward. So he was away for two weeks and I was desperate, so I hacked off my beautiful long hair with scissors and I dressed all in white, and when he walked in the door, I was sitting cross-legged on the floor reciting the Precepts. Actually I'd never memorized the Precepts. I was just making it up. But he wouldn't have known that. He wasn't that . . . you know, connected to the Lord. He asked me what had happened, and I told him I'd become a nun and I couldn't have contact with a man for three months. By dinnertime he was drooling like an octopus. And that night, once I'd rescinded my vows, I had the best hammering I'd ever experienced in my life."

"Mair," I said. "I really don't think this is relevant."

"Really?" She smiled as if remembering the intimacy of that night. "I think it's relevant. If it hadn't been for that homecoming present, you wouldn't be sitting here at this table."

"Why wouldn't . . . ? Oh, my God. You aren't . . . ?"

"Nine months later my little angel of heaven arrived in the world. The child conceived of passion. That's why you have so much fire in you, daughter."

"Fire? I was the result of you impersonating a nun. I'll go to hell."

"Don't be silly, child. We were husband and wife. Couples often resort to role-playing."

The revelation was too much. As if I wasn't already messed up, now I had to analyze how religio-erotic blackmail might have affected me. I looked across the table where Noy and Mamanoy were sitting open-mouthed like catfish on ice at Tesco. And that was when Mair dropped in her non-sequitur of "Would anybody like some mixed-friends ice cream?" Followed a few seconds later by the bang. At first I thought it was something exploding in my head, a brain overload perhaps, but everyone looked around, so I knew they'd heard it too. We all rushed outside. Always a good idea when someone's firing mortars at you. But I imagine, like me, they assumed it was the electricity distribution box, which blew up often. Instead, we saw gray smoke coming out of Mair's shop and being immediately dispatched on the wind.

Grandad Jah and Arny made the women-folk stand back 'cause we were all so fragile and needed protection. They walked into the shop through the smoke, and Arny grabbed the nice red fire extinguisher that had stood beside the door unnoticed for a year. He was trying to figure out how to follow the Chinese instructions to make it foam.

"Arny, don't bother," I said, pushing past him. "There's no fire."

A blast of some type had sent cans and packages flying to the back wall and ripped apart two shelf units. Ground zero was our refrigerator, which now looked like a paper lantern after a wind-tunnel experiment. Something mighty powerful had torn that up. The shop was open-fronted with a pull-down metal shutter. We had moved to an area where people tended not to lock their doors, so we'd got into the habit of leaving the shutter open while we were eating. If some rare customer should happen by, he or she could alert us by beating a stick on the zinc watering can suspended from the rafter or just leave the money on the counter. It was that kind of place. All this by way of explaining that the shop was wide open and anyone could have tossed in an explosive without even slowing down their car . . . or their black SUV.

In a place like Maprao you didn't have to wait for the evening broadcast on public radio. News spread like urine in a public swimming pool. First on the scene, as ever, was Captain Kow. I swear he has some sort of radar antenna inside that dirty gray baseball cap he never takes off. Then there was Jiep, the rice porridge lady, and Chat from the used-bicycle dealership, and Loong, the coconut pulp grinder, and Ari, the monkey handler, without his monkey, and Auntie Sakorn and her fourteen-year-old pregnant niece. Very soon the entire village was standing around staring at our bombed-out shop. Someone with a sidecar on their motorcycle had kindly given Constable Tawee a lift. The volunteer village constables were semi-serious police whose main function was to fine locals for betting on card games. Hardly a day went by when some group of fishermen's wives wasn't betting away their husbands' income. As he rarely left the police box, I imagine Tawee had to rely on gamblers with guilty consciences turning themselves in. He wasn't qualified to do any investigating, but he did have a cell phone and I was sure he'd called the real police. "Real" being relative, in our case.

This presented two problems for us. I called Grandad Jah to one side.

"The gun?"

"What about it?"

"You have to get rid of it."

"I do not."

"You know who did this, don't you?"

"Yes."

"If we accuse them, the gun story comes out. It'll be our word against theirs. We all saw them pull their knives, but if they find the gun . . ."

"They won't."

I glared at him.

"They won't," he repeated.

The only competent officer at the local police station was Lieutenant Chompu, and he was warm and snug in my pouch. He'd be no problem. Whoever else they sent to investigate our explosion would merely ask the questions as they were laid out in the regulation manual. All I needed to do was get to the witnesses and make sure we all told the same lies. Arny was our weakest link. They wouldn't need interview room violence to break him down. If they raised their voices, he'd confess — even if he

101

wasn't responsible. I found him squeezing pilchard cans back into shape and reminded him he was interfering with a crime scene. He pouted. I grabbed his thick arm and led him outside.

"Arny," I said. "Grandad Jah didn't shoot at the body snatchers."

"He didn't?"

"No."

"You know I'm not very good at this?" he said.

"I know. But this is family, and I need us all to stick together with this one. Do you really want to see Grandad locked up in chains in the Lang Suan prison, the hand-cuffs chafing his old flaky wrists? His body riddled with rat- and flea-bites from the communal bedding? Abused in the shower room by perverts with fetishes for . . . skinny and ignorant old men?"

He thought about it.

"No," he said at last.

"Then you didn't see him shoot at the body snatchers."

"OK."

And I knew I was pushing my luck, but I needed one more small lie from him. This one was for me.

"And Noy and Mamanoy? They don't exist."

"They don't?"

"Not at all. We weren't having lunch with them today. We still don't have any guests. In fact, if you moved our truck over, I bet we could squeeze their car under our carport too. Put one of those silver gray plastic covers on it and nobody would even notice it was there."

My little brother looked uncomfortable. He lowered his voice.

"There's something suspicious about them, isn't there?" he said.

"Yes. But if Pak Nam's finest come by in force, it might just frighten them away and we'll never find out what the Noys have been up to. It wouldn't surprise me if they were in their room packing as we speak. And what ever mess they've got themselves tied up in will only get worse if they flee past the entire population of Maprao in their unregistered car."

"I should tell them not to panic."

"Good boy. Tell them to go for a blustery stroll along the garbage-strewn beach, like good tourists, and not to come back till the excitement's died down. Tell them . . . I don't know. Tell them we don't want to lose our only paying guests of the month. Don't, and that means, *do not* tell them we think they're suspicious."

The last witness tampering I'd have time for was Mair. I knew everything would depend on who or where or when she was at that particular moment, but it turned out she was way ahead of me . . . or somebody.

"Sissi, darling," she said. "You know I've never condoned dishonesty in any of my five children."

"Yes, Mair."

"But this is a family matter. It's my father's life."

"I didn't see him fire a gun," I said.

"What? But you were standing right there."

"No, I mean, wink wink I didn't see him fire it."

"Oh. That's right. You didn't. It was a tern."

"What was?"

"A tern, disoriented by the northeasterly wind, was thrown into the side window of the big black car, which caused the glass to smash. It had been flying so fast it might have been mistaken for a bullet. A tern flying at high speed makes a similar sound to .41 caliber gunfire."

"Either that or we don't know anything about a broken car window."

She gave that a lot of thought.

"Yes," she said. "That might work too. If

it happened, which I doubt it did, it didn't happen here. Good. Then there's the situation with the older and younger Noys."

"I've never heard of them."

"Is that a wink wink?"

There were eleven police officers permanently attached to the Pak Nam station. Nine of them came to investigate our explosion. Life could be dull for crime fighters down here. The charge was led by Major Mana, who had obviously been having a slack day in his Amway direct-sales dealership — which afforded him the time to investigate a crime at last. Alighting from the truck with him were constables Ma Yai and Ma Lek and a skinny officer with a Nikon, all of whom I was acquainted with. Then came the fat fellow with the cheap toupee, with whom I was not but felt I needed to be.

Right behind the truck were two motorcycles carrying two uniformed officers apiece. The only one I recognized was Lieutenant Chompu. He was riding pillion with his arms locked around the good-looking young driver.

"Little Jimm," said Major Mana for everyone to hear. He was middle-aged, shiny brown and short. Yes, I'd once rejected his clumsy attempts to seduce me, but I'd also made a name for him on a case a few months before. He owed me a favor. But he had a short memory and wandering hands. "You know? Ours was a very peaceful little district before you and your family turned up here."

His hand was already kneading the small of my back.

"Right," I said. "And look. Here we are blowing up our own shop just to mess with your statistics."

"I'll be the judge of that," he said, the sarcasm sliding past him like an oiled eel.

They set to work, although most of them seemed to have been assigned gawking duty. Chompu was chief interviewer. We sat together on my porch. He led with:

"Nice one, Jimm."

"I know who did it," I told him.

"Well, hooray. That makes our jobs just that much easier. Who?"

"A couple of goons from the SRM. They came to pick up the head nobody's investigating."

"And why would they want to damage your shop?"

"They were rude cretins with knives. They threatened us."

"And did you make a complaint to the

106

police about that threat?"

I laughed, then he laughed. Reporting a threat to the Pak Nam police would have been like reporting a mosquito bite to the provincial health authority.

"We chased them off, so I imagine their noses were put out of joint."

"How?"

"How what?"

"How did you chase them off?"

"Well, there was me, Arny, Grandad Jah, and Mair. We outnumbered them."

"A fearsome foursome indeed. I'm surprised they haven't already brought out a comic book about you all."

"Don't make fun. We can be pretty frightening. Look at Arny."

"Ooh, I have."

"Right. If you didn't know he was a hamster . . ."

And talking of animals, out of the corner of my eye I saw Sticky carrying something large and dirty in his mouth. He was heading toward the crime scene. I had a bad feeling about it. I called out to him, but he didn't exactly know his name yet.

"Give me a minute," I said to Chompu. "Go interview Mair."

I went after the dog, who looked back over his shoulder and started to run. Running for me was as alien as discipline was to him. But I felt there was a need. I swore I could make out the shape of a handgun wrapped in rag. Sticky was heading straight for the major. He stopped directly in front of him, dropped his booty, and barked proudly. The policeman turned around to find Sticky staring up at him and drooling. Like most southerners, the major was wary of strange dogs. He backed up. Sticky nudged the package closer.

"Will someone call this mutt off?" said the policeman.

"Looks like he brought you a present, Major," said Constable Ma Yai. "Hey, little fellow. What you got there?"

He bent down to pick up the package, and Sticky snapped at him. Ma Yai recoiled. I arrived at that moment. There's something slow-motion about me running. I threw myself to my knees and grabbed the gun and the dog. Over the sound of Sticky yapping, the major asked:

"What is that?"

"Hairdryer," I said. "It's a game we play."

I laughed. They laughed. Sticky barked. It was pretty clear the dog had been Eliot Ness in a previous life. It probably really pissed him off that he couldn't make words anymore.

■ ■ ■ ■

"You buried it?"

"Yes."

"That was your grand idea for hiding the gun?"

The police had gone, and I had Grandad Jah cornered in the toilet block. He'd been unclogging a drain. It was a good feeling to be reprimanding him for screwing up. I didn't get the chance that often. He nodded. His overconfidence had given way to humility at last. All at once he was forty-five kilograms of decaying osteoclasts, and I felt like a bully.

"Well, consider yourself lucky our local police force can't tell a magnum from a hairdryer," I said. "I bet they raid a lot of beauty salons."

"Idiots."

I knew it was too much to expect an apology from the old man. I sat on the sink and heard a crack. Time to think seriously about that diet. With the monsoons, I'd stopped cycling, and every meal, every flagon of Chilean red, every mini–Mars Bar was setting up home in my hips.

"So where do you think it'll go from here?" I asked.

"The police will bring the two hoodlums in for questioning. They'll deny they threatened us. They might or might not mention the gun, but my guess is they won't."

"Why not?"

"Because we don't look like gunslingers, so the police would laugh at 'em. And they don't have any evidence."

"Thanks to me."

He ignored that.

"They'll probably come up with an alibi," he said, "and technically the police would check it out. But knowing our lot, they'll probably accept it and apologize to the hooligans for taking up their valuable time."

"Not Chompu."

"I admit the queer boy does have skills. But we don't know they'll assign him to the case."

"They don't have cases, Grandad. What else has happened down here for the past couple of months? They weed the station flowerbeds, use up their petrol allowance by driving round smiling at girls, and set up random barricades to extort money from truck drivers who think seat belts are for sitting on. Oh, and they practice marching. They have to assign it to Chompu. He's the only one who can spell."

"These police don't know how to deal

with hard nuts like those two thugs. There's only one recourse," Grandad snarled.

He cracked his knuckles. It sounded like tiles shuffling on a mah-jong board.

"Oh, Grandad. No."

"There's only one thing those types understand."

"Please."

"Street justice."

I'd been afraid that might happen. Our own geriatric Judge Dredd had recently formed an alliance with an equally honest and subsequently vilified ex-policeman from the south called Waew. Together, they had wreaked revenge on an evil-doer and got away with it. Vengeance was a drug that made Viagra look like aspirin. I suppose I should have reasoned with him, told him how dangerous it was to be messing with villains like the rat brothers, but Grandad's well past his use-by date. When you're beyond seventy, nobody's really surprised when they find you facedown in your fried rice. Probably better to arrive in nirvana with a slit throat and stories.

"Whatever," I said.

I was about to take the truck into Pak Nam in search of the elusive Burmese community that Lieutenant Egg had failed to engage.

I'd reversed out of the carport and was crunching my way into first. It's an old truck. But in my side mirror I saw an excitedly pretty face. I squeaked down the window and said hello to Noy.

"The coast is clear," I said.

Mother and daughter had been hiding out in the woods at the far end of the bay for an hour for no particular reason. None of the police asked whether we had any guests.

"Jimm, I just wanted . . . to tell you . . ."

She was out of breath. The wind did that to you. Filled you up with so much air you couldn't get it all out. I'd been expecting a story. They'd had enough time to come up with a good one. I'd thought something like . . . I don't know . . . vengeful husband or boyfriend perhaps. That would have worked. Ours was a matriarchal family, so that would probably have twanged at our heartstrings. But what they conjured up was a disappointment. Noy ran round the front of the truck and put herself in the passenger seat. She was trapped now. There were no handles on the inside.

"I hope you don't mind," she said.

"Not at all."

I switched off the motor, and the truck shimmered to a standstill.

"I imagine that you and your family are

wondering what people like us are doing here," she said.

"You're not on vacation?"

She giggled.

"I'm sure you didn't believe that," she said.

"If our prime minister can make spring rolls on national television, nothing would surprise me."

"The fact is . . ." she began.

I've noticed how often people say "the fact is" before launching into fiction.

"The fact is my father is one of the leading activists against the yellow shirts. You do know about the situation in Bangkok?"

I guessed nobody had informed her that I'd been an almost prize-winning journalist at a national publication. An army was rising up to oppose the yellow shirts, with the backing of the satellite-dish tsar and his billionaire family.

"I think I saw something about it on TV," I said.

"Well, he . . . Dad was very vocal against the yellows. We tried to convince him to keep a lid on it, but he's a very principled man. He spoke up in public accusing the yellow shirts of dragging our democracy into the dirt. He . . ."

"Yes?"

113

"He received threats. Not against him but against us. His family. They said they'd kill us."

"The yellow shirts said that?"

"Right. As he loves us, and I'm sure you understand why I can't divulge his name, he sent us away from Bangkok. That's why we're here. That's why we removed the number plates. That's why we're avoiding the police. I'm so sorry we couldn't tell you this. But we still have to be very careful. The yellow shirts can be evil."

"Right."

I could imagine the scene. Auntie Malee, the exporter of traditional coconut cakes, calls together Bert, the brake lining supplier, and Lulu, the barista, and orders a hit on Noy whose father had dared voice what half the country had been complaining about publicly ever since the yellows sauntered into Government House. So the Noys flee. And they head in exactly the wrong direction, south, yellow-shirt central. Come off it, girl.

"You must be terrified," I said and put my hand on hers.

"We are," she said, looking at a string of beach cabbage that had blown over from the sand and wrapped itself around our wipers. "But when you told us the police were coming, we sensed that you could feel our anguish. We decided we could trust you and wanted you to know the truth."

"Well, I appreciate honesty. We all do."

"We just wanted you to understand that we've done nothing wrong. Nothing illegal. We are victims."

"I feel for you, my sister."

She took back her hand and placed her palms together. She folded herself low to my left kidney like a scullery maid addressing a royal in a very confined space. She smiled and tried to leave the truck, only to realize there were no handles. I ran round to let her out and watched her walk off toward her cabin. It had been a performance worthy of a raspberry. But one thing was certain. These two were no grifters. They couldn't act their way out of a prawn cracker packet. It was time to see what dirt Sissi had come up with. The Noys had done something bad. Very, very bad. I wanted to know what it was.

5.

ALL MY JEANS ARE FILLED

(from "Love Me Tender" — ELVIS PRESLEY)

It's hard to describe our nearest town, just as it's hard to call it a town and keep a straight face. Think of any crossroads you know, then squeeze it to a point where two cars can barely pass one another without slapping wing mirrors. Remove traffic lights and stop signs from your thoughts. Add the chaos of handcarts and sidecars and people walking in the street because the pavement has cars parked on it. Then imagine you're standing in the middle of the cross. North you'd see a few cramped wooden shops selling nothing anyone would ever need. Likewise to the south. Dead end to the southeast where the road terminates at the river. Too bad if you're new to the district and travel in that direction at any speed. The Pak Nam Champs Elysées, route 4002, heads west. It's there you can find the 7-Eleven, the post office, the bank, the market, the district office, and the best darned lady finger banana seller in the country. You cannot, however, find decent cappuccino, pizza, wine, cheese, ice cream, black forest cake, or cherries — all those things that make a civilized society. This was truly a hardship posting for a girl who grew up in a multicultural metropolis.

I pulled up in front of the old ice factory at the docks. The sound of ice being crushed resounded like strikes at a bowling alley. I'd had to ask directions. The factory was in a cleverly concealed turn-off before the cul-de-sac. When you were driving into town, you could see the harbor from the road bridge. It made a good photograph. The sun glinting off the water as the triumphant fishing vessels returned with their catch. A few tourists stopped there. That and the concrete battleship were our only photogenic spots. But being down here was different altogether. The hastily put together hovels all around me spoke of poverty and disorder and neglect. Temporary accommodation for temporary people. Clunky wooden fishing boats gathered around the concrete piers, two or three abreast, like polite pigs at a feeding trough. On the jetties, people worked. I don't mean they went through the motions with one eye on the overtime clock. I mean they toiled. They sliced and gutted and bagged and hauled and lugged. There was a different pace to life. An urgency. It was a bit eerie really.

I stepped out onto the dirt parking lot. There were people all around, but nobody stared. Nobody so much as turned their head. All right, I know I'm no head-turner, but there's this world standard of inquisitiveness, isn't there? "Who is this broad-hipped, short-haired stranger?" "What does she want with us?" Down here at the docks, nobody cared. I looked at my hand to see whether I'd become invisible on the drive over.

There was music playing. Women joking. Men shouting. And I understood not one word. And all at once I knew how Dorothy felt. I wasn't in Thailand anymore. The Toyota Mighty X had come down in the land of the Munchkins. I was only five minutes' jaywalk from the town post office, postcode 86150, but I was completely in the wrong country. Nobody had been able to tell me exactly how many Burmese there were around Pak Nam as the majority weren't registered. But I'd certainly found myself in a hub. I needed a guide. Chompu had given me a name. He said I should ask at the open-air ice works for Aung.

I walked up to a big-boned woman whose face was caked in yellow-brown paste. I'd seen it a lot, but I'd never actually understood the concept. You splatter the gunk all over yourself as protection from the sun. The sun, as we all know, ages us prematurely and makes us unattractive and therefore unmarriageable. But I doubted that the effects of that nasty old sun would have been noticed much before our thirtieth birthday. And by then we should have been wed. After twenty-two, the odds started to stack up against us. So why, I ask, would you want to spend your most alluring years plastered in a vomit-colored death mask? It's like those poor Muslim girls who have to squeeze all their sexuality into a two-by-eight-centimeter eye-letterbox slot of opportunity. I'd tried that "if you're a nice person, men will find you attractive" routine, and I'm afraid it gives men far too much credit. They want something to show their mates. You have to have at least one selling point. I have my lips, which Mair often reminds me are sensual. The Burmese throwing huge blocks of ice in a crusher had breasts. They drew attention from her face. I know it's a little catty of me to say this, but perhaps, in her case, the powder mask did her a favor.

"Excuse me," I said. "I'm looking for Mr. Aung."

She didn't so much as look up. I rechecked my invisibility. I was there.

"Mr. Aung?" I said.

I didn't want to be ignored again, so I put my hand on the next ice block on the conveyor. I tried for eye contact. She shrugged and looked away.

"Do you speak Thai?" I asked. The ice blocks were jamming up behind me and my hand was getting an ice ache, but I wasn't about to give in.

"Do . . . you . . . ?"

"No speak," she said.

Good. Contact.

"Mr. . . . Aung."

She pointed toward the nearest dock.

"Two . . . one . . . seven . . . one," I think was what she said.

"Two one seven one?"

She nodded. I thanked her and tried to leave, but my hand was stuck to the ice block. I may have screamed a little. Meeting Mr. Aung with a chunk of ice clutched to my chest would have made a bad first impression. Obviously I wasn't the first person to stick myself to a giant ice-cube because she had a plastic bottle of lukewarm water beside her that she sprinkled on my hand, and like magic, I was released.

I presumed 2171 was the number of a boat. They each had four digits in white paint at the front. The front of the boat is either the bow or the galley. I never did remember boating vocabulary. I knew you had to pass an oncoming ship to the starboard, but I didn't know whether that was left or right. Fortunately, I'd never have to learn it because I had no intention of being on the sea in any kind of vessel whatsoever. At high school I sat out swimming lessons because Mair had knitted me a swimsuit. I kid you not. Hand knitted. It was like a suit of armor. If I'd so much as stepped in the water, I'd have sunk like a rock. I did eventually learn to swim, but that had led to a number of other traumatic experiences in water. So I gave it up, and as a non-swimmer I fully intended to be a non-boat passenger.

I asked the nearest Burmese if there were any Thais around. He said yes, then walked off. At the same high school where I didn't learn to swim, I also didn't learn to speak Burmese. They had a very small part-time elective course. Instead, I went on to intensive English, memorized hundreds of pop songs, joined a student exchange to Australia, watched a lifetime of American movies, and fell in love with Clint Eastwood. And what good did that do me? Here in Maprao, even my Thai was a mystery. Southern Thai dialect was like listening to sausages popping on a grill, and now I learned there are more people here speaking Burmese than standard Thai. I was a minority.

"Can I help you?" came a voice.

I turned to see a dark-skinned man in shorts. Only shorts. His torso was decorated with grease smears, but that was a body without a gram of fat. A worker's body. On top of it was an untidy head; hair sheared and uncombed, a wispy haphazard beard, a recent scar dividing his left shoulder in two. But, my word, he was adorable. His smile went straight to my womb.

"I'm Aung," he said.

He put down his spanner and *wai*'d me. I *wai*'d him back.

I said, *"Ming ga la ba,"* the only Burmese I knew. I hoped it meant good day. He probably didn't even know I was speaking Burmese because he continued in Thai.

"How can I help you?"

"Your Thai is very good."

We said that to Westerners all the time, but we didn't really mean it. We didn't really expect that much from the wealthy whities. But we tended not to compliment menial day laborers from neighboring countries, even if they were fluent. But Aung was fluent and gorgeous.

"I've been here twenty-four years," he said, and smiled again. "I must have picked it up."

I'd obviously reached that hormonal juncture in my life when every second man I met was a sex object. Aung conjured up feelings in me I hadn't felt since university. I wished he'd put on a shirt so I didn't have to stare at his pectorals. But he continued to stand there, sweating wonderfully.

"I . . . I . . ." I said.

"Yes?" He smiled.

"I'm a journalist. I was hoping I could interview you about the problems the Burmese community faces in Pak Nam."

"No problem," he said, which surprised me for some reason.

"Really? When would be a convenient time?"

"I work till seven," he said. "Any time after that is fine."

"Would tonight be too soon?"

"No."

"Sissi, he's so . . ."

"Yes?"

"So natural."

"Jimm, we're all buds of Mother Earth."

"No, we're not. We start off natural, then we're tutored in the arts of pretense and deception."

There was a pause, and I wondered whether we'd been cut off.

"That comment wouldn't be directed at me, by any chance?"

Damn. Why was everything about her?

"Shut up, Siss. No. It's him. He's raw. If he'd hit me over the head with his spanner and dragged me off to his cave, I wouldn't have made a whimper."

"OK. So you've got the hots for a Burmese. Welcome to the bottom of the barrel. I'm happy for you."

I wondered when the Burmese stopped being equals. Everyone hated them. It was as if you got yourself a shitty junta government and it was a reflection on the whole population.

"I'm going to marry him," I said, just to be cantankerous.

"Yeah, right. So do you want information about your Honda City, or do I have to listen to tales of migrant lust all night?"

"You already found something?"

"It's not that hard."

"What do you know?"

"The car was registered in the name of

Anand Panyurachai. I looked him up. They're not an online family at all. No Facebook, no Twitter, not even e-mail accounts, as far as I could ascertain. That's really odd for a young girl in the dot com age. So I had to go down the slow track. The prehistoric route. National records. A program put together by orangutans. I started with the census and found where they live, and I worked outward from there. There's a program that allows me to align and cross-reference the —"

"Sissi, I've got to meet my Burmese in ten minutes. Can we just cut to the chase?" I'd always wanted to say that.

"All right already. I just wanted you to appreciate how much love I put into this assignment."

"I appreciate it."

"Father, Anand. Owns a small engineering company. Some gambling problems. Rumors they were living beyond their means. He seems to have sorted that out. No outstanding debts. Mother, Punnika. Middle school principal."

"Any political connections?"

"He's a registered democrat. He's helped with campaigning. Nothing fanatical. Couldn't find anything for the wife."

"And the daughter?"

"Right. Now here's where cross-references went bananas. Once I put in her name, I was bombarded. Daughter, Thanawan. Twenty-four. Nickname, Bpook. Number two in the nation in 2003 in high school mathematics. Number fourteen nationally in chemistry. Top fifteen percent in English, History, Thai language, Physics and Geography. Girl's a genius."

Who'd have thought it?

"Didn't you have to be overweight and dowdy to excel in high school?" I asked.

"She won a scholarship in 2004 to study in the U.S. Georgetown. Washington, D.C. And in the sciences, no less: they have very high standards."

"And she got through the course?"

"Barely."

"What?"

"It's really odd. She squeezed through on Cs and Ds. It was as if they were carrying her for four years. Every year the faculty had to get together to decide whether to kick her out. She was the class dunce. Some of her professors tried to convince her to save her money and go home. They were certain she'd bomb her finals."

"And did she?"

"Straight As. A-plus in four subjects. A-minus the lowest. Top scorer for the year for that program. It pumped her GPA up to somewhere approaching respectable."

"How?"

"That's what the faculty wanted to know. Clueless for four years, then a sudden spurt. The university didn't like it. They convened the Honor Council and interviewed our girl. They hired a private detective to investigate."

"Wasn't that a bit excessive?"

"They had a reputation to maintain. They take academic dishonesty very seriously. They were sure she'd cheated, but they needed to prove it. She was interrogated. There may have even been a lie-detector test at one stage. I accessed the personal files of the detective. In the end they decided to give her an oral test in the subjects she'd excelled in. A sort of resit of the examinations and thesis topic, but with a committee asking the questions. They checked for bugs and transmission devices and put her in a soundproof studio and bombarded her for three hours."

"And?"

"Got 'em all right. Nobody could understand it. Given her high school results, they had to assume she'd been suffering from some mental disorder for four years and then suddenly got over it. But whatever the reason, she's kept her mouth shut. At the end of it, they had no choice but to give her a degree."

"Happy ending."

"But . . ."

"What?"

"She didn't turn up to receive her diploma. Vanished. No record of her leaving the country."

"Obviously she did. She's here."

"From Washington to Pak Nam Lang Suan. Every young girl's dream. But just to make sure it really is her I'll send you a photo to your phone. It was from her school yearbook."

"I get a strong feeling we're missing some vital information."

"And I'm afraid the Internet can't fill in that gap. The last I have for her is the university newsletter listing the students who didn't collect their diplomas, and a modest little hacking of the central airline registry that told me she wasn't on the passenger manifesto of any flights out of the country. Right now, she only exists in your resort. The trail has gone cold. But I can tell you that both her mother and father resigned unexpectedly from their jobs."

"How do you know that?"

"A cunning little invention called the

telephone. I called their places of employment. Nobody has any idea where they are."

"So Dad vanished too? Damn. I wonder where he went?"

"Have you checked the boot of the car?"

"Yes. Grandad went through it. It's empty. No bloodstains."

"This is a darned fine mystery, Jimm. Too bad I won't be around to solve it for you. On Thursday the good ship Sissi will be setting sail for foreign shores."

"Good. So I have two more days of free research assistant."

I met Aung under a lamppost beside the District Electricity Authority building. He'd said he couldn't give me an address because his domicile didn't have one. He'd have to guide me there in person. He was standing back in the shadows when I drove up, and he stepped into the light like a dishy cabaret singer. Unfortunately, he was now dressed, but his hair was just as unruly as earlier. A feral beast. My insides felt like a newly opened soda bottle. I was wearing a dress with a pattern that trivialized my bottom but positively yelled out how nice my legs were. My shoes had half-heels, just enough to take me up to his height. My sensual lips were within smooching distance.

He smiled and I wanted to throw him up against the Electrical Authority sign. But he was too fast for me. He headed off along the main street. Eight P.M. and not a car in sight. Pleasure city. After passing the council hall, he ducked down an alleyway, and I followed him into a labyrinth of little dwellings. The belly of Pak Nam. We passed poky concrete row houses with the doors open so anyone could look in to see families watching TV, small fat people sitting cross-legged on the floor drinking beer, teenagers patching motorcycle tires. Then down tighter and darker paths, where a girl could never feel safe. Where at any moment a rough man might turn around and throw his arms around her.

But he rounded one final corner and stood bathed in a moody yellow light from another open doorway. He smiled and kicked off his shoes. I joined him on the front step, and a little girl of about two came at me from out of nowhere and lifted the hem of my dress above her head. I have to say it was fortunate I was wearing underwear because there were a dozen people in the room looking in my direction. They all seemed to think my indecent exposure was funny, or perhaps, like the Thais, Burmese used laughter to camouflage embarrassment. I wanted to punch the little girl in the nose but was aware that this would be an inopportune moment to do so. I'd get her later. I unfastened my shoes, and Aung introduced me to various members of the Burmese community who had turned up in honor of my visit. Then I met Aung's pretty wife, Oh, and their five children.

"Have you eaten yet?" Oh asked me. Her Thai was just as Thai as that of her husband. I wasn't sure of the etiquette. Should I say yes or no? I tried no. It was a winner. The women retreated joyfully to the back area, which I assumed housed a kitchen. There were only two rooms, divided by a wall that didn't make it all the way up to the ceiling. It was a minimalist terraced garage of a place. The walls were painted with watered-down pink undercoat, and the electrical wiring was all visible. There was a large poster of Aung San Suu Kyi and a smaller one of our own royal family on a skiing holiday. The floor was tiled with non-matching squares, and there was a stack of bedding, presumably for seven, in one corner.

I heard a gas range pop and the clatter of pots and dishes.

"I invited some members of our community committee," said Aung. The men were all still with us, and they were folding themselves down into a circle on the floor. In jeans or shorts I'm fine with sitting on the ground. But I was wearing a dress. I felt stupid. But what the hell? They'd already seen my Macro Huggy Rabbit bikini briefs.

"That's good," I said and negotiated a position that was demure but totally uncomfortable. Another half hour and I'd be paralyzed, and they'd have to carry me out to the truck.

If you didn't count the disappointment, it was a splendid evening. I was pleased that I could still enjoy myself without alcohol. Aung and Oh seemed comfortable together. They somehow made you feel that living in a sub-divided brick dog kennel was the answer to a dream. After a while I'd learned to ignore the TV channel-hopping from the next room, the even louder Mo Lum country music tape from the place behind, the howling dogs, the screaming babies, the drunken arguments. I felt like an anthropologist doing research on twenty-first-century slum culture. But like I said, it was a good night. The committee members were all interesting and smart, and we talked and laughed a lot. All the while I took notes.

There were some 5,400 Burmese in and around Pak Nam. Half of them were here officially. This meant they had sponsors and

ID cards. The rest paid fines to the police whenever they were rounded up and gave their cell phones or any jewelry they were foolish enough to be wearing. As part of the conditions for their employment, the Burmese were not supposed to have cell phones. They couldn't own or drive motorized vehicles. The legal Burmese had access to the thirty-*baht* health care services, but the kids weren't accepted at local schools. Legally the schools were obliged to take them, but in reality they had nowhere to put them and no teachers to teach them. So they ignored the law.

I had so much interesting data I even considered actually doing a story on it. But what Thai publication would give a monkey's about the harsh living conditions of the Burmese? Nobody would read it. And it wasn't even big enough for the world press. These people had told me about humiliation, degradation, corruption, and racial prejudice. But what the world wanted was violence on a huge scale. To get into *Newsweek* these days, you needed celebrity break-ups or genocide. But now I had my chance. The younger kids were asleep on the tiles, and I decided to tell everyone about my head. I described the discovery, the collection, and the refrigeration of my uncle what's-his-name. During the telling, passed on through the buzz of translation from Aung and Oh, I noticed some disquiet in the ranks. There were glances. Looks of guilt. I'd obviously trespassed on some hallowed ground. But at the end of my story nobody had a comment to make. I didn't even get the obvious question, "Why did the police and collection crew automatically assume the head was from a Burmese?" The hair, the skin color, the earring — they all pointed to a Burmese fisherman but didn't eliminate a Thai. Or was I missing something?

"Have you heard of other Burmese bodies or parts thereof being washed up on the beach?" I asked.

Again the stares. Again the feeling I'd overstepped the mark. The shaking of heads. One man, Shwe something, long-haired, mustachioed like a seventies folksinger, looked me straight in the eye and spoke . . . Burmese. His wife tried to interrupt, but he ignored her. The other men shouted. But he continued to speak to me and nobody translated. I watched it like a bemused viewer at her first Australian Rules football game. No idea what was going on. At last they all stopped, and all I could hear was a cacophony of slum life around us. Our room was quiet.

"What happened?" I asked.

"Nothing," said Aung.

"That was a long noisy nothing, Aung."

He gave me a smile, but there was nothing erotic about it this time.

"Just a small domestic disagreement between husband and wife. She thought he was flirting with you. It happens."

"Not to me," I thought. My research was finished for the night, but I was getting tired of being lied to. What I needed was to get Shwe alone. We'd see how his wife liked *that* basket of mackerel.

6.
It's Been a Hard Day's Night, I Should Be Sleeping on Kellogg's

(from "A Hard Day's Night"
(LENNON/MCCARTNEY)

There's something you need to know about the monsoons. They come. And they blow. And they go. It's not like a Robert Louis Stevenson story, where the biting wind blows blood-numbing sleet off the ocean for three months at a time. The southern monsoon season is more like a security guard at a gold necklace shop. Day after day nothing happens. Then suddenly two masked robbers burst in, firing guns and banging the guard over the head. They scoop up the necklaces and they're gone. Then it all goes back to nothing again. I got that one from Mair, but it's one of my favorites.

When I got to bed that night, there was no wind at all and the surf was soothingly soft. The first monsoon had passed and we were back to nothing. That was too bad because I needed a distraction. I needed crashing waves to drown out my thoughts. My brain was trying to convince the rest of me that I was over the hill. That I would never again feel the strong arms of a lover around me. Never again have a man snore in my ear. That, like the salt virgins of Xanadu, my vagina would seal itself up and I would become a fossil. The antidepressants weren't working. Or perhaps they weren't strong enough to counter my mega-midlife crisis. I took another two, washed down with Chilean red, and lay my head on the pillow. I couldn't be bothered to clean my teeth again, so I knew they'd be mauve in the morning. I needed a man, desperately. I needed to be admired, wanted, complimented, desired . . . loved. How difficult could that be? Village head Bigman Beung desired me, as did Major Mana. So there were precedents. I wasn't totally repulsive. All I needed to do was transfer that desire to a man with skin rather than scales.

Since I am a Thai woman, my culture discourages me from making the first move. But my culture is eroding as fast as the Gulf coastline. And I am a Thai woman raised by a liberated, free-thinking hippy mother. Unlike most Thais, I never fit in with groups.

Relationships with my friends, whom I always felt were wary of my un-Thainess, evaporated on the last day of high school and then again the day after my university graduation. I had been encouraged to embrace the modern world and follow my instincts. Mair wouldn't have thought twice about being the aggressor when she was my age. Enough of being the tick on a blade of grass, hoping some hairy creature might brush past me. No, sir. Tomorrow I would go after my prey. It was a good plan and I felt confident. I might have even found sleep about then if it hadn't been for the head-board of my mother's bed banging against the wooden wall of her cabin.

I was in the new, barely used meeting room at the Pak Nam police station. They still hadn't removed the plastic wrapping from the chairs. It had taken me a while to get up to the second floor. I had been passed from man to man like a baton on my way up. Loitering was the activity of choice there. Officers old and new were leaning and sitting and standing at every corner, like statues in an ancient mansion. Nobody seemed to have a job. Those I knew, like Desk Sergeant Phoom, quickly introduced me to those I didn't, summarizing my entire life in twenty seconds and ending with the ubiquitous "She's single." But as they knew I was a reporter and therefore educated, "She's single" here was not intended as an invitation to date me, more a sorrowful postscript much in the vein of "She only has two months to live."

I was discreetly removing chair plastic with my nail scissors when Chompu threw open the door of the meeting room. He entered diva-like with the back of his hand on his forehead, slamming the door behind him. In order to get into the police force, Chompu had pretended to be straight at the interview, just as many other successful gay policemen had done before him. Some even married and produced children to compound the effect. But my Chompu had wanted to make a stand for camp. He believed that openly effeminate men had a role in the modern Thai police force and should not have to disguise what nature had given them. Consequently, he'd been transferred thirty-eight times in his career, and here he was at rock bottom. There was nowhere else to be transferred to. So Chompu could be himself and nobody really cared.

"Bad day at the office?" I asked. It was only nine A.M.

"They treat me like a dishrag," he said. "Honestly. I'm the only one actually working here, and nobody appreciates me. They've got their catfish ponds and their Five Star fried chicken concessions and their Amway — and who in their right mind would buy foundation cream from a man who plucks his nose hair in public, I ask you? — and actual policing is a troublesome diversion for most of them."

He plonked down in a padded chair I'd already liberated from plastic.

"Why didn't you want to meet in your office?" I asked.

"I don't have an office anymore. Not to myself, anyway. They put him in there — Egg, the fat man with the cat carcass on his head."

"What's he doing here?"

"Requested a transfer, they say. But pray tell me why anyone would ask to move here. He was in Pattani before."

"Well, excuse me, but that might just explain why he'd want to move here. Are you joking? Pattani? Muslims on motorcycles shooting harmless Buddhists. Buddhists on motorcycles shooting harmless Muslims. Pick off five of ours, and we'll pick off six of yours. Schools torched. Primary school teachers assassinated. It's the world center of cowards with weapons. Kill anyone as long as there's no danger of getting hurt yourself. It's the symbolism. They no longer value human life down there."

"Have you entirely finished?"

"Yes."

I hadn't really. There was so much I had to say about the deep south.

"Well, Señora Evita, if you'd been paying attention, you'd have noticed I didn't question his reason for leaving Pattani. I asked why he'd want to come here to Thailand's own Pyong Yang when there are so many better moves he could have made. I sneaked a look at his transfer papers. He specifically requested Pak Nam, but he has no family connections here."

"Has he got a girlfriend?"

"Do you have no shame?"

"I'm not applying. I was just . . ."

"I know. I'm just being catty. Sorry."

"You don't like him, do you?"

"Well, apart from the fact that his short-wave radio is on ALL the time, you know what he did? You remember those darling little button ferns I had on the desk? He emptied them out the second-floor window, dirt and all."

"No!"

"Can you believe it? He said if he wanted

to be in the jungle, he'd take a job with the border patrol. I'd nurtured those ferns. They were like children to me. Of course, they died immediately. They weren't used to the harsh world outside."

I took a tissue from my bag and handed it to him. I was just in time.

"He's a bully," I said.

Chompu nodded and wiped the tears from his eyes.

"I'm afraid of him," he said. "He talks so rudely to me. I daren't go in the office now."

"You've got a gun."

"You think I should?"

"Can't hurt. Most bullies are just friendless cowards. Nobody would miss him."

"Oh, but he has friends."

"How would you know?"

"Because according to the statement, he was having lunch with his buddies at eleven thirty yesterday."

"Were you doing surveillance on h—Wait! What statement?"

"The statement that was included in the investigation of your bombing. It was a hand grenade, by the way."

"Why would . . . ? Don't tell me he provided an alibi for the rat brothers?"

"They're off the hook."

"I could see they were friendly when he

came by our place the day they picked up the head. But why would he give them an —"

The door swung open, and Constable Mah Lek sauntered in with a tray of coffee cups and iced water.

"Sorry, folks," he said. "Had to wait for the water to boil. It's an old kettle. Sugar in the pot. Coconut cookies, but they're a bit old too."

He set his wares down on the table between us.

"Everything OK?" he asked.

"I'll recommend the service here to every criminal I know," I said.

He laughed and left us to it.

"Where were they supposedly having lunch?" I asked. "There'd have to be witnesses to corroborate it."

"Don't bother. They were at Egg's house. Just the three of them."

Convenient. Egg and the rats alone.

"He has a house?"

"On the way to the hospital."

"So he has other means. Like someone else I know."

"Don't lump me together with his type. My means are from a family heirloom."

"Accrued over hundreds of years of hon-

143

est dealings with the common people, no doubt."

"Don't mock the wealthy. The only difference between your family and mine is that we were successful at business. We were competent."

"No argument there."

We sipped our Nescafé, and I wondered why instant coffee was classified as a drink.

"All right," I said at last. "Then we need a counter-witness who saw them in Maprao at the time of the explosion. You were interviewing the bystanders. Did anyone see the SUV?"

"No."

"Come on. We have twenty cars and trucks passing a day. Surely someone saw a big black wagon pass through."

"Not one."

"All right. Then they were driving one of their own cars. Did anyone see a strange slow-moving vehicle cruising the village?"

"No."

"A motorcycle with both riders in helmets?"

"No."

"Come on, Chom. You and the Keystone Kops were talking to the crowd for an hour. There were fifty-odd people there. Surely someone saw something? I watched Constable Mah Yai filling out a case form. Somebody was making a statement."

"Not about the bombing."

"Something else? What?"

"You know Ari?"

"The monkey handler? Who doesn't?"

"He filed a complaint."

"I bet it wasn't relevant."

"Someone's kidnapped his monkey."

If I was the UN, I'd pick up the phone and request a Thai/Burmese simultaneous interpreter. Twenty minutes later I'd have a girl in my office with a Ph.D. in both languages. I wasn't the UN, and I had no idea how to conduct a clandestine interview with Shwe the squid dryer. He supervised a team at Grajom Fy that laid out sandfish and baby squid on bamboo racks to dry under the hot sun. With the arrival of the monsoons, sunny periods were few, so the workers had to hurry out with their trays and be prepared to hurry them back under cover when the rains came. I know it sounds trivial, but some twenty thousand fish are sun-baked there every day. Someone was making a lot of money out of the operation, and it wasn't the Burmese.

There was just the one NGO working out of Pak Nam, and that was Rescue the

145

Orphans Thailand. It was a branch of an international organization called Rescue the Orphans World that reputedly did some good . . . somewhere. I had yet to find that place. In my cynical mind they were every bit as bad as the SRM and a dozen other acronyms and initialisms that claimed to be doing more than they were. They misled and leeched off the backs of other projects and took a lot of photos of things they weren't responsible for to send back to the ignorant church folks in the West. ROT was brazenly Christian. With every pill, every textbook, they'd issue a reminder to the orphans that if it wasn't for the great white God, they'd be illiterate or starving or dead. So howsabout a hymn?

But ROT was also one of the three places downtown with A/C (7-Eleven and the bank being the other two), so I strolled into their office. I'd heard they had a Burmese working there who spoke English. There were four desks, and they were all empty. A tall man in a yellow T-shirt, yellow trousers, and a yellow peaked cap was sitting on the floor cutting out yellow paper chains. Yellow seemed to be in this year. He looked fearfully in my direction.

"Hello," I said in English.

"Sawat dee," he said badly in Thai.

He remained seated on the ground, perhaps believing I'd come to the wrong place.

"Do you speak English?" I asked.

"Yes."

"I need to speak to a Burmese worker.
Can you translate for me?"

"Yes."

I wondered whether this was one of those
gag scenes where the person you're speaking to only knows the word "yes."

"Where did you learn your English?" I
asked.

"I graduated from the University of
Rangoon many moons ago. I was an English
major. Not frightfully useful in my present
circumstances, I might add."

All right, he could speak. He sounded like
a leftover from the British Raj, but he could
speak. My problem then for the next fifteen
minutes, as we locked the office and drove
my truck to Grajom Fy, was shutting him
up. He was his own favorite subject. I could
tell you all about his life, but it would really
be a huge chunk of unnecessary narrative.
So all you need to know is that his name
was Clive. His portfolio in Pak Nam had
nothing to do with orphans. He was here to
initiate AIDS-awareness programs for the
Burmese community. AIDS was still good
charity, and even though there were far

147

more pressing problems for the Burmese in Thailand, AIDS was what got Iowan and Indianan church folk dipping into their pockets. So, despite the fact he had no medical training and couldn't speak Thai, his command of the English language for some reason made him the ROT representative in Pak Nam. In his yellow ROT uniform the Burmese could see him coming half a kilometer away, but I wondered how they viewed him. With his education, I imagined he'd be something of an outsider. And would Shwe be comfortable with Clive as an interpreter?

We found Shwe among the vast spread of sunning tables laying out sandfish on racks like neat torture victims. All began well. The two were acquainted. They exchanged smiles and greetings. Shwe nodded curiously at me and told Clive a quick story, which I'm certain involved my underwear. Clive's brown cheeks turned claret. We retired to the shade of a huge deer's ears tree and sat on large plastic buoys.

"What would you care to know?" Clive asked, still too embarrassed to look me in the eye.

"Last night I was asking a group what they knew about Burmese bodies being washed up on the beach. Shwe had something to say, but the others there wouldn't let him tell me. I want to know what he knows."

Clive's translation and the subsequent discussion in Burmese took some time, and I thought I was about to be excluded until Clive sighed and looked at his knees.

"Well, goodness," he said. "One is never too old for an education. I am flummoxed to learn of these things. It would appear that there have been numerous disappearances from amidst the Burmese. All unexplained. A husband would fail to return from his toil in the plantation. A workmate might stop by his associate's dormitory only to discover the door open and the bedding unperturbed. A fishing boat captain might be overwhelmed that a good and steadfast mate had failed to turn up for his shift. In the past year alone there have been thirty such incidences of whom he knows."

"Were they reported to the police?" I asked.

Clive passed on the question.

"In the case of a Burmese being registered and having a Thai sponsor," Clive said, "the employer would go to the police station to report that one of his workers had vanished mysteriously. The response would invariably be that the Burmese are a notoriously unreliable race and the worker probably found some other place of employ that offered a more substantial stipend. There was, however, no explanation as to why he would be of a mind to leave behind his clothes, possessions, and, in some cases, his Burmese ID card and money."

"Is there a theory as to where these missing workers may have gone?" I asked.

Another dialogue.

"There are tales," said Clive. "Seafarers' yarns about deep-sea slave ships. Vessels whose crews work under armed guard, never paid. Subsistence rations. Torture and cruelty. Out at sea for a month transferring their catch to smaller boats. No way to tell of their plight. And in case of a mutiny, a bullet to the head."

"Or a machete to the neck," I added.

"Quite so. Nobody has ever returned from such cruises."

"So, if nobody returns . . . ?"

"Hmm. I shall inquire."

The Burmese chatted. In the middle of their conversation Shwe's left leg started to play the Thai national anthem. He laughed and rolled up his trouser cuff. There, taped to his calf was a cell phone in a holster. He switched it off. He obviously wasn't about to calmly hand over his phone to the police. Necessity was the mother of invention.

"There is no cement evidence," Clive said. "But the slices fit together to make the cake. The account from a drunken Thai crew member. The sight of a man being bundled into a truck. Missing Burmese. Body parts found on a beach . . ."

"So there have been other parts?"

"Again, rumors."

It wasn't any type of tale a journalist would touch with a long bamboo pole. The Internet was full of this stuff. Not a shred of evidence.

"Why wouldn't Aung want me to hear this?" I asked.

"For the same reason you won't write about it," he said.

Shwe smiled.

He was right. I was a journalist in spirit. There might be facts I could follow up on, statistics, hospital records and the like, but I wouldn't get much from the Burmese. Why would they want to bring a rock face down on themselves? Who'd volunteer to have his precarious life crushed by getting involved in an investigation into a bunch of unsubstantiated claptrap? The missing were missing. The dead were dead. The police didn't care. Protect yourself and your kin, that's the way of it. I asked whether Shwe knew anything about the head on our beach. He said he didn't, but he'd ask around.

I drove Clive back to Pak Nam, and he was pleasantly quiet. I assumed this was his inauguration into the horror of life for the poor fisherfolk. This wasn't the yellow-paper-chain world, or the world of asexual hand-puppets telling each other to use a condom. This was the world where people got eliminated. There was no evidence, but I could tell that he believed what he'd heard. When he stepped out of the Mighty X, I asked him how he knew Shwe.

"I consult with him from time to time," he said. "He used to be the head of urology at the East Yangon General Hospital."

"So what's he doing here drying fish?" I asked, although I was sure I knew the answer already.

"The poor blighter has a son back home with muscular dystrophy. In his old job he didn't make enough to medicate the boy. This pays twice as much."

All this excitement and it wasn't even lunchtime. Just as well because I was supposed to be the one making it. I don't know how I ended up with kitchen duty, but it was by far the hardest job in the household. Mair looked after the shop, which was currently Kosovo. Arny minded the chalets, all but one of which were empty. Grandad Jah watched traffic. I made breakfast, lunch, and dinner and solved world problems. You can see where all the pressure fell in our family.

I pulled into the car park and saw a crowd standing around the latrines. Nobody was doing anything. They just stood by the concrete block, staring like tourists at the pyramids. It didn't occur to me at first, but as I walked down to the beach, I noticed some geometric anomaly with regard to our public loos. The entire block was leaning at a thirty-degree angle. When I reached the scene, the problem was clear. The sea had claimed the entire beach right up to the crest. The water was scooping out the foundations of our toilet block wave by wave. We weren't talking tsunami here. This was a deceptively gentle rise of the tide. To my left, the polite surf was already lapping at the top step of the front cabin. The plants bobbed up and down in their plastic pots. The picnic table was sub-aqua. In the four hours since I'd left, our resort had become Venice. Captain Kow was right. Earth was in the process of wreaking revenge on its abusers.

As King Canute discovered to his chagrin, there isn't a lot you can do to turn back the sea. We stood and watched. Our kitchen, farther inland, had a thirty-centimeter wash, and the carport was a quay. But this was a kindly reminder from Mother Nature that we lived beside several trillion liters of water. If it wanted us, it could have us any old time. I stood beside Mair as the toilets dipped another four degrees.

"Should I get buckets?" she asked.

I laughed and she smiled. It wasn't inconceivable that one day our entire resort would become Atlantis and they'd make TV documentaries about us. But today all I could think of was Grandad Jah unblocking the U bend on a toilet that was now deep beneath the surf. Like I said, the monsoons had a sense of humor.

We had lunch that day crammed around the bamboo table on the veranda of my cabin. I hadn't had a chance to tell anyone my findings about the Noys. Noy genius had embedded herself beside Arny. I had no idea what chemistry would draw a future Nobel prize scientist to a man who shaved his buttocks. She was so in love with him I didn't have the heart to mention that my brother's fiancée would be back from Hong Kong the next day. I really didn't want to tell her that Kanchana Aromdee, three times national bodybuilding champion, could easily rip Noy's skinny arms out of their sockets. And

I didn't want to point out that Arny was not flirting with Noy in the least. Didn't even understand the concept. He was just being his sweet, honest self. But, in fact, I knew I'd have to point all this out because Noy, alias Thanawan, had enough problems already and the last thing she needed was a broken heart. I'd wait for an appropriate moment.

"What do you intend to do about your toilet block?" Mamanoy asked.

"I was thinking we might issue snorkels and goggles to customers asking to use the bathroom," I said.

"I must say you're all taking this remarkably calmly," she said.

"You know where your cheeks are, but that doesn't stop you biting the inside of your mouth from time to time," said Mair, looking out to sea.

We all nodded. None of us had any idea what that meant, but our guests had obligingly learned to surf my mother's squalls. They were becoming family. I wanted them to stay. Having found out what had happened in the States, I knew I'd never sleep again if I couldn't make some sense of it. I didn't want to scare them off by asking directly. I needed a ploy to squeeze information out of young Noy drip by drip without

155

her realizing what I was doing.

In order to obtain their trust, I decided to share my Burmese findings with them. Severed head stories aren't always the best accompaniment to a meal, but the Noys appeared to take them all in *bon goût*. I went on to list the indignities our Burmese neighbors were experiencing day in day out in our land of smiles. Then I even added the myth of the slave ships and the alleged execution of mutineers. By the time my tale was told, all eyes were on me, and only I had a full plate.

"Serves 'em right," said Grandad Jah.

"For what?" I asked.

"Turning against the British," he said.

I was surprised the old man knew the first thing about regional history.

"Stick with the Brits," he went on, "and you've got a royal family at your back. Can't beat royalty for political stability."

I wondered whether to point out that Thailand had entertained no fewer than thirty-nine prime ministers since 1932, seventeen of whom were planted after military coups. But you never won an argument with Grandad, even when you were right.

"The Malays stuck with the Brits," he said. "The Indians. The Australians. And look at all them. Democracy is government by the people. These countries aren't run by halfwits in tin hats bleeding their countries of all their natural resources and treating their citizens like unpaid coolies. If they'd just stuck with the Brits, we wouldn't have any Burmese on Thai soil. Not a one. We'd be sending our laborers over there to build high-rises and roads."

Grandad was a man who generally dribbled words sparingly. On the few occasions he let the floodgates open, you appreciated those dribbly moments that much more.

"That's really sad," said Mair.

"Just pay attention to the lessons learned from history," said Grandad.

"They can't even count," said Mair.

We all paused.

"Who can't count, Mair?" Arny asked.

"The Burmese children," she replied. "And they're so adorable in their little clothes and powdery cheeks. It hadn't occurred to me that they weren't in school. I shall build one."

"Mair, you aren't nearly connected enough for a Nobel prize, and will you stop spending all this money we don't have?" I pleaded. "We can't even afford to clean up the shop or salvage the latrine from beneath the mighty ocean, let alone set up a school."

"It shouldn't cost much," she said, her mind already seeing the smiling faces sitting in the front row, the hands raised, the queue for the pencil sharpener. "We could hire ourselves a little teacher. A Burmese teacher wouldn't cost very much. And we could drive over to Ranong and buy books, and I could teach Thai once a week, or sewing."

And off she went, describing her Burmese school, the Noys smiling and offering suggestions, Grandad Jah grumbling that nobody ever listened to him and collecting the lunch plates, Arny smiling like the little boy whose mother told fantastic stories to three little children with no father. And me, unappreciated, carrying the worries of the world. I reached into my pocket, palmed two antidepressants and washed them down with the last of my Coca-Cola. And to my utter surprise, with my mother sitting to my left yakking on about blackboard paint, a familiar sound emerged from Mair's cabin next door. It was the sound of a headboard clattering against a wooden wall.

7.
THEY SAY LOVE IS MORE OR LESS A GIBBON THING

(from "I'm a Believer" — NEIL DIAMOND)

"Are you out of your mind?" I asked, and immediately knew it was a silly question. Of course she was.

Grandad Jah and I sat opposite Mair, who was seated on her bed with the monkey sprawled across her lap.

"What in the world possessed you to kidnap a monkey?" asked Grandad.

"She needed me," said Mair.

"She told you that?"

"Not in words."

"Well, that's a relief."

"She told me with this," said Mair. She lifted the animal's left leg and rolled her over. The monkey's back was diced with welts, some quite fresh. Her hair was patchy, and there were sores everywhere. Ari, the monkey handler, used to bring her once a month to collect coconuts from our trees.

The first time they'd arrived I'd been relatively amused by the animal's skill. But from then on, it was just a monkey on a rope and I can't say I paid much attention. I'd go to the truck when it was all over, count the nuts, and take our share of the profits. It looked like only Mair had taken any notice of the monkey.

"Mair," I said, "we had seven policemen here, and you had a kidnapped monkey in your room."

"I didn't kidnap her. I rescued her. And why should the police search my room? We were the victims, weren't we?"

"Why didn't you tell us?" I asked.

"I didn't think you'd let me keep her in the room. But I was sure it couldn't have been much of a secret. She was causing such a fuss. You certainly heard the noise."

"Yes, but I thought it was . . ."

"What?"

"Never mind."

"What are you planning to do with it?" asked Grandad.

"There's a gibbon rehabilitation project in Phuket," she said. "I was thinking of sending her over there."

Grandad Jah stood, cracked a few bones, and walked over to get a closer look at the monkey, who bared her teeth at him. Mair monkey-whispered and the animal melted back onto her lap. I imagined her doing the same to me when I was a snarling two-year-old.

"One," said Grandad, "this isn't a gibbon. It's a macaque. And two, Phuket's six hours away. You going to put it on the bus?"

"I haven't been in a hurry to think it through, Father," she said. "She still hasn't recovered, and I'm not going to send her anywhere till she's better. Now stop picking on me."

I left my mother and grandfather to it. There really was nothing I could do. We had a monkey. And I secretly cursed that monkey for stimulating my libido under false pretenses. But an incontrovertible process had begun that first headboard-clattering night and now I had an itch to scratch. There was only one man in Maprao who came even vaguely close to my "type." I'd been married for three years to a man who wasn't my "type" at all. I'd dated a platoon of men who weren't my "type." And I'd arrived at the conclusion that perhaps my "type" and my "realistic options" were so far removed I might have to compromise.

Ed the grass man was leading the field in my compromise chart. He was younger than me, which perhaps played on some fantasy I'd never admit to. He had dreamy chocolate eyes and . . . No, look. I don't aspire to writing romance fiction. Forget what the tall slim stack of muscle looked like. I was desperate. He was divorced. And it wasn't a coincidence that it had been Ed the grass man there with me in my erotic dream. So, why not? As I rode in search of him, it hadn't occurred to me how totally against character and culture and common sense this potential seduction was. I was being led by a force much greater than my brain. I'd taken the bicycle in search of Ed. I figured all that pedaling might calm my ardor by the time I found him. It wouldn't do to appear too needy. Lust may have addled my mind, but it hadn't damaged my common sense. I had a condom in my bag. It made me feel terribly naughty. This would be an encounter never to be forgotten but not one to be remembered every nappy-changing, school-uniform-darning, prison-visiting day for the rest of my life.

I missed Ed at his house, at the boatyard, and at the orchard whose cut grass bore his precisely manicured signature. But I found him at an empty building site, where he was assembling a fitted wardrobe. He was certainly a versatile young man. The bricklayers and electricians and cement renderers had completed their tasks, leaving Ed to finish the woodwork himself. Destiny had placed him here in front of me in a future bedroom.

"Ed?" I said, and in my mind's eye we crashed into one another, locked in a passionate embrace. Our lips mashing one against the other. He looked up from his chiseling and wiped sweat from his eyes.

"Jimm?"

Everything was going so well. I sat on a metal grinder carry-case and crossed my legs. I was wearing shorts. Nothing erotic, but he was a man. Just the sight of skin drove them insane.

"What do you want?" he asked.

"Just to visit," I said.

"How did you know I was here?"

"I asked at the boat dock. They laughed mischievously when they told me. Honestly. Men."

There was a long pause.

"That's a very nice fitted wardrobe," I said. "I had no idea you were so good with your hands."

He nodded.

"Do you want to take a break?" I asked.

"I don't know. I have to get these frames

done by four. They're bringing in mirrored doors."

"Just a quick break," I said, and licked my top sensual lip. "A break . . . to remember."

He put down his chisel at last.

"Remember what?"

"Remember the time, not so long ago, when you came to me with a proposal."

"Is this about when I almost asked you out?"

"Almost, yes. Rudely interrupted by me. You see? It was too soon, Ed. I didn't know you then. Ha, I barely knew myself."

"It was seven weeks ago."

"Time enough for me to let down my defenses. It was so obvious you found me attractive. I wasn't ready then. But, Ed . . ."

"What?"

"I'm ready now."

"What for?"

"For you."

I reached out my hands to him. It was the moment. Our fingers would touch and the electricity would course through us. I could already feel a tingle.

He just stood there.

"I'm engaged," he said.

"What?"

My hands dropped to my sides.

"I found somebody. We're engaged."

The cement floor beneath my feet gave way, and I dropped fifteen floors to the nuclear bunker. I landed on the wiring board of the strategic defense system and started a war.

"What?"

"You've said that already."

"I know, but . . . not even two months ago you were suffering because your wife ran off with a glazier and you wanted me."

"And you said no."

"You give up that easily? How can you be so . . . indiscriminate?"

"I didn't want to be alone."

"So you ask everyone on your list till you get a yes?"

"It's a bit more complicated but, yeah, something like that. But thanks for thinking of me."

"Thanks for . . . ?"

I burned off a lot of frustration on my pedaled escape from that unfinished house but not nearly enough to prevent a slide-show of Hong Kong and Taiwanese male movie stars flickering in front of my eyes. I even looked sideways at an elderly farmer with no shirt who was tugging his cow beside the road. I might have even stopped and talked to him if my cell phone hadn't sent out a chorus of "Mamma Mia." I stopped the bike under a tree and looked at the screen. It was Sissi.

"You not left yet?" I asked.

"Jimm, listen. Whatever you do, don't open that packet of trial antidepressants I sent you."

I was exactly in the mood for the teens at the Pak Nam Internet shop. They could obviously tell I'd have gladly bumped them on the head with my personal mouse if anyone had attempted to stop me getting on to my regular computer. Even the craggy-faced shop owner desisted from his preachy "We do have a queuing system here, you know?" The last time he'd tried it I threatened to call the school board and tell them about all the young boys here who spent their homework time surfing for big-eye-contact-lens Japanese idols in bikinis. That had shut him up. Just about anything I needed a computer for would have been more important than that. And this evening I had two very important reasons for getting online.

First, I sent an e-mail to my friend Alb in Bangkok. He ran a sort of unofficial Australian news agency. He made big bucks out of those scandalous Aussie celebrities arrested

166

in Thai resorts. He specialized in drug orgies, but he had a nose for all kinds of sin. I'd first met him when we were both investigating a pop singer pedophile holed up in a five-star hotel in Chiang Mai. We staked him out together and kept in touch as we followed the subsequent trial and suicide. We were good friends.

Alb, I wrote. *What do you know about slave ships in the Gulf of Thailand?*

I pressed SEND. He was an e-mail addict. Even if he wasn't at his desk, he'd have his iPhone set on Taser buzz. He kept it in a small pouch hanging from his belt, like a sporran, so I knew there was something kinky about it. While I waited for an answer I Googled FLIBANSERIN. I got eighty thousand results almost immediately. The first site I clicked had the headline VIAGRA FOR WOMEN. I said "shit" eleven times in English, but the word was obviously on the high school vocab list because everyone looked at me. I read on.

AFTER THE FIRST ROUND OF TESTS THE BOEHRINGER INGELHEIM CORPORATION HAD BEEN DISAPPOINTED THAT ITS WIDELY TOUTED ANTIDEPRESSANT FLIBANSERIN HAD NO ANTIDEPRESSANT QUALITIES WHATSOEVER.

THEIR CHEMISTS MADE SOME SLIGHT
ALTERATIONS AND SENT THE DRUG
FLIBANSERIN II FOR A SECOND ROUND
OF TRIALS. BUT UNEXPECTED FEED-
BACK BEG —

Alb had answered. He could wait.

UNEXPECTED FEEDBACK BEGAN TO
FILTER IN FROM WOMEN WHO'D TRI-
ALED FLIBANSERIN I. THEY WERE
CLAIMING THAT SINCE THEY STARTED
TO TAKE THE DRUG REGULARLY THEY
HAD DEVELOPED RAVENOUS SEXUAL
APPETITES.

"Oh my word."

WOMEN AS OLD AS 76 WERE . . .

I couldn't read any more. I was so embarrassed. I was a love junky. I'd thrown myself
at a gay policeman, a happily married man,
and just a few hours earlier I'd forced myself
on a grass cutter. The story would have
made the rounds of the entire district by
now. They'd write things about me on the
walls of public toilets. Fathers would bring
their teenaged sons around for their first
experience. I'd end up an old hag in mesh
stockings and a push-up bra beckoning

passing drivers into the resort. What had I done?

I clicked Alb.

Lots, he wrote. *What do you want to know specifically?*

I typed *Everything* and sent it.

I looked around the Internet shop. Some of the boys looked away embarrassed. They'd heard. I was dirty laundry.

"We saw the harlot in the Internet shop last night," they'd tell the teacher in the morning.

Alb replied. *We should chat.*

And we chatted on Gmail for half an hour. Alb had heard all the same rumors. On the Andaman coast out west he said there was indisputable evidence of kidnappings and failure to pay salaries. There was an island, he said, that a bunch of Burmese fishermen had escaped to. They'd been there six months. Nobody knew what to do with them. They didn't have papers. They were illegal aliens. The Burmese junta wasn't about to send a pleasure boat to pick them up. Nobody else wanted to take responsibility. *Now, if they were Swedish,* he wrote, *then we'd have a story. But what you've got is disposables. It's like the big tsunami that hit Thailand in 2004. If it had just swallowed up Thais and Bangladeshis, there'd have been a*

169

couple of days of press in the West. "100,000?
How tragic. Anyone know what the cricket
score is?" But that same tsunami hit five-star
resorts and took out German sportsmen and
blond fashion models and Italian executives.
And there was outrage. Millions of dollars
were donated. It could have been us, they
cried. Someone tried to sue God.

So, fifty Burmese on an island? Slaves in
deep-sea vessels? Summary killings of little
brown men with no culture or religion to relate
to? Collateral damage in the harsh world of
the peasant, my dear. Investigating it would
be expensive and what do you end up with?
Couple of columns in The Age *that eighty*
percent of readers skim over on their way to
the comics. No, Jimm. We get a lot of tip-offs
but, quite frankly, nobody gives a toss.

A twelve-year-old with fake, pink mouth
braces — which had mysteriously become
all the rage with teens — leaned over me
and flashed his queue number. I was so
upset that I let him have my seat. Now this
was actual depression and I didn't even have
anything anti to take. And perhaps the worst
part of this whole affair was that the effects
of Viagra-fem were getting stronger. Just
how long would I have to wait for it to wear
off? Until it did, no man was safe.

We had two new guests for dinner that night. The sea level had dropped sufficiently for re-entry into the kitchen, so I made spaghetti seafood. One of our bamboo picnic tables had been washed away. Not far away. We could see it rocking back and forth some way out, like one of Robinson Crusoe's failed escape attempts. Mair refused to allow Arny to swim out to retrieve it. She said losing another nephew to drowning would be too much to bear. The other four tables were still where we'd left them. From table two there was a clear view of the sunken latrine, nose down in the sand. Grandad Jah had turned a spotlight onto it, and the effect was every bit as spectacular as Pak Nam's own concrete battleship. The night was calm. The sky was starry. The beach garbage looked almost picturesque in the shadows.

Joining us all the way from Hong Kong was Arny's fiancée, Gaew. If you were to project a slide of Miss Thailand World onto a brick kiln, that's what Gaew looked like. The hurricanes had yet to offer up a wind that would blow her off her feet. But we all loved her bubbly personality and sense of humor, especially my mother. And Gaew seemed every bit as pleased to see Mair as she was to be re united with Arny. My brother grinned like a lovesick donkey at everything she said. Noy picked up on this interaction and remained subdued all evening. Gaew picked up on Noy's subjugation, added to it the girl's innocent beauty and youth, and decided it wouldn't be a bad idea to hold my brother's hand all night and feed him fried squid with a fork.

Our other guest that night was Captain Waew, retired from Surat Thani police force. He was as round as Grandad Jah was anorexic, as short as me, and worryingly twitchy. He had so many tics you'd doubt he could ever be truly still. He ate sparingly, spoke frugally, and smiled at everything. He was the reinforcements called in by my grandfather. I felt so much better to see he had back-up.

The grenade attack on our freezer had destroyed our frozen fish and most of our beer supply. The bottles had shattered, but the cans had merely been blasted across the room. The beer that accompanied our supermarket seafood therefore was in Salvador Dali cans, which exploded foam at every opening. After an hour we all stank of Leo. By then we hardly noticed the arrival of the subtle black curtain of clouds being pulled across our sky. While everyone else was getting plastered, I called on my superhuman ability to be unaffected by alcohol when a good story was at stake.

With bladders filling fast and their owners running off to rooms to empty them, I worked my way around the table like a clever Pac-Man, sliding into vacant slots until I found myself beside my prey — Noy.

"Are you having a good time?" I asked.

"They seem so happy," she said, staring at Arny and Gaew, her words slurred. She was pickled.

"Love. What can I say? Blind as a beefburger."

She didn't laugh.

"She's . . ."

"Older than your mother?"

"Yes."

Noy was swaying. I don't know how many abstract beer cans she'd been through, but I was certain she was just about to say things she'd regret. I leaned into her ear.

"Tell the truth, I'd like to see him with someone younger," I said. "But she's so worldly. She's been everywhere. Can you believe she studied in America?"

That was a lie. I was fond of lies.

"Well, so did I," slurred Noy.

Bingo.

"You don't say? He loves women with overseas experience."

"I have it," she said. "I have overthere experience. And what an experience. You know? You know what I was?"

Drunk was what she was. About to pass out, I'd bet. I needed a few more clues before I lost her completely.

"What were you?" I asked.

"I was . . ." She looked around, not focusing on anything or anyone — perhaps only the memory.

"I was a rental."

"Like Hertz?"

"Excac . . . ex . . . actly like Hertz. Driven into the ground, dented and dumped. Used. That was me."

She put her arm around me and belched.

"Sorry," she said.

"No problem."

"All used up," she sang. She was fading now. I had twenty seconds left at the most before her lights went out. "And what . . . what would they have done to me after the gas tank was empty? Put me in the scrap metal, that's what. So, Jimm, that's why."

"Why what?"

Mamanoy had seen her girl talking to me and was on her way over to us.

"Why what what?" Noy asked.

"No, you said, 'That's why.' "

"Right. That's why." She got clumsily to her feet and raised a fist. "That's why I stood up to them. Why I told them it wasn't right. It shoul . . . should have been me."

Then in English she said, "The monitor lizard knew nothing."

Her mother caught her just before she collapsed.

"She isn't very good with alcohol," said Mamanoy. "Talks absolute rubbish after the slightest amount of beer. I'd better get her back to the room."

Ex-Captain Waew saw an opportunity to manhandle a nubile twenty-four-year-old and propped up one side of Noy while her mother took the other. I watched them fade into the shadows.

"Well, how confusing was that?" I asked myself. I couldn't think. Beer made my brain stodgy. If I'd been drinking Chilean red, I would have had an insight by now. Casa de Easter might give me brimstone hangovers, but it did wonders for my imagination. Noy had told me something important, but I didn't know what.

When the captain returned from Noy's cabin, he joined Grandad Jah at another table and I knew they were up to no good. I wasn't having it. I went over to them and squeezed in between the old fellows.

"Jimm," said Grandad, "go and play somewhere else. This is grown-up talk."

He sometimes forgot I'd grown up too.

"OK, old policemen," I said. "Here's the deal."

"Jimm!" snarled Grandad.

I didn't want to break Grandad's face in front of his colleague, but I had a lot on my plate, not least of which was the feel of Captain Waew's strong forearm against my side. Just how evil were those pills?

"I know what you two are up to," I said.

"Jimm, do not interfere where you aren't wanted," said Grandad.

"If you do anything to the rat brothers, I'm going straight to the real police. I'll tell them everything, including the gun."

Grandad Jah looked at his friend apologetically.

"She's young," he said.

"I may be young," I agreed, "but I'm not stupid. I know why your co-avenger is here. And I need your combined expertise on a much bigger case. I want to know whose head that was on our beach. It's possible he was beheaded by slavers, and they got away with it. They've probably been getting away with it time and time again. I want you to focus your minds on something more important than revenge against a couple of lowlifes. I know you aren't that fond of the Burmese, but they're people. They have rights. And they believe nobody cares about them here in Thailand. That's because nobody does care about them. I don't think that's fair. I want justice for our day laborers. But I tell you what. The rats are connected to all this somehow. And once we've uncovered the kingpins, you can do whatever you like with them. Or perhaps you aren't up for a large-scale operation."

The two old men were silent for a while. A squall had started to gust the rain off the Gulf. Large drops hit the straw roof over the table and the napkins blew away. Mair and Gaew hurried to clear up the dinner things. Captain Waew smiled at Grandad.

"Mitt," he said, "she's a child of your loins right enough."

"I taught her everything she knows," said Grandad.

We had the beginnings of a task force and a downpour.

It was Thursday morning and I had to go to market to scrounge for food. The Pak Nam covered market, once the heart of this metropolis, where lovers met and movies were shown on the weekends, was now a huge dilapidated warehouse of a place with a few stallholders hanging on for dear life. There was no logic behind what fruit and vegetables would be available at any given time. Like the deep-sea catch from the night before, the abundant fresh produce was targeted by the gluttons of Bangkok, whisked away in huge refrigerated trucks before our sleepy heads left the pillow. Like temple dogs, we had our choice of what scraps were left. I often returned home with a sprig of what could conceivably have been weeds and a plastic bag full of something local and covered in dirt.

I'd hardly slept the previous night as I wrestled with the ravages of withdrawal. The beer had sedated me till about two when I sat bolt upright in a cold sweat, like they only do in movies. I reached for my anti-depressants, but I'd flushed them all down the toilet. I lay back and relied on the strength of my will to get me through the next four hours. I did a lot of thinking but no sleeping at all. I wondered what effect a rubber toilet plunger might have on sub-merged pills. I wondered whether Ed's friends were drawing lots to see who'd get me first. I'd listened to the rain that clat-tered down on my concrete roof all the way till dawn.

I drove home through the pouring rain with our humble food supplies and noticed how the little ditch at the back of our place had become a stream. It was quite picturesque. Now I understood why there was a bridge. Until now it had served no purpose. I could imagine a big-eye-contact-lens Japanese bikini girl standing there with an umbrella. We could make it a tourism feature. Tourists loved features. I parked in front of our burned-out shop and marveled at how the village women had rallied around Mair. The ladies of the co-op were mopping frantically and sorting out the salvageable from the hopeless. Despite the steady rain, Captain Kow was sitting on his motorcycle in a flowing purple plastic poncho. He looked like a morning glory. I needed a seafaring man to explain to me the politics of deep-sea fishing. Kow, the squid-boat captain, seemed to spend an inordinate amount of time in front of our shop selling fishballs from his motorcycle sidecar. I wondered whether "Captain" was just his first name. I think he was surprised when I walked up to him. If he'd had more teeth, he'd probably have a nice smile. His nose was a little broken, but his eyes were smoky gray, and time and weathering had shaped him a good face.

"Captain Kow," I said, and saluted as was my witty way.

He saluted back, as was his.

"Nice weather for dolphins," he said.

For some reason this made me think of all those creatures that have never experienced dryness. Fancy that, being permanently wet. That in turn made me think of whales washed up on beaches, creatures who obviously associated dryness with death. On our beach we had a lot of fish washed up. They all had that "who put that beach there?" expression. But nobody rushed out with damp blankets and iced water to rescue a mackerel. There were no SAVE THE MACKEREL bumper stickers. My philosophy was that if you were too stupid to realize you were swimming on dry land, it really didn't matter how enormous or endangered you were. Mother Nature has a way of dealing with the dumb. Meanwhile, Captain Kow was yakking on about the weather conditions. Something about rain and two weeks and flash floods. I interrupted him.

"Captain Kow? I was wondering whether I could sit you down sometime and ask you some fishing boat questions."

His gray eyes lit up.

"It would be an honor," he said.

I booked him for ten o'clock in my room.

I was offloading my fruit and vegetables when I felt a presence behind me. I turned to see Noy under a green umbrella. She looked pummeled, all puffy and red-eyed. I loved to see beautiful women in those paparazzi photos taken at the supermarket when they looked just like you and me. Noy was the type who should really stay away from Leo beer.

"*Pee* Jimm," she said.

Pee. Older sister. Good. Respect. I liked it.

"Yes?"

"I . . ."

There was probably more to that sentence, so I waited.

"I wanted to ask you . . . about last night."

"Yes?"

"I . . . my mother said I was talking to you . . . a lot."

"You don't remember?"

"I drank a lot of beer. I'm not used to it."

"I could tell."

"Did I . . . did I say anything?"

Now perhaps you can see why I was one of the country's top crime reporters. My chance had arrived.

"You told me a lot," I said.

"About?"

I was getting wet. I took her arm and led her to the plastic awning.

"About everything," I said.

"No." The muscles of her face tensed. "I . . . I wouldn't have."

"Georgetown. Science. The exam."

She was a white girl. The type of girl sheltered from the harmful rays of the sun from birth. Coated in creams. Barred from garden games. But I swear that white girl dropped through three more shades of white right there in front of me.

"It's not possible," she said.

"Then I must be psychic. Listen, you told me. It doesn't matter. You've landed in the safest place in the country. We all like you and your mother. We want to help. You can stay here as long as you like. What happened in America doesn't bother us. Everything's fixable."

"You don't understand."

It was true. I didn't. I knew the what but not the why. But I wasn't about to tell her that.

"I think it's quite evident," I said.

"No, Jimm. This is serious. This isn't a sinking latrine. These are dangerous people. If they found out you were helping us, they could . . . delete all of you. There'd be no evidence that you ever existed."

I felt a tingle of excitement. I wasn't sure that I *had* existed for the past year, but this was incredibly dramatic. I took her shaking hand in mine. She was truly terrified.

"Pbook," I said.

"I told you my name?"

"Just that. No surname. No connections to your real life. Your family's identity is still protected. And only I know the truth. I haven't told anybody else. It's just me and you against . . . them. And I'm a great ally to have."

All she knew about me was that I was a cook in a beaten-up resort at Earth's end. But she was desperate for a friend. She fell against me and took me in her arms and sobbed into my shoulder. In my current condition, even that was a little exciting. But the longer we stood there, the more her anguish seeped into me like a computer virus. It was overwhelming. What could possibly have happened to this poor little bird?

"I like to see girls bonding" came a voice.

I looked up and there was skinny Bigman Beung leaning against a coconut tree with his arms folded. His uniform was drenched. It was some type of archaic police suit. Noy stepped back and wiped her tears with her hands.

"What do you want?" I asked.

"Reminds me of a video I once saw," he said. "Except there was less clothes and more baby oil."

"I asked you what you're doing here."

"You need to ask when I'm clearly dressed in my sanitation department uniform?" he said.

I smiled at Noy.

"We can talk later," I told her. "Tell your mother you really have no reason to leave here."

She returned my smile, collected her umbrella, and headed off into the rain. Bigman Beung observed her bottom.

"Leaving, is she? Such a waste. Still, I can probably return to the image of you two smooching at a later time. Perhaps when I've had a few drinks. Meanwhile, I have an ecological disaster to avert."

"Our latrine?"

"How did you guess?"

"Ooh, I don't know. Tons of human excrement escaping into the Gulf from our three-seater toilet block? Would that be it?"

"I have a camera. There are grants available. Combination of natural disaster and hazardous waste. Worth a million *baht* if I take the snaps from just the right angle. You want to come down and pose in front of it?"

"It's underwater."

"You're right. It would be a swimsuit photo shoot."

"No."

"Too bad. Please yourself."

He headed off down to the beach. I called after him.

"Beung."

"Changed your mind?"

"That day I reported the head, who did you phone?"

"The M code?"

"Yes."

"New fellow at the Pak Nam station. He's responsible for all Burmese matters. Lieutenant Egg. He called us village heads to a meeting and told us about the hotline. Any body or body parts washed up on our beaches that we suspect might be Burmese we were to contact him directly."

"What does the M stand for?"

"Maung."

8.
OUR LOVE IS LIKE
A CHIP ON THE OCEAN

(from "Rock the Boat" — WALDO HOLMES)

Maung was the generic term the rude Thais used for Burmese. It was like calling all Australians Bruce. It was just another show of disrespect. I sat down with my task force, and the three of us went over everything we thought we knew about the Burmese fishermen. It didn't take long. We needed professional input to understand exactly what was happening out there in the deep Gulf. Ten minutes later, that information arrived. There was a knock on the door. I opened it to the gappy grin of Captain Kow. I noticed Grandad's haunches rise like a mad dog, so it would help to point out at this juncture that Grandad and the squid-boat captain weren't on speaking terms. I have no idea why. Of course, Grandad Jah could count his close friends on one finger, whereas the number of people he irritated would fill the national football stadium. So, whatever had come between them was probably his fault. Captain Kow was a very laid-back type, and most other people seemed to like him. In fact, Grandad was the only one who didn't. Having them together in a small room was going to be a challenge to my refereeing skills.

Over the next half hour, the captain proved that he was every bit as knowledgeable about maritime matters as Grandad Jah was about road transport. That didn't stop Grandad arguing and making nasty comments. But Captain Kow gave no indication of being rattled at all. He rode the interruptions like a man in a rubber dinghy and calmed us all with his soft sing-song voice. I noticed that he directed most of his attention to me, as if we were the only two in the room. He was given perhaps to unnecessary detail, but the gist of his talk was this.

The Gulf of Thailand is 350,000 square kilometers and is 80 meters at its deepest. Until the sixties it was rich in all different types of fish. The local markets were full of cheap anchovies and mackerel. Thence developed the deep-sea trawler industry . . . instant huge profits leading to overfishing. An average catch of 300 kilograms an hour in 1961 dropped to 50 kilograms in the eighties, 20 today. All that was left was called "trashfish," supplied to the anything-will-do factories. Most affected were crabs, sharks, rays, lobsters, and all the large fish. With the decline of these predators, the trashfish and squids and shrimps — the bottom plankton feeders — increased. Commercial squid-fishing vessels primarily used purse seines — which the captain told us were a type of fine net used to encircle the shoal — or scoop nets. Powerful lights were used to attract the squid to the surface, where they were more easily captured.

From the seventies there were various regulations introduced as to when the boats were allowed to go out, what nets they could use, and where the spawning grounds were. Anything over seven meters had to register for a license and pay an annual fee. Currently the big boats weren't allowed out for the first three months of the year, and anything over fourteen meters had to stay beyond the 3,000-meter mark for the rest of the year. But the policing of those waters was poor, and most of the bigger boats ignored the regulations.

"So, in other words, what you're saying is the bigger boats can do whatever they want," said Grandad Jah, if only because he hadn't said anything for ten minutes or so. "So, none of what you told us is helpful."

"It always helps to know what the rules are, so you can tell how far they're being bent," said Captain Kow.

There was a short Q and A on communications, crew numbers, and registration necessities, which Kow handled well. Since the squid-boat captain wasn't a member of our task force, I thanked him for his input and showed him out. On the veranda he touched my arm, smiled as much with his eyes as with his mouth, and set off into the downpour as if he hadn't noticed it was raining. I could visualize him on the deck of his boat, rocking and rolling and hauling in the nets. It was a romantic but thankfully not erotic image.

Back in the room the two old men were engaged in a hushed conversation. They looked up at me like chipmunks caught in a headlight beam. It was a bad sign. I had to rein them in.

"Whatever you're planning, stop," I said.

"It was nothing," said Grandad. "We were just agreeing that those SRM boys would have a lot to tell us if we just put a bit of pressure on them."

"You are not going to torture the rat brothers," I told him.

"It'd save us a lot of time in the end."

"No."

"So what are we supposed to do?" he asked.

"Look," I said. "We know Egg's set up this elaborate system for clearing bodies off the beaches. When he met up with the village headmen, he specified Burmese. Now, why would he do that? He's not selling spare parts. He has the body snatchers take them off to the SRM and stick them in a broom cupboard. There are no investigations. The victims remain nameless. What reason could he have other than protecting the slavers who throw their unwanted Burmese overboard? If it was an accident on a legal boat, the captains would report missing crewmen. They'd have to account for the Burmese they hire legitimately. I think you two should go talk to the Thai boat owners. I don't mean interview them. Just find out where they eat or drink or play pool and get into casual conversations with them. See if you can pick up any rumors about deep-sea vessels. Make a few —"

"You don't need to tell us how to extract information," Grandad Jah snapped.

Right. All those illegal parking interrogations fine-tuned a policeman for situations like this.

"You're right, Grandad. Sorry. I'll find out what I can from the police and take another stab at the Burmese. I think the more I can get them to trust me, the more they'll open up."

Before concluding the proceedings, I decided to tell the two old fellows everything I'd learned about the Noys. I thought all their years of experience might help solve that mystery too. They seemed far more interested in that story than in keeping a few Burmese alive. But they agreed we needed to go ahead with caution so as not to frighten off the two women. The old men grabbed their umbrellas and walked off in the direction of the truck. I gathered my wet-weather gear with a view to taking the motorcycle into Pak Nam. Grandad had reminded me that I was young and could withstand a soaking far better than they could. Pneumonia, you know. I was closing my door when, through a curtain of rain, I spotted Arny in front of his cabin. He was sitting on a deck chair flanked by the dogs.

"Hello, little bro," I said.

"You're up to something," he said.

"I'm always up to something," I reminded him.

"You and Grandad and the old policeman. You're doing something. I want to know what it is."

"Why?"

"Why?"

I jogged across to his cabin, shook my hair dry, and sat on the balcony railing. As always, Gogo turned her rump to me. I don't know what I ever did to that dog.

"Yeah, why?" I said. "Why do you want to know? If I tell you it's nothing, you'll get upset because you'll assume we're lying. If it's something, you'll get upset because . . . well, because it's something."

"You make me sound like some emotional disaster."

I thought it best not to respond to that.

"Is it about the grenade?" he asked.

"Indirectly."

"The head on the beach? The Burmese slaves?"

"Possibly."

"Why won't you tell me?"

I didn't know how to break it to him. Honesty had its good points, but in the wrong hands it could be cruel. I really didn't want fragile Arny involved in all this. Just by looking the way he did, he was likely to get knifed down there by the docks. I went the honesty route.

"Arny, you're a wimp."

To my horror, he burst into tears. It was

awful. Even the dogs backed away in embarrassment. Surely I'd insulted him worse than that in all our sibling years together. This was about something else. I knelt down and put my arm around his thick neck.

"Arny?"

"I think . . . I think she's going to leave me," he said through the tears.

"Gaew?"

"Yeah."

"Don't be ridiculous. You two are great together. You're engaged, aren't you?"

I brushed away his tears with the back of my hand, sorry I didn't have a tissue for his runny nose. He'd waited thirty-two years for this first love. It was a bit late in life for a first dumping to go with it.

"It was . . . was so right at first," he said. "I loved her. We almost had sex so many times."

"I know you . . . You what? I thought you said . . . ?"

"We did all the foreplay. She wanted to . . . you know . . . but I said no. It has to be just right. You know?"

"Of course."

"But I think . . . I feel she needs more from me. She wants me to be more of . . . ."

"A man."

"Yes."

"She said that?"

"No, but . . ."

"You feel it."

"Right. She's a big Jackie Chan fan."

That threw me.

"You do know he's only thirty-seven centimeters tall?" I said.

"But he's so macho."

"So you feel you need to make a statement."

"Right."

"By getting involved in our battle with the slavers."

"Is that all right?"

I wasn't sure.

"You might have to — I don't know — hit people. Dodge bullets. Face danger."

He paled.

"I can do that," he said with no conviction.

Against my better judgment, I yielded.

"All right," I said. "You're on the task force. Don't let me down."

He started to cry again. This time with happiness.

Before I could get to the motorcycle, I got a call from Sissi.

"Hey, Sis."

"I'm out of the condominium."

"Well done."

"I'm in a taxi."

"I knew you could do it."

"It smells."

"That's the scent of reality."

"I just wanted to remind you that you won't be able to avail yourself of my services for a week."

"I shall survive."

There was a pause.

"Are you sure?"

"Barely. How are you feeling?"

"I'm surprisingly excited. And you can keep your eyes on the road, you pervert."

I assumed that wasn't directed at me.

"There's something you need to remember before you leave the country," I said.

"What's that?"

"You never stopped being beautiful."

There was another long pause, and I knew she was smiling.

"I'll call you from Seoul," she said.

"Bon voyage."

I sometimes wondered why they hadn't come up with a new *bon.* Nobody voyaged anymore. At last I made it to the motorcycle and was about to head off when Mair ran out of the shop holding some kind of deflated pink football bladder.

"Monique," she said, "where are you going?"

"Pak Nam."

"I need you to go via Lang Suan."

"Hmm, a mere thirty kilometers out of the way in the pouring rain. Why not?"

"It's an emergency," she said. "I want you to stop by Dr. Somboon's place and ask him to take a look at her."

She held her handful aloft and there it was. Something.

"What is it?"

"A puppy."

"Not again. Is it alive?"

"Do you think I'd ask you to take a cadaver to the vet?"

"Mair. We have too many dogs already."

"Child, every rule book has a final page. But the kindness bus has no terminal."

She dropped it into my poncho's detachable hood, which I'd just been about to attach. The animal was hairless and riddled with disease.

"Where on earth did you get it?"

"She came to me, darling. Like all the creatures do. Like Mohammed, she floated down the river on the bulrushes. I pulled her from the water and gave her resuscitation."

I cringed at the thought of Mair applying

196

mouth-to-mouth to an almost-dead dog.

"And look," Mair went on, "she survived. All the sick and dying creatures of the earth will find their way to me."

I had no choice. I folded the creature into the poncho pocket, still wrapped in the hood, and left Mrs. Noah standing in the rain waiting for the giraffes to arrive. I stopped at the bridge, surprised at how quickly the humble stream had swollen to a gushing torrent. I wished then that I'd bought an iPhone when I still had an income back in Chiang Mai. Discovery Channel paid well for home videos of natural disasters and I sensed the Gulf Bay Lovely Resort was about to become one.

"What's that moving in your pocket?" Aung asked.

"Dog," I said.

"Beer" was feisty for a dying pup. She was mad at all the shots Dr. Somboon had speared her with and the pills he'd forced down her throat. I couldn't blame her. I'd named her Beer because the vet was drinking a can of Singha when I arrived. I think he'd had a few. It was just a stop-gap name. I couldn't imagine her surviving the night. Not in this weather. To his credit, Aung didn't ask me why I had a dog in my pocket.

He wasn't shirtless today, but he was soaked to the skin and his T-shirt stuck to his muscles like paint. I fought back my urge to rip it off him with my teeth.

"Aung," I said. "I know you don't trust me."

Throw that line at a Thai and he'd be on his knees denying it. Aung's expression said, "Yeah. You got me."

"But here's what I think," I continued. "I think Burmese are being kidnapped and ferried out to deep-sea vessels, where they're enslaved, ill treated, and killed if they make too much trouble. I think the head that arrived on our beach was just one example. I think you and your community know about this, but you feel helpless because you aren't able to do anything about it. I think you all live in fear that one day it'll be you or your wife whisked away."

A long silence followed.

"So?" he said.

"That's all I get? A 'so'?"

"Look. Even if you know. Even if you have proof. Even if you're out there on the big boats taking photographs. What do you think you could achieve? What Thai prosecutor really wants to go to the trouble of prosecuting Thais for crimes against the Maung? We're dispensable."

"Well, that's one thing we can achieve. Make you less dispensable. Put names and faces and family backgrounds to the slaves. Talk to loved ones. Show that —"

"Nobody would give you a name."

"OK. So I'd make it up. Photoshop a loved one. Hell, who's going to rush down here to prove me a liar? Aung, this is Thailand. We manipulate public opinion all the time. The masses feel what Channel Nine tells them to feel. If I couldn't splash up a wave of sympathy for the poor country boys chained to the oars of a galley, I wouldn't be much of a journalist, would I now?"

"Who do you work for?"

Damn, the man just refused to get caught up in the splendor of the rhetoric. And he'd hit another nerve.

"I'm freelance. That means I can work for anybody."

"Or nobody."

I was starting to see why we hated the Burmese.

"All right. Here's the deal. My family and I are going to fight this. We had a grenade thrown at us because we refused to give in to bullies. If you aren't into human rights, fair enough. Somehow we'll get evidence and somehow I'll write about all this and somehow it'll make the eyes of the world. And I do this with you or I do it without."

Clint would have put some background music in there. Violins rising to a cello and kettledrum crescendo is my guess. All I had for emphasis was the belch of a tugboat horn. I hoped it would be enough for Aung to sense my sincerity.

"Good luck."

"That's it?"

"You'll need it. You don't know what you're up against."

"So I can't count on any help from you?"

"I didn't say that. I'll give you information when I can. As long as it's off the record."

"That's big of you. All right. Information. Give me some now. Explain how your people are lifted from the street in broad daylight without anyone seeing."

"Are you serious?"

"Sometimes."

"Then why do you think nobody sees?"

"Thais down here may be stubborn, proud to a fault, but they have a sense of justice. If they saw someone being bundled into a truck, they'd do something about it."

"Not if that truck was brown and cream with a flashing police light on top."

■ ■ ■ ■

"What's that in your pocket?"

"Dog."

"You don't say. How does it breathe in there?"

"I lift the flap from time to time."

"If it's a shih-tzu, I'll take it off you."

"You like shih-tzus?"

"Who doesn't? Those broken little Chinese noses. Those pus-filled squinty eyes. And they do so attract the boys. 'Ooh, what a lovely little doggie.' "

I was having lunch with Chompu at Pak Nam's famous chicken and rice restaurant, called The Chicken and Rice Restaurant. The chicken and rice were average, but the sauce — passed down through Yunnan dynasties — was what brought in the customers. They traveled from as far away as Lang Suan to eat there. The place was never empty.

"Even so, it appears to be quite agitated," Chompu observed.

"Look, will you stop whining about the dog? It's a survivor. I'm asking about the Pak Nam constabulary picking up Burmese off the street."

"Happens all the time."

"Ha. You admit it."

"Hard to deny. Random ID checks. Work cards. It's policy."

"To harass?"

"You know? With the right interior decorator, they could really make something of this place. I'd go Japanese. Bamboo on the wall. Short-legged tables with —"

"Chom!"

"Perhaps we harass a tad. But nicely."

"Why?"

"Well, those without work permits hand over a fine."

"Which is signed for, paid into the police fund, and sent to the police ministry in Bangkok, naturally."

"Which goes directly into the wallet of the harassing officer to be spent on base desires such as karaoke."

"And you think that's OK?"

"We aren't paid very much, you know? And it's better for them than going to jail. Paying the fine is the penalty they opt for when they decide not to go through legal channels. They know the risk."

"I have witness statements that Burmese were stopped on the street and bundled into police vehicles, never to be seen again."

"Uh-oh. Hold the Pulitzer. That isn't exactly a secret either. It happens every day, darling. After our random stops, if the migrants don't have work permits and don't want to contribute to our pleasure fund, they're invited into the truck and whisked off to immigration in Ranong. We have to keep up our quota. We'd look suspicious if we didn't have any illegals at all, wouldn't we now?"

"How many?"

"Six to a dozen a week."

"So what would you say if I could prove these vanishing Burmese had work permits and sponsors?"

"I'd say, 'Bring me the witnesses.' And you'd say, 'Ooh, they aren't comfortable speaking to the police.' And I'd say, 'Mm, I'm not surprised, considering they're all figments of your imagination.' "

"Don't you be so sure."

"Oh I'm sure. If they were Thais, they'd have no idea whether the Burmese we picked up were illegal or not. So that leaves only the Burmese themselves. And the only way one of them would step up and accuse the Royal Thai Police of kidnapping a fellow countryman is if he was certifiably insane. In which case his statement would be inadmissible. Ta-daa! I rest my case."

"All right, so — and this is hypothetical — if I could prove a legal Burmese was kidnapped by the police and sent to the deep-sea vessels, would you file the report?"

"Let me see now. You're asking whether a smart, virile young police officer, a-k-a me, who carries a burden of sexuality that makes his tenure in the police force tenuous if not feeble, would pursue a criminal case against his friends and colleagues in order to bring justice to the citizens of a country none of us particularly likes?"

"Yes."

"Having thus outlined the negative aspects of such foolishness, all that remains is to inquire as to what, if any, the positives might be."

I told him about the pride that could be felt by adhering to moral and professional standards, and when that didn't work, I told him he'd get Egg out of his office and his ferns back.

"With no career, I wouldn't have much need for an office, would I now?" he reminded me. "And do you have this hypothetical witness?"

"Not yet."

"Then I don't have to hypothetically commit my career to the garbage pail, do I now? Get back to me when reality steps boldly from the shadows."

"You don't think I can do this, do you?"

"I don't think you should."

"Why not?"

"Just a hunch. But if we're talking about slavery and murder and decapitation, I doubt this is a sideline of the local embroidery society. Your foes have already tossed a grenade into your midst."

"Do you want to make my life safer?"

"How could I do that?"

"I'm planning to break into Lieutenant Egg's files. I'd bet he has a metal filing cabinet right there beside his desk."

"With a lock."

"OK. So I sneak in there and find all his files relevant to missing Burmese. And I steal them."

"And what would I have to do to make your life safer?"

"Break into it yourself."

He squealed a little and the customers looked around.

"There is no way," he said. "He's a beast. He'd beat me to death."

"Chom. You're supposed to be in that office. He'd never know. Any policeman worth his stuff could open one of those files with a bobby pin."

"Heavens. I haven't worn a bobby pin since the good old days."

"I'll lend you one of Mair's. You can find

a time when he's out of the office. Take the files down to the copy room. And replace the originals before he gets back. Nobody would need to know you were involved."

"He never announces where he's going or for how long. He could walk in any minute."

"Then I'll distract him."

"Just how would you go about that?"

"Sissi?"

"This is she."

"Are you still in the country?"

"Yes. But I'm considering applying for political asylum in Korea."

"Why? What's happened?"

"Do you remember telling me there wouldn't be any middle-aged ladies with expensive perms marching out to the airport to throw themselves down in front of my jumbo?"

"Yes."

"Well, I wouldn't recommend fortune-telling as your next career move."

"No way."

"I'm at Suvarnabhumi. They're every-where: retired pilots, middle-aged women in bulging sweatpants, tropical-fishshop owners. It would appear your yellow-shirted yuppies are in the process of laying claim to our national airport. Bangkok's middle classes are on the rampage. A fearsome mob. There's a backgammon game going on as I speak."

"Are they stopping any flights?"

"Not yet. Seoul is still up there on the departure board. But my faith is dwindling. I'm having a karma attack."

"They wouldn't. I mean, they aren't going to. Don't worry. How did they get in?"

"Same way they got into Government House. They whispered sweet nothings into the ears of the heavily armed police on the barricade. Told them who was funding the invasion, I wouldn't wonder. Reminded them of the oaths they swore at school and strolled right on through the lines. Your average policeman is overcome with guilt when aiming his gun at a terrorist who looks and sounds exactly like his primary-school teacher — and probably was."

"How long before your flight?"

"Somewhere between forty minutes and infinity."

"Do you want something to take your mind off it all?"

"Anything."

"Can you get online?"

"Of course. I'm traveling first class. They'd fly in Bill Gates if I asked."

"You obviously haven't flown first class

for a while. But do you think you'll have time to do me one quick favor?"

"Probably more than enough."

"Do you think you could access Bpook's class lists for the duration of her course at Georgetown?"

"That's all?"

"Yes."

"I could probably do that on my iPhone with my eyes closed."

"Big head."

"How do you think that would help?"

"I don't know. I'm wondering if there was some relationship issue. What if she had a boyfriend studying with her, someone who was taking advantage of her?"

"Isn't that the role of boyfriends anyway? I doubt there'd be a cross-reference of relationships in the public domain."

"No, but we can see what names come up often in her classes. She said she was a rental, dented and dumped and used."

"You want me to check call-girl agencies around D.C.?"

"You don't think . . . ?"

"She wouldn't have been the first."

"Well, OK. But I doubt she'd have used her real name."

"The Web sites post photos of their girls these days. Prostitution's come a long way."

"She said, 'The monitor lizard knew nothing.' "

Sissi laughed. I knew why. The Thai word for monitor lizard is *heea,* and, oddly, it's the dirtiest word we've got in our language.

"Male or female?"

"She said it in English so there was no gender. But somebody's really upset her. If it was the call-girl thing, it might be a friend or relative that got her involved. Could have been a boyfriend pimping her out. But I don't know. She doesn't seem the type. She's got the looks, but she's missing the tough edge. She seems so innocent."

"They pay extra for that."

"I know."

I knocked on the door of the office that was formerly that of Lieutenant Chompu.

"Come in" came a gruff voice that clearly wasn't his.

I entered and found Lieutenant Egg sitting at Chompu's old desk, the one with the bullethole decals across the front. Chompu was at a sort of card table off to one side, working through a pile of files. The annoying short-wave radio was on, the volume too loud.

"I'm looking for Lieutenant Egg," I said.

"That's me," he said.

I've never understood how men with bad toupees can be unaware of exactly how ridiculous they look. I wonder if they gaze lovingly at themselves in the mirror and visualize their heads twenty years earlier before the bald bugs started gnawing at their roots. Lieutenant Egg really looked as if some flock of small birds had built a nest on top of him. But the rest of him was all brawn, so I doubted anyone dared make fun of him. He was a rough-looking man, not to be reckoned with.

"My name is Jimm Juree," I said. "I'm a journalist doing a piece for *Thai Rat* about the police and their relations with the Burmese."

"Why come to me?" he asked.

"Major Mana said you were responsible for Burmese matters."

"So?"

He looked pointedly at Chompu, who hadn't yet emerged from his paperwork burrow.

"So I'll be looking at officials at every level, from village headmen, through medical and emergency personnel. I need to know what the attitude of the police is."

"I don't think —"

"The major believes it would be valuable for his station to have this story told. He said it might dispel some widely held myths that there's any anti-Burmese sentiment in the police force."

"The major said that?"

He probably would have done if he'd been here and not off selling herbal hair conditioner out of the back of his Pajero.

"Yes."

"All right. No names to be printed. I haven't got much time. Grab that chair and bring it —"

"I'd rather do this just the two of us."

"That's all right. Loo-ten-ant Chompu can skip out and pick daisies somewhere. Isn't that right, Loo-loo? Got some embroidery to do?"

Chompu blushed.

"Ah, the major had me set up my recording device in your meeting room," I said. "There are refreshments there as well."

Lieutenant Egg slapped his palms on the desk.

"This better not take long," he grunted.

"Ten minutes. Fifteen at the most," I said.

The lieutenant slammed shut the file he was working on, picked up his radio receiver, and stamped past me and out the door. I raised my eyebrows to Chom.

"Fifteen minutes at the most," I mouthed and tossed him a pack of bobby pins before following the lieutenant along the corridor.

After taking a long time to settle down and test the recorder, which was being temperamental, I finally asked Egg what his role was when dealing with the Burmese community. I wanted to ask him to turn off his short wave, but I didn't want to antagonize him. He summed up his duties in about four sentences and leaned on the desk, ready to stand.

"Is that all?" he asked.

I couldn't think of any more questions, but I knew he'd walk if I didn't say something.

"Why you?" I asked.

"What?"

"Why did they make you the representative for the Burmese? There are a lot of officers of the same rank. Why you?"

"I'm an expert," he said.

"On . . . ?"

"Burmese issues. I'm fluent in their language. I know more about their history and culture than most of the uneducated peasants you meet over here. I'm a sort of ambassador, I suppose you might say."

As opposed to a diplomat. He was distracted by movement in my rain cape, which hung from the door.

"What is that?" he asked.

"Dog," I said.

I got the feeling he thought I was lying.

"So you were also liaising with the Burmese when you were stationed in Pattani?" I asked.

He glared at me.

"How do you —"

"Major Mana."

"Yeah, I was organizing cross-cultural events. Awareness training for new arrivals. That kind of thing."

"Well, that's just wonderful. I admire men who care about ethnic problems."

"Right. Other officers — they don't care so much. But I'm very sensitive to the problems the Maung face."

Ten minutes and counting.

"And fluent in Burmese. Wow. Where did you learn that? I've looked at the textbooks. It seems unfathomable. I reckon you have to be some kind of genius to pick it up."

I got a brief gloat out of him.

"You know, here and there," he said. "Some people just have an ear. What can I say?"

"I hope you don't mind me saying that you seem to be a very special human being, Lieutenant. An officer of the law. A linguist. A social worker. I've a good mind to rewrite this just as a feature on you."

Mistake.

I'd gone too far too soon. I could see him shut down. He stood and went to the door.

"None of that," he said.

"I don't have to use your photo."

"Nor name. Nor the story."

"Why not?"

He was already halfway out the door.

"I like to keep my altruistic side private. Modest that way, I am."

"Couldn't you . . . ?"

But he was gone. I looked at the time on my phone. Twelve minutes. Depending on how long it had taken Chompu to open the cabinet, sprint downstairs, make copies of all the relevant files, sprint back up and replace them, then return the cabinet to its original state and rearrange his hair, I thought twelve minutes would be just about enough. That was if everything went according to plan.

I walked along the corridor to their office, where I found Egg standing with his hands on his hips, staring down at his filing cabinet where a nylon police-issue jacket, the type Chompu had been wearing to lunch, was hanging by one corner, wedged in the top drawer of the metal cabinet. Chompu sat at his desk wearing a smile that had seen better days.

9.
WE WILL IRON EACH OTHER

(from "Islands in the Stream" —
THE BEE GEES)

The water in the stream behind our resort had risen above the banks and was spreading slowly. The sea in front of us was rising gently, now creeping beneath the door of hut number one. The gray sky sent down a steady sprinkle of rain. It was a humble invasion but one that would eventually drown us all. In Chiang Mai, our wise country folk built houses on stilts to keep their families cool in summer and dry in the rainy season. In the south, everyone built at ground level and laughed in the face of floods. It was the Rambo response to disaster. "Come and get me, nature!" "It's only water," they say here. "We'll be dry in a week." They may have been right, but I'd already watched a table/bench/straw roof set float off to the horizon. Our toilets were shipwrecked, my vegetable patch was being eaten by fish, and our new home, our only livelihood, sat on a sliver of land between the devil river and the deep gray sea.

I had to leave the motorcycle up on the road beside Captain Kow's because our carport was waterlogged. The water reached the top of the Noys' Honda wheels, but at least it was still there. That meant they must be too. Mair and Gaew were in the shop. It was an impressive sight. The ladies of the co-op had done an astounding job. They'd cleaned up and repaired and repainted. They'd replaced the smithereens of wooden shelving with neat bamboo racks, and the place looked every bit as good as it had before the blast. Admittedly, it hadn't looked that great before the blast. And all this they'd done without the aid of electricity. The power was off all over the district. A little drop of rain and "pop" goes the transformer. I went over to Mair and reached into the pocket of my poncho. I carefully pulled out little Beer. I swear she was about to spit at me until she noticed Mair standing in front of her. And before my eyes the dog became lovable. I offered her up in the plastic hood, but my mother took hold of the puppy in her bare hands and held it to her bosom. She stroked its head and gave it a kiss. I had to look away. I wondered whether Mother Teresa had a daughter who didn't care that much for lepers. Probably not.

"There," said Mair. "See? She'll be just fine. Do you want to introduce her to her brother and sister?"

I couldn't think of anything worse. Between them, they'd probably insult her, then eat her. Mair had too much faith in natural dog bonding.

"No, Mair. I've done my duty for the day. You serve her up yourself."

"Fair enough."

She kissed me on the forehead with the same mouth that had kissed the dog-of-the-living-dead. But what could I say?

"Your policeman friend phoned," she said. "Twice."

I'd forgotten that Chompu had Mair's cell phone number. I'd turned off my phone the minute I'd fled the Pak Nam police station. I suppose it was good news he was still able to press the numbers. It meant not all his fingers were broken. I know I should have stood by him. I should have told Lieutenant Egg it was me who forced Chompu to break into his cabinet. But I needed to keep that newsman's distance. The crime editor at the *Chiang Mai Mail* — when he was still sober

— had told me, "You can only write about a gold shop robbery if it wasn't you that did it." It was conceivable he was speaking literally, but I was young and impressionable and I tended to prefer to see him as a wise seer speaking in fables. The lesson learned was that the journalist had to remain aloof, report the crime with enthusiasm but not to the point that she becomes a part of the investigation. It had been one of the most profound moments of my journalistic education, not at all diminished when the editor's brother was convicted of robbing a gold shop. Evidently, his masked accomplice had escaped. The editor had me write up the report. It was my first by line. A moment and a moral I'd never forget. I had faith that my cunning Lieutenant Chompu would have come up with a viable excuse as to how his jacket was trapped inside the other lieutenant's cabinet. The true answer probably fell somewhere between darned bad luck and stupidity. But it wasn't my call.

"Grandad not back yet?" I asked.

"Goodness," said Mair. "He's been dead for forty years. What kind of a sick question is that?"

"I meant *my* grandad."

"Oh, that one. No."

"Have you seen the Noys since breakfast?"

218

"Now that's a story," she said. "Usually they don't make it far from their cabin. Can't say I blame them with this weather. But it's nice to see they're getting more adventurous. They made it all the way to Pak Nam today."

They'd escaped?

"Mair, are you sure?"

"Of course I'm sure. I got a call from Boung at the bank. The power was out there too, so the ATM wasn't working. You know? A bank is rather like a block of soap when there's no electricity. All that useless equipment. I bet most of the girls there can't do sums in their heads."

"So, the Noys?"

"They couldn't use their credit cards, could they now? And it wasn't their bank. They could have had our bank phone their bank to get confirmation, but I imagine our Noys would be wary about making contact with anything connected to their real lives, wouldn't you? A few phone line traces and, zoom, helicopters descend on Pak Nam Lang Suan, men in black parasailing down wires."

"Why did the bank clerk phone you?"

"To verify I knew them and would vouch for their credit card."

"Wait! How did they get to Pak Nam?

Their car's down there in the carport."

"Another story. Boung saw them pull up in front of the bank on the back of the drinking water truck."

"The man who delivers the bottles here?"

"Supachai."

"So they really were escaping."

"You know, I bet they were avoiding paying their bill."

"Mair, the deposit they left would have been enough to put Arny through law school. No, they were afraid it wasn't safe here anymore."

"The latrines?"

I hadn't told Mair the details of Noy's peculiar education in D.C.

"They don't trust us," I said.

"To be frank, I don't blame them," she said. "I don't trust us either."

"Well, it doesn't matter now, does it? They'll be long gone."

"I doubt that."

"Why?"

"I refused to vouch for them."

"You did?"

She grinned as if she'd done something spectacularly naughty.

"Mair, why?"

"They're obviously in some sort of trouble. They're so desperate they ditched a

perfectly good car and fled in the rain
wedged between plastic bottles. They were
so unworldly they thought the local passenger truck to Lang Suan would accept a
credit card. Ha! I can see Visit's face now."

"The driver?"

"Could I really launch such a sweet couple
into a world that had painted them into a
corner like this? With black paint. Emul-
sion. Matt. No. It's apparent they need al-
lies more than exits. I got Boung to pass the
phone to the mother, and we had a little
chat."

"So, where are they now?"

"They're on their way back here. I asked
Nat at the post office to bring them with
the mail."

"Do you know the names of everyone in
Pak Nam?"

"Don't be silly."

"Do you honestly expect them to come
quietly?"

"The world can be a daunting place when
you have no money. You ask all those poor
people in Bangladesh. Especially when it's
raining."

"Does Nat have a car?"

"Motorcycle with a sidecar. One of the
Noys will have to sit at the rear with the
mail pack on her shoulders."

I was desperately sad the Noys had chosen to run away from us. I thought we'd established some sort of trust.

"They'll be wet to the bone," said Mair. "Why don't you go and make them something nice and hot for their lunch? They probably haven't eaten anything since breakfast."

There she was. My mother. Her mind seemed to be leaking directly into her heart. As the former shrank, the latter swelled. Or perhaps she'd always been this way and I'd been too self-absorbed to notice. She seemed quite surprised when I threw my arms around her neck and sniffed the sweet perfume of her cheek. The animal in her arms growled.

"I named it Beer, by the way," I said. "The dog."

"What a lovely name." She smiled. "So bubbly."

I was in the kitchen putting together something hot and welcoming and trying to call Sissi back on my hands-free. Multitasking had always brought out the Mr. Bean in me. In fact, doing just two things at the same time invariably led to accidental crossover from one to the other. The phone rang before I was able to get my call through, and I didn't bother to look at the screen.

"Easy on the MSG," I said.

"Solid advice."

"Chompu?"

"Surprised I'm not dead?"

"I'm delighted, Chom. What happened?"

"You scarpered, is what happened."

"A controlled retreat. At the spur of the moment that was the course of action I decided would benefit us both. It was instinct. Come on. I know you came up with some wonderful story to explain away how you got your jacket stuck in the cabinet drawer. You're brilliant like that."

"It wasn't my jacket."

"See? Who'd have thought of that?"

"No. I mean it wasn't my jacket. You and Egg had been gone barely a minute. I broke into the cabinet quite brilliantly, and there I was on my knees ferreting through drawers when I heard the door handle squeak behind me. I turned in fright, trembling, expecting to see Egg's pistol aimed at my head. Instead, there was Sergeant Major Tort, who handles all the accounts for the police stations in the region. The sergeant major is generally on a tight schedule because he also has a catfish farm that takes up a lot of his time. He can't wait for this or that officer to get back from the field to hand over his expenses sheet, so he has access to all the locked cabinets. The desk sergeant gives him a bunch of keys when he arrives. Egg's time sheets were in his files. I took the papers I thought would be relevant down to the copy room and returned to find the major still at it. I put back the original files and secreted the copies in my Nok Airways baby-blue backpack. Subterfuge successful! I even allowed a smug expression to creep onto my boyish face.

"That's when the sergeant major got his jacket stuck in the drawer. He'd put back the budget file and slammed the drawer shut and the jacket zipper got itself wedged in there somehow. He hadn't even locked the thing. He heaved and he hoed and tugged for all his worth and could not get that jacket out. The scene was playing beautifully for me. If only he'd stayed there tugging away. But, to my horror, he deserted the jacket, calling it 'the type of cheap flashy crap the police were so fond of handing around' and he left. A minute later Egg arrived and you ran away."

"I assumed . . ."

"That I was Inspector Clouseau?"

"So you have them?"

"The files? But, of course, *ma chérie*."

224

"And Egg bought the whole stuck zipper story?"

"Unequivocally. Haven't you?"

"Of course I . . . Wait! Is it true?"

"Does it matter?"

"That is exactly why I love you so dearly, Lieutenant."

"Ah, if only you were a New Zealand rugby player. Do you want me to bring you the files?"

"No. I'd like you to read through them first. If there's anything suspicious in there, you're the man to spot it."

"Very well."

"Chom. You were sensational."

"I know."

I had another call waiting. It was Sissi telling me she had the class lists and was sending them to my e-mail. The flight to Seoul had been delayed an hour. The yellow-shirt spokesman had announced that this would be a temporary measure while their own people took control of the airport.

"I'm not sure how much faith I have in a traffic control tower manned by clothing retailers," she said.

I could see her point, and I'd run out of "everything will be fine" comments.

"Can't you kick up a stink?" I asked.

"No need for that, little sister," she said.

225

"The rebels didn't face fire from the police, but you should see the flak flying from all the disgruntled passengers. There's nothing like an airport full of stroppy foreigners to test the unity of an insurgent army. It's a joy. I'm watching a group of British darts players poking some poor baroness in the bosom with their fingers."

"You're taking it all very calmly," I remarked.

"Can't fight fate, Jimm. When the ides are against you, there's nothing you can do but sit back and enjoy the show."

"Look, Sissi. I can't get to my e-mail right now. As you have a little while before your flight, perhaps you could . . ."

"Already started. I see eight Thai names on the lists. It looks like it might have been a scholarship program or something. Only one name so far that I've found on all the lists. It's someone called Chaturaporn — male. But these are early days. And I have a feeling I'll have endless free hours for research. There's just been a delivery of table tennis tables. They seem ominously well prepared."

"You know? If all else fails, you could always come down here for a bit of a holiday."

"Wade knee-deep in stinky beach garbage

and trip over body parts? That would be something of an itinerary. I'm surprised Club Med hasn't picked up on it."

" 'No' would have been fine."

"Yeah, sorry. I don't think I'll make it. Besides, I seem to be caught up in a little ruck of Thai history, here. I can tell my grandchildren all about it."

"Well, you stay out of trouble."

"Not on your life. I've just emerged from solitary confinement. I'm planning to get into as much trouble as I possibly can. I read there were couples who met during the occupation of Government House and fell in love and got married there. Just think. I have all these men around me who can't get away. After a few weeks I might even start to look attractive to them."

"It sounds to me like you don't really care about Korea."

"Care? Certainly I care. But this might even work out better. The gala's foreign guest of honor held captive by desperate terrorists in an airport siege. They'll be burning candles for me. I'll be a martyr to the cause of self-deception. They'll name a brand of *kimchee* after me. I'll end up with the key to the city of Seoul."

"If you don't get killed."

"The only way I can see getting killed here

is in the rush for the Ladies'."

"In that case, I hope your flight gets canceled."

"Thanks. Gotta go."

For the first time since we'd arrived in Maprao, I had back-to-back call-waiting. It was just like the good old days. Aung was hanging on. I wondered if he'd decided for us to get together before the effects of the antidepressant wore off.

"Aung?"

"You really want to help?"

"Absolutely."

"Shwe. They've taken him."

I sat in Aung's little living room with Grandad Jah, Arny, and Ex-Police Captain Waew. Aung seemed uncomfortable to have so many Thais in his house. He'd almost fled through the back door when he saw us arrive en masse at the front.

"Aung, it's me," I'd called out. "This is my family. We're here to help."

Once we were all seated on mats on the floor and had been served lukewarm water in six different drinking vessels, Aung's wife, Oh, left us to it. I don't think it was a matter of this not being a woman's business. Even without the benefit of understanding their language, I could tell she was distressed. I got the feeling she'd attack her husband with a wok as soon as we left. She was a mother of five children, and her husband's decision to bring in the Siamese was inviting danger.

"So, what happened?" I asked Aung.

Once more the Burmese looked nervously at Grandad, who'd not opened his mouth since our arrival. I hadn't introduced him as ex-police, so there had to be some scent about him.

"At about one o'clock," Aung began, "Shwe was on his way back to his lodgings. The rain hadn't let up, so there was nothing they could do at the fish-drying plant. Shwe was walking alone along the road by the fruit orchard when a police truck pulled up. Shwe was used to this. He stopped, *wai*'d — the police like it when we *wai* — and reached for his ID card. One of the policemen pulled out a gun, so Shwe dropped to his knees and put his hands on his head. We learn . . ."

He looked at Grandad Jah.

"We learn all the hoops to jump through for the police. Usually, it's just a game that we're encouraged to lose. But this time they bundled Shwe into the back seat of the truck and didn't even look at his ID. And they drove, not west to Ranong immigration, but north along the coast road to Sawee. There, they dragged him out of the truck, searched him, and locked him in a concrete shed with six other Burmese. None of them could speak Thai, so they had no idea what they'd been arrested for. Five of them had legitimate work permits and sponsors. Like Shwe, they'd been picked up off the street in broad daylight. Shwe knew in his bones that this was connected to the slavery rumors."

"How could you possibly know all this?" I asked.

"Shwe kept his cell phone taped to his lower leg," said Aung. "He was sick of getting his phones permanently confiscated by the local cops. Body searches generally miss the back of the leg. So he had his phone with him. He called me and told me what had happened."

"And he's still in Sawee now?" Captain Waew asked.

"Yes," said Aung.

"Do we have enough information to pinpoint the place they're being held?"

"No. One of the detainees knew the district they were in because she'd been there before. But not the exact location."

"They have women there?" I asked.

"Two in that group."

I wanted to ask why, but I feared what the reply might be.

"Are you still in contact?" I asked.

Aung shook his head.

"Here's the problem," he said. "Shwe's phone battery is really low. With all the power outages, he hasn't had a chance to charge it. He's got . . . I don't know . . . a few minutes left at the most. I told him to turn it off and only get back to me if he finds out their exact location."

"That was smart, lad," said Grandad, much to everyone's surprise.

"But it means that all we can do is sit around and wait," said Waew.

"Right," Grandad agreed. "And what then? Even if we know where they're being held, are we expected to go and raid the place? Us?"

Aung's face seemed to confirm the hopelessness of it all. He'd feared as much. What the hell could we do about it? Who was there to report to? I felt I was letting him down.

"Shwe said there were two policemen in the truck?" I asked Aung.

"Yes."

"Did he describe them?"

"That wasn't so important. He had a few minutes on his phone."

"Of course."

But it did mean there were other police officers involved. Egg wasn't alone in all this. If the kidnapping took place at one, it meant Egg wasn't in that truck. He was in the interview room with me. I started to wonder whether the whole station was involved. I also wondered whether anyone would bother mentioning seeing a police truck passing through Maprao a few seconds before our shop was bombed. Was it us against the police force?

Aung promised to phone me the moment he heard from Shwe. We secretly hoped that wouldn't be too soon because we weren't prepared to deal with such an eventuality.

10.
SOMETHING IN THE
WAY SHE MOOS

(from "Something" — GEORGE HARRISON)

As we were already in Pak Nam, I diverted us via the Internet shop. It was the worst possible time to be there. The place was crammed with Zelda warriors and online car-jackers and big-eyed Japanese searchers. We needed subterfuge, and my task force hounds needed exercise. Grandad Jah walked in first, like the head reservoir dog, and flashed his ID, putting it back in his pocket before anyone had a chance to notice it was his Lotus supermarket discount card. Arny and Waew fanned out behind him to make it look like a raid.

"All right. Everyone away from the computers," said Grandad.

Chair legs scraped and teenage arms rose.

"Who are —" began the owner.

"Haven't you been warned, son?" Grandad asked, looking rudely through the documents on the young man's desk. Waew began facing all the kids against the wall. Arny . . . looked menacingly uncomfortable.

"You think we don't monitor what goes on in places like this?" Grandad asked. "You want to see a list of all the illicit Web sites accessed from right here? Don't you know there are laws in place to prevent minors looking at filth and radical rantings?"

"I don't —" began the owner.

"No, you don't. But ignorance doesn't keep you out of prison, boy. Come on. Outside, the lot of you."

You'll notice Grandad hadn't actually claimed to represent any official body, but he had that presence. While everyone was marching out, I snuck inside and hijacked a computer that was already online.

Alb, I wrote. *I desperately need an NGO working with Burmese that has some political and financial clout. Funding from overseas preferred. Urgent.*

While I waited, I printed out Sissi's class lists on the communal printer. As I looked casually through them I noticed something odd about the names. Most of them were followed by an "m" or an "f" to denote gender. In the first semester, the Chaturaporn that Sissi had spotted on all

Noy's lists was tagged as male. But in the second and subsequent semester, that had been changed to female. Given my own family history, it wasn't unthinkable that Mr. Chaturaporn had opted for gender reassignment, but I doubted anyone would leave a country with the best sex-change clinics in the world and go to Washington for a snip. It could have been a mere clerical error, but I'd get Sissi to follow up on it later. I was checking the weather forecast for the Gulf when Alb's reply arrived.

Contact Piper Porterfield at Hope for Myanmar, he wrote. *I hear she's been sleeping with George Soros, the philanthropist. Lot of aid money to spread around for the Burmese cause. She's got nice tits too.*

Men. Was there any hope for them? Fortunately, rather than a bra cup size, he'd added her phone number. I called. She picked up almost immediately.

"Piper."

I told her who I was, where I was, and what was happening. I didn't know whether she could speak Thai, so I did this in my pronunciation-challenged English. All the time she kept quiet, and I wondered whether she'd put the phone on her desk and gone out for dinner. But I kept going all the way

235

to Sawee and the seven incarcerated Burmese.

"Can you hear me OK?" I asked.

There was a pause and a sound like the tap of a keyboard.

"Just the seven?" she asked.

I think I preferred her when she was quiet.

"Yes."

"It's just that that is rather small fry."

She had a Lady Di accent.

"Just how many people need to be kidnapped and killed before we can increase the size of the fry?" I asked.

"Thousands disappear every year," she said. "Refugees wiped out by the junta on their way to Thai camps. Children nabbed from construction site slums. And lots of et ceteras. I get reports such as yours every day. Your situation is every bit as tragic, of course, but the resources needed to resolve the matter would far exceed the benefits."

I didn't know whether I admired her honesty or hated her for it.

"Benefits obviously meaning something more important than keeping people alive," I presumed.

"Yes, look, I'm sorry. In my line of work I tend to trivialize death. It helps. The benefits I'm referring to are the factors which help to change world opinion. Burma has no natural oil to rescue from tyranny, so we have to rely on slowly creating a mood of outrage at the social level before we can hope for international intervention. Once we have political support, we may be able to save more lives than we can with a small police action in the forgettable south."

"I thought you had a budget for things like this."

"We do. But our directive is to maximize these situations. To take an issue and humanize it at an international level. Touch as many hearts as possible. We did a sea rescue once, but it was so isolated and over so quickly that we barely made a ripple in the world press. It was a very expensive failure."

I was punched numb for a few seconds. When I came around, I asked, "Do you have a counterpart at the Thai Police Ministry?"

"Certainly. We fund their Division of International Day Laborers."

With all that money you'd think they'd come up with something more catchy than DIDL.

"And what do they do there?" I asked.

"They distribute information to the press. Collect relevant reports from the police data bank."

"Any of them have guns?"

"What are you getting at? They're all

qualified police officers."

"I mean, do they ever leave the office and go out and shoot people?"

"Not . . . no, not shoot. There are officers attached to the unit who are involved in casework."

"But they could be called upon if massive public outrage was being waged. They could rush to a scene if it was in the public eye and guaranteed a world audience?"

"I suppose . . . yes."

"Good. Then this conversation wasn't a complete waste of time. I'll get back to you."

The trouble with a cell phone was that if you slammed it down, you'd break your own jaw. It seemed the bigger the organization, the less they dealt with actual people. And don't even get me started on the UN. All I needed was a few thousand dollars for high-powered weaponry, and we could do the rest ourselves. Blow those slavers out of the Gulf. But no, I suppose that would be just too difficult for the silly cow to write up in the annual report.

I collected my printouts and my family and Captain Waew, abandoned all the street-bound nerds, and returned to the truck. We were on our own, tactically, but I didn't want to break that news to the task force. It was a desperately lonely feeling.

Giving up suddenly felt like such a good idea. While Grandad drove us very slowly home through the drizzle, I looked around at my cohorts. Arny had joined up because he wanted to impress his girlfriend. Grandad and Waew were on board because they wanted to get revenge on a couple of hoods. None of us was particularly fond of the Burmese. Once the Viagra had worn off, I doubted I'd have any personal interest at all. So what was it? Why could I not shake this urge to do something suicidal? The rain smudged my side window, and I looked into its patterns. I saw the posturing of the rat brothers and the homophobic bullying of Lieutenant Egg, and I thought back to why I'd become a crime reporter. If the crooks were crooked and the cops were crooked, who was there left to bring justice to our corrupt world? Who could we respect? Where was the shoulder angel who twanged on the conscience of the undecided youth? Who else might argue that the words *graft* and *dishonesty* and s*elfishness* were not necessarily inspirational? Who else but the press? That's why I'd become a journalist, and that's why I'd turned to crime writing. To shore up our flimsy status quo. To challenge the view that the bigger the crime the lower the chances of arrest.

Victims of trafficking and imminent execution shouldn't be on their own with no hero to fly in and rescue them. But out there on the high sea there were only the seagull and the prawn to witness the crime. It was a vast lawless outback. It was impossible for a criminal not to be overwhelmed by that feeling of invincibility. Who cared what he did?

Me.

I'm not sure anybody noticed that explosion of moral dignity inside the cab of the Mighty X. I felt it was time to inspire a team spirit.

"OK, everyone," I said. "Let's get serious. What do we have to go on?"

I'd forgotten all about the old boys and their afternoon detective work. As they hadn't mentioned anything I assumed they'd had no success with the Thai boat owners. So I was surprised when, with a twitch, Captain Waew said:

"Common opinion is that it's the Bangkok boats doing all the illegal stuff. There were two new concessions added out of the blue last year by senatorial decree, or whatever it's called. That means that despite long-standing agreements with the Fisheries department limiting the number of contracts, every now and then you get some influential figure handing out deals to this or that nephew or cousin. They'd lease big boats and take them deep into the Gulf. They'd reap as much profit as they could before the next election when the contracts were revoked by the next minister, who'd go on to replace them with his own relatives."

"Did you manage to get the names of any of the boats?" I asked.

"The contact didn't know any specifics, so I phoned the Department of Fisheries. They'll fax me a list of all the newly registered boats over the past year. The local trawler owners aren't at all happy about outsiders coming in, ignoring all the no-fishing zone markers, using dragnets over young coral and just generally making assholes of themselves. The big-boat captains that come from down here in the south, they aren't averse to bending the odd rule, but they've all learned from experience what overfishing has done to their industry."

"This might be a stupid question," I asked, "but isn't there anyone policing the sea at all?"

"I found an old seafarer who told me all about the Coastal Patrol," said Grandad. "Except he called them the Postal Patrol. They have two boats to police an area of two thousand square kilometers. And they don't have much of a budget for fuel, so they rely on donations."

"Don't tell me," I said. "From big-boat owners."

"That would be correct."

"So if they don't go after the big boats, what do they do?"

"Splash around in the shallows hassling the small-boat fishermen, from what I can make out. Fine them for minor infringements."

"While the big boats break the law with impunity," said Waew.

"It all seems . . . I don't know . . . too big for us," said Arny. Never one to pass up an opportunity for pessimism.

"I think it's doable," I said.

"How?" asked Grandad, turning to give me a prolonged Grandad Jah glare, even though he was driving.

The Mighty X really shouldn't have had a back seat. The expression "4-Seater" was only a selling point. I suppose if you had two mine-victim passengers, it would be the perfect vehicle. But anyone with legs had to wrap them around the seat in front. With Arny taking up half the cab all by himself, we were an intimate foursome in that small space. You could smell the lack of confidence.

"I don't know what it is yet," I said. "But I know there has to be a way."

When we got back to the resort, the sea had retreated somewhat, but the Neo-Mekhong river out back was wide enough for paddle steamers to ply their trade. Only the side walls of the bridge were visible above the surface. A hundred years ago all this water would have found its way unimpeded to the sea, but idiots like our predecessors had built for sea views and filled the land and limited the runoff from the hills to ninety-centimeter pipe segments that burrowed under driveways and palm plantations and houses. Monsoon water didn't have that type of patience. If you've gotta go . . .

We parked the truck on the hump in the road fifty meters from the resort, and I splashed down to the kitchen. I was on dinner duty, of course. With the tide at its lowest, I no longer had to wade from the larder to the stove. The power had been off all day, so the menu was decided on what smelled best in the dark refrigerator. I was just one step ahead of putrefaction. The day's events had caused me to be absent for the Noys' return on the postal motorcycle earlier. I'd called Mair from the truck, and she told me the two had eaten sparingly and were sorry they'd tried to escape. So I decided to create an evening meal that was both nutritious and welcoming. Thankfully, gas was not subject to the whims of nature. I was halfway through my famous spicy ginger chicken when Sissi phoned.

"What's happening?" I asked.

"I'm into the semi-finals of the table tennis tournament. It appears it's one of those skills you never lose."

"I thought all your muscles had atrophied from years seated in front of a computer."

"You're so yesterday. For six months I've been seated in front of the computer on a stationary cycle. I've probably been to Shanghai and back since May. I had to get in shape for Seoul."

"You bored?"

"It isn't quite as intense as I'd hoped."

"Is your flight canceled?"

"Everybody's flight's canceled."

"Are you allowed to leave the airport?"

"They have a fleet of yellow-shirt shuttle buses. You can go anywhere you choose in Bangkok free of charge."

"So, why are you still there?"

"Where would I go in Bangkok? It's an awful place."

"You're still banking on having something to tell the grandchildren, aren't you?"

"I'm keeping a notebook diary. So far, the only excitement has been the barging and yelling from the disgruntled passengers and my table tennis victories. I might have to embellish."

"So, are you free now?"

"I have another match in twenty minutes. A baggage handler. Strong wrists. Lovely smile."

"All right. Never mind the table tennis. You remember the coverage of the Iraq war? A journalist a million miles inside the desert. Not a communication tower in sight. And he charges up his laptop computer and files a live report. And it's all wobbly and the words don't all connect up, but there he is, live in the middle of nowhere."

"Technology's come a long way since then."

"So, would it work if you were, say, in the middle of the ocean?"

"Same principle. As long as you're on the BGAN network with multiple voice and data interfaces, including WLAN connectivity."

"All right. I have no idea what you just said. I don't actually need the serial numbers and stock codes. Where do I get hold of one?"

"Can't you just video it?"

"No. It has to be live."

"Then you'd need a multi-user satellite phone with extensive functionality. Thane and Thane do a really top —"

"All right. Where do I find one?"

"You don't just stroll into an appliance store and pick one up. You certainly won't find one on the shelf at Tesco Lang Suan. They usually have to be ordered. When do you need it?"

"Tomorrow. Maybe sooner."

"I sense another menopausal, heterosexual mad rush to the head. Take a deep breath and tell your old sister exactly what you have in mind here."

Dinner was served with a very fine cardboard cask of Chilean red in the room of our friends from Bangkok. Because I didn't want to overwhelm them with too many annoying visitors, I told the rest of my family they weren't invited. This was my game. Beneath the shuddering light of an oil lamp, with the rain still pattering against the glass of the windows, the Noys looked drained of their natural beauty. Since there was no electricity, they hadn't showered or blowdried or freshened up from the day's ordeals. They'd assumed an unmistakably helpless demeanor, like the last two polar bears on the last block of glacier. They didn't attack their ginger chicken with the enthusiasm I thought it deserved. I felt like I was eating for the three of us.

Between bites, I asked, "So where did you think you'd go from here?"

Neither answered.

"You realize how insulting today's little drama was, I suppose?" I added. "It was a bit late to stop trusting us. If we'd been likely to turn you in, you'd have been busted long ago."

"That wasn't the reason," said Noy. "We did. We do trust you. We love you, even. We feel safe here. We didn't want to leave."

"Then . . . why?"

"We were afraid for you," said Mamanoy. "We were afraid they'd find us, and harm would come to you because you'd been sheltering us."

I so desperately wanted to know who "they" were, but I was supposed to know the whole story already. If I admitted ignorance now, they'd clam up.

"They're not as powerful as you think," I guessed.

"How would you know?" asked Mamanoy.

Good question.

"Because power is an illusion. Most people who act tough are just . . . acting."

"Not these. They have people looking for us. Professionals."

"How could you know that for sure?"

"It's the way powerful people work. You lose face, so you have to let your associates know you've 'fixed' the problem. Not doing so would be a sign of weakness."

"So you think running and hiding is the answer? When would it all end?"

"When somebody's dead," said Noy, calmly.

None of us was eating.

"You really think . . . ?"

"Yes. I know what they want me to do. When I refuse, they'll have no choice."

Whatever happened over there in the States had followed them back home and traumatized them.

"They've already sent a message," said Mamanoy.

"What sort?"

"We left two cats behind. Before we fled, we asked the neighbors to take them in. We thought they'd be safe. But som-somebody went to the neighbors' house and killed our cats."

"What? But that could have been some random psychopath," I said.

I knew no end of people who would gladly torture cats.

"The neighbors had three cats of their own. They weren't touched. The next day some people went to their house claiming to be local police officers investigating the cat killings. But the neighbors hadn't reported it to anyone. They told the men they didn't know us. They said they just noticed the cats weren't being fed and took them in. The officers left a phone number and told them to get in touch if they had any contact from us."

"How do you know this?"

"The neighbors are actually close to us. The husband is in e-mail contact with my husband. He writes from his office."

"And what machine does your husband write from?"

"He uses Internet cafés," said Noy. "We all have notebooks, but we've agreed not to use them with cell-phone dongles. Neither do we use our cell phones. Once every two days we call him from a pay phone. Here we used the one at the end of the lane. It's underwater now. We usually call him at a land number in —"

"Shh," said Mamanoy, and blushed immediately.

I smiled.

"I'm so sorry," she said.

"No problem," I replied.

Once paranoia sets in, it's hard to keep it under control.

"We knew they'd be looking for a mother, father, and daughter, so we went in different directions," said Noy. "We came down Highway 41. After Hua Hin we started traveling at night on back roads to avoid highway cameras. We'd find small resorts like yours to rest in in the daytime. We'd drive past, remove the plates, then drive back. We didn't want anyone reporting our registration details. We only stayed at places that didn't insist on seeing our IDs. On the day we came here, we'd been driving all the previous night. We'd stopped at two resorts where they said they had to write down our citizenship card details. They said it was the local regulation."

"Well, you're here now," I said. "And I don't want you pulling any more stunts like today. Now think back. Did you do anything in Pak Nam to draw attention to yourselves?"

"No," said Noy.

"Tell me exactly what you did there."

"We waited for the passenger truck and realized we didn't have money. We'd given your mother the last of our cash for the room here. We hadn't taken the car because we couldn't buy petrol."

"Where was the last place you used your credit card or ATM?"

"Hua Hin."

"That's four hundred kilometers away. Technically they could have traced you to there. All they'd need is someone at the bank to check the records. Either way they'll probably have assumed you were heading south. So, since Hua Hin?"

"All cash."

"We underestimated the costs of food and petrol," said Mamanoy. "We should have taken out more. Enough to get us to Malaysia. We hoped we could use the ATM today and be on a bus before they could trace it."

"So in Pak Nam, you tried the ATM and it was down. You tried to get money on your credit card, but they needed a guarantor. The bank phoned us. At no stage did anyone note down your card number or ask for personal details?"

"No," said Noy.

"Good."

"Not at the bank."

I gasped.

"Somewhere else?"

"I did send a letter EMS while we were waiting to be delivered back here."

"How did you pay for that?"

"We didn't. I told the manager I'd left my

wallet at your resort. When we arrived, I borrowed the money from your mother. We'll pay you back."

"I hope you didn't put your actual name in the sender box."

"I left it blank on the EMS form."

"Good. The post office can track that. That's why it costs extra. When the power comes back on, they'll type the details onto the computer."

I was getting as paranoid as them. I mean, who was going to hack the post office express delivery details?

"Tell me you didn't give this resort as your return address."

"Of course not," said Noy. "I put c/o the post office."

"Well, that's something, I suppose."

"Mair!" I shouted. I could hardly hear myself. There was a backhoe twenty meters away digging an escape channel for the flooded river. The local administration had decided my vegetable garden would be the perfect spot for it. Mair was on the veranda of her hut surrounded by creatures like some kindly lady in an old Disney animation. The three dogs were wrestling with her. Sticky had taken an immediate liking to little Beer and seemed to be unaware of how diseased she was. Even antisocial Gogo was tag-teaming with Mair. The monkey lounged on the rattan table above them, unpeeling tiny lady finger bananas. A toad hopped unimpeded across the deck. Two daring parakeets sat on the railing opposite, waiting for dropped bananas, and a whole parliament of ceiling lizards hung above, ever hopeful that the electric light might be switched on. The paraffin lamp attracted, then fricasseed any insects that made it through the drizzle.

"Mair!"

Gogo growled. The others ignored me.

"Yes, child?"

"Do you have the number for your friend at the post office?"

"Nat? Of course I do."

"Can I have it?"

"It's in my phone."

"Where's your phone?"

"Phuket."

"Phuket?"

"I'm assuming so. I contacted the gibbon rehabilitation center at Bang Pae. I'd taken some pictures of Elain here, and I wanted them to see her. See if they'd agree to take her on."

"So naturally you put the phone in the envelope so they could take a look."

"There's probably a way to send the pictures separately, but I couldn't for the life of me get them out. So I'll let them sort it out in Phuket."

"Did you, at least, turn it off?"

"The phone? Naturally. Do you think I'm completely useless? I'm sure animal activists will be able to work out how to turn on a telephone."

Sticky was mating with Mair's foot. He had an impressive erection for a young fellow. I had to turn away.

"Mair, I think the dogs are getting too excited."

"Well, somebody didn't take them for their evening walk, did somebody?"

"Mair, I'm a little bit bogged down here with stuff."

"I forgive you, darling."

"Have you seen Captain Kow around?"

She twitched.

"No. Why should I have?"

"I just want to talk to him."

"He won't tell you anything."

I tell you. Weird is a difficult concept to get your head around. If I ever wanted to waste a few years on a Ph.D. I'd probably look at signs in early life that point to the inevitability of Alzheimer's. Mair had always been that fringe character. Like me, her school and university mates had liked her, I suppose. She was funny, friendly, but too odd to join those cliques that linger later in life. The old school network didn't have a seat for Jitmanat Gesuwan. Her communist jungle years put her in touch with like-minded outcasts, most of whom sought respectability once the armistice was agreed.

Mair never really lusted after respectability. That's what I'd loved about her. Her joy. Her total disregard for Thai etiquette. Not caring what people thought of her. She'd been so unlike all the other mothers. She'd turn up at parent–teacher meetings in shorts and a T-shirt and boots. Unmade up. Unadorned. Unencumbered by shallow considerations. No show at all. And if the headmistress said something stupid — and they all did and everyone in the hall would know it — it would be Mair's hand in the air. Mair's voice saying what everyone thought. Damn, I loved her at those meetings. I didn't care that I was the daughter of the odd woman. I'd push it to its limits. My trademark dark brown nail varnish, for example. If anyone else had tried that, they'd be dragged in front of the discipline mistress. But me? I was "the daughter." I needed tolerance. They probably had teachers' meetings just about me. I was top in most subjects, so the mother–daughter relationship hadn't retarded me at all. It just made me culturally dubious. If Mair had been Chinese or *farang* — a white foreigner — the faculty would have had no problem at all in labeling me. Ostentation was commonplace in foreigners. My defect lay in the fact that I was Thai, born of Thai parents from a long, inexhaustible line of Thais. They put the accident of me down to my mother. Neither of us fit. We'd gone our own ways. Me, into the unquenchable fascination of study. Her, into — wherever she was now. She came back to visit us on Earth from time to time, but I knew she had a happier place. I just wondered whether I was headed there too.

The monkey, aka Elain, climbed down from the table and started to pick imaginary ticks out of my mother's hair.

"I've rented a room," said Mair.

"For what?"

"Our Burmese school."

"Mair, we don't have —"

"Don't worry. It was only a hundred *baht* a month."

"Oh? What type of room can you rent for cheaper than a three-pack of toilet rolls?"

"Well, when I say room, perhaps I mean space. It's the unused back corner of the ice works down at the docks."

The same factory I'd visited earlier.

"Wouldn't that be a bit noisy?"

"It's a start. And to start badly is better than never to start at all."

That was, of course, so not true.

I doubted whether my TV would have been much more entertaining had there been power. I lay on my bed staring at it anyway. The screen reflected the tiny glow of the mosquito coil burning on the floor beside me. Beyond the window was a sort of final blackness. It suited my purpose: a clean slate.

Here we go.

The Noys. An upper-middle-class family. Father a successful businessman. Mother, the head of a large suburban middle school. Daughter, as bright as the Big Dipper. She gets a scholarship to study in the U.S. She struggles right up until the final year, when suddenly she outscores everyone on her finals. Far from being elated, she runs away without collecting her degree and reappears in Thailand, where her entire family is forced to flee, pursued by some mysterious "they." If I didn't have such a problem with clichés, I might, at this point, have told myself I was missing something. So I didn't.

Even though I obviously was. I wondered whether the father's gambling debts had something to do with it. But how would that follow Noy to the States? I wondered whether Noy really was hooking to pay her way through school. What if, suddenly, she got serious about her studies and — I don't know — missed a date with some Saudi oil sheik? But how many D.C. pimps had a network that would hound the Noys all the way back to Thailand? And what about the mysterious sex-change boyfriend? How did the clerical department of one of the country's top universities stuff that one up so badly? That, I decided, was the place to start.

I flicked on my all-night rechargeable electronic hurricane lamp — made in Taiwan. *Guaranteed eight hours of almost daylight.* The picture on the box showed Saddam Hussein and his officers in an underground bunker, plotting by the light of the Shinomax. It momentarily bathed my room in an impressive warm light before fading down to dim. It was just enough to help me thumb through the pile of handouts Sissi had e-mailed me from Chiang Mai. She'd pretty much cleared out the Georgetown files. There were financial records, course registrations, and what I was looking for, the student lists. I found the name Chaturaporn on all of Noy's class files. He did indeed begin his academic life as a Mr. before reappearing as a Ms. by semester two. That would have remained a mystery to me had I not come across the list of deposit receipts from overseas students. I paused only to boggle at the cost of overseas study. No wonder my local education department sent me to Sydney Tech. Financial records rarely thrilled me, but that one list provided two fascinating discoveries that sent shudders through my knees.

First was the reason the clerks had initially classified our Ms. Chaturaporn as a man. They had condescendingly assumed that anyone from Thailand couldn't spell. Admittedly, we can't. But that wasn't the case in Chaturaporn's fee receipt. The name was not Mr. Chaturaporn but ML, Chaturaporn. The clerks had taken the liberty to adjust the spelling, but anyone who grew up in my country would know there was no error. The *ML* was an important clue. It painted the scenery an entirely different color.

I was about to put down the bank transfer details and move back to the lists when I noticed the second startling piece of information. According to the receipts, ML

Chaturaporn had received her deposit via the Bangkok Bank Corporation. It made me curious about who had funded Noy's study. But I certainly wasn't expecting what I found. The wire had been from exactly the same account. The bank details for both girls were identical. And there, like that first ever orgasm from a totally unexpected donor, the stars burst before my eyes. I had it. I wanted to shout. I wanted to call the *Chiang Mai Mail* to remind them what a great head of the crime desk I would have made. But, of course, I could not announce what I had learned. I could, however, confront the lawbreaker.

My Shinomax offered little more than a gray puddle of light to guide me to the Noys. It felt like midnight in Transylvania, but my phone told me it was only 8:37 P.M. Candles still flickered behind the Noys' curtains. I knew what crime they'd committed and had an idea who was after them. I had to admit they were totally screwed. I didn't bother to knock. The Noys were on their beds, reading by candlelight. With no fan to cool them, they wore the flimsiest of sleepwear. But I didn't let their gorgeousness distract me from my task. They didn't seem at all flustered by my arrival.

"Sorry, ladies," I said, and sat down at the

end of Mamanoy's bed. They both knew the story, so I guess my purpose there that night was to confirm that I knew it as well.

"Here's the drama as I see it," I began. "A straight-A student is hired by a family to be a study friend to their eldest daughter while overseas. Of course, they didn't employ you for your social skills. You were there to attend every class together with your new friend. Perhaps we should call her . . . the duchess. I was confused that the registrar's office had her listed as a male in the first semester, then changed to female in the second. It didn't seem like the kind of error a university clerk would make But our Ms. Chaturaporn had indeed intended to write ML. As you know, it had nothing to do with gender. It was the abbreviation of *Mom Luang*. ML Chaturaporn was a member of the aristocracy. Her father, I imagine, is a very powerful man, I'm sure you know that. You were a shadow student to a little duchess. And in return for you kindly keeping their daughter company, they agreed to pay off all your father's gambling debts, unmortgage your house, and rescue you all from the threat of poverty."

"Jimm, I don't think —" Noy began.

"And all you had to do was switch ID cards before the tests or when you handed in the papers. I wouldn't even be surprised if you switched names for the entire time you were there. Your faces were similar enough. And heaven knows, we Asians all look alike. Now, the rest of this — you can just stop me if I'm wrong. Your duchess was an average student with no motivation. But her family expected excellence from her. It's a system that goes way back. So many of her ancestors had traveled the same route. Brainbox study buddy. No risk. The daughter passes with honors. The shadow either fails in the end or, if she's very lucky, squeaks through with poor grades. The sponsor has to do the very least to keep the shadow in class right up to the final semester. She can't fail too many courses before then or they'd send her classmate home. But in that final term she doesn't need the shadow anymore, so if she's of a mind, she could just not attend any classes. Send the shadow home with no degree at all. No problem. Who cares?"

The Noys said nothing. Their faces contorted in the candle flickers.

"But, Noy," I said, "you cared. You were an excellent student. The material was easy for you. You loved the courses. You devoured them. But at the end of each semester, you'd reluctantly hand over your student

ID card and accept whatever grade she'd deign to eke out for you. And what was she doing while you slaved over books? She was in the nightclubs, wasn't she? Driving the BMW around with her high-society friends? And I bet she didn't show any respect at all. Not a word of thanks after those A grades. You were the maidservant. You labored for her. You and your family were taken care of financially, so why give thanks, eh?

"And it built up in you," I continued. "All this injustice. You knew the duchess was intent on failing you. She hardly attended classes that final semester. You were a brilliant student, yet people looked down on you as a dunce. And after three years of it, you were Mount Etna. The humiliation bubbled up inside and you blew. You marched into those exam halls, turned up with your term papers, and brushed past the outstretched ID card of your duchess. And you hammered everything that final semester, just like you did the entire course, but this time the honors were in your name. You'd stayed on for the Honor Council inquiry, passed the extra oral tests, suffered the humiliation of the lie-detector test. And all because your foolish courage would have meant nothing if they'd stripped you of your degree. You were in a red funk. A mad rush of blood. And it wasn't until it was all over that you realized what you'd done. What danger you'd put your family in. You probably called your parents then and told them. It was no small matter. You'd broken a contract. But, more important, you'd broken the face of a dynasty. You'd destroyed a century-old tradition. And, Noy, do you know what?"

"What?"

"Good for you, is what. Screw the tradition. You're a bloody heroine. It was one in the eye to the classes who believe their heritage allows them to break the rules. Left to her own devices, the little duchess probably failed the final semester, and they're still conducting an inquiry to see where she went wrong. As far as they're concerned, she was a top student who suddenly went bad. They'll invite her to resit those last finals, but for reasons you and I know, she'll have to decline. She still doesn't have her degree, does she?"

Noy blushed and sighed. There was a long period of silence that seemed appropriate.

"They came to see me in the dormitory," she said. "A couple of Thai goons in safari shirts . . . in the middle of D.C., I tell you. They asked me if I wanted to see my parents hurt. It would be a shame, they said, if they were to have an accident. The goons were very matter-of-fact about it. They told me all I had to do was go to the dean and confess that I'd switched my ID card with the *Mom Luang*'s. She hadn't noticed I was a cheat. That, in fact, all my final semester scores should have been hers. Of course, I would have been thrown out of Georgetown in disgrace. My name . . . my family name would have been dirt. So I ran. I jumped on a Greyhound bus and headed south. I don't know why. It was all a little bit overwhelming. I was starting to get paranoid that they were after me. I was certain there'd be some way of checking passenger lists on aircraft out of the country, so I decided to leave overland. I met up with a tour group of Taiwanese students, and somehow, in the confusion that happens at borders, I got lost in the chaos when a large group came up against an underpaid immigration officer, and I arrived in Mexico in a tour bus. There was no record of me entering the country. I flew home from Mexico City. I think that was what gave us the time to get away from our house. They were still looking for me in the States."

"I respect her for what she did," said Mamanoy.

"You lost your jobs and your house," I said.

"We'd already lost them," she said. "My husband's debts . . . Noy's time in America gave us a sort of stay of execution. That was all. They paid off our bills as part of the deal, but they're in a position to put more pressure on us. My husband would never get work in his field again. He has accepted full responsibility."

"Oh, what a wonderful man. Frankly, I'm amazed that you're still together," I said.

"Love is —"

"Yeah. Don't bother."

"Being a family is all we have."

"Being a family's really going to make everything so much better on the road and in hiding for the rest of your lives."

"Do you have a better solution?"

"I can fix this," I said, with more confidence than I was actually generating.

"How?"

Good question.

"I'll get back to you on that," I said. "We have time. You'll be safe here for the foreseeable future. We can work together on a strategy."

They didn't look inspired. They still saw me as the cook. They didn't know I had contacts beyond Maprao. I had skills. But I did not reveal my secret identity just then. When the time was right, they would see my super-self.

11.
GIVE ME MY PORPOISE WHEN YOU GET HOME

(from "Respect" — OTIS REDDING)

The uneventfulness of the following morning made it all the more remarkable. At three A.M. the power had returned, and all the lights we'd forgotten to turn off and the utilities we'd forgotten to unplug came to life. There ensued the act of putting them all back to sleep. We'd awaken later to a cautious normality. The natural erosion caused by the backhoe ditch had turned our garden into the Grand Canyon. Water had gushed out onto the beach, and the rear flood waters had subsided. The tide had ebbed to leave one end of our latrine block embedded in the beach, as if it had dropped from space. The sky was clear, and the only reminder of the monsoon was a brisk wind blowing off the Gulf. The Noys sat on their veranda playing pre-breakfast mah-jong with Grandad and Captain Waew. Mair and the ladies of the cooperative continued with their exemplary renovation of the shop. Arny worked out by raking beach wood into pyres, which, if they ever dried out, would one day make spectacular bonfires.

Captain Kow announced that the small boats would be able to venture out that day. As they'd been docked during the temperamental tempest, he had no fresh fishballs to sell from his motorcycle sidecar. Undeterred, he was there bright and early in front of our shop with an honest sign saying THREE-DAY-OLD FISHBALLS — NOT THAT DELICIOUS. It was hardly surprising he sold not a one. I'd invited him to join us for breakfast. As always, he seemed flattered. Grandad Jah seethed, like the alpha old man, at the table but said nothing. And once everyone else was full and gone, I led the captain to my balcony. He admired my mobile shell collection.

"How far out can the little boats go?" I asked.

"Depends on the waves," he said. "Two meters maximum for most of us."

"But if it's calm?"

"Go all the way to Vietnam or until the diesel ran out. Why?"

I'd decided the previous night to tell the captain everything, from the head on the beach to the slave ships to the suspected involvement of the Pak Nam police force. He listened intently but didn't seem all that surprised.

"It's not just here," he said, when I was done.

"What's not?"

"The slavery. Happens all around the coast. Except the recruiting's done by agents over on the west. They put crews together, take their down payments, make promises, then vanish. The Burmese do a three-month stint, then queue up for their salaries only to be told that the wages are all handled through the agencies. It's in the contract — in Thai. As the agents have all shut up and shipped out, that's three months of free labor and nothing for the Burmese to send back to their families. Happens all the time."

I blame Buddhism, you know? Get yourself a soft religion and you can forgive yourself almost anything. No shame. No guilt. I'll do my penance in the next life. No worries. I wondered whether Captain Kow was one of those *mai pen rai* characters. One of the "no problem, let's not get worked up over nothing" majority.

"I imagine you're going to do something about it," he said, and smiled.

Damn. I wish I could have put some teeth in that gap. I knew it would have been a grand smile if it hadn't been so vacant.

"I'd need help," I confessed.

"I could get about ten, maybe fifteen small-boat men together, I suppose."

"You could? And why would they co-operate?"

"They don't like the big boats much. And they owe me favors."

"And why would you cooperate?"

"Me?" He laughed. "I like your style, Jimm. I like your spunk. You're a credit to your mother. I'd be proud to be there beside you."

You tend to assume old men are flirting when they overdo the rhetoric, but Captain Kow's eyes sparkled and I really got the feeling he was up for the adventure.

"You got a plan?" he asked.

"Sort of," I replied. "Do I have to tell you it?"

"Too true you do."

It was almost lunchtime when Lieutenant Chompu called me from the police station.

"At last," I said. "How long does it take to read a few documents?"

"Ooh, what dominance," he said. "I love a forceful woman. If it had been just words, I

271

might have finished yesterday evening. But it wasn't that simple. Our Lieutenant Egg uses his own shorthand, the type of which I'd never seen. It amounts to leaving out all the vowels and tone markers. So every word was a puzzle."

"But you cracked it?"

"I have a reputation for inserting my key into otherwise impenetrable locks."

"But the documents?"

"Yes, those too. I have entered his devious world, young Jimm."

"And did you find anything?"

"Not really."

"Chom!"

"Not a complete failure, however. I found no fewer than eleven official reports in normal script for beached bodies and body parts. These were cases he'd personally taken on. His success rate in finding relatives and solving the cases was — as far as I could see — zero. All 'Case closed, probably Burmese, domestic dispute.' "

"But he's only been here in Pak Nam for a month."

"Right. These reports go back six months to when he was stationed in Pattani. Your personal head is number eleven. It's his first up here."

"So if he's cleaning up, he's following a boat."

"Or a fleet. I checked out the movement of deep-sea vessels from Pattani to Lang Suan around the time of his transfer. There was a total of four that changed registration and fishing zones. One was a mackerel trawler bought by a conglomerate in Prajuab. But three others always traveled together. Same owner. Same catch records. They're now operating out of Pak Nam, but they spend most of their time at sea and transfer their catch to smaller boats. This deep-sea fleet has five local boats registered to collect and deliver. Doing good business, by all accounts."

"So somewhere out there are three big boats that don't come home much. I bet that's them. There I was imagining one slaver ship. Sneaking up on it in the dead of night. Surprising its sleeping crew. But three? You've just changed the odds."

"You mean from 'don't even think about it' to 'very don't even think about it'?"

"Why do I not feel a deep sense of police cooperation?"

"Jimm, there are three boats bobbing fifty kilometers from the nearest impartial witness. They'll each have burly, unshaven ex-convict types with automatic weapons patrolling the decks. They would have already massacred so many random Burmese that they'll not even consider murder to be a negative thing. They'll have spotlights on their boats, radar even. I have no idea how you'd sneak up on them without being cut into little bloody pieces. My love remains undying, but my cooperation ended with this report."

"You aren't even going to tell your boss?"

"Tell him what?"

"That . . ."

No. He was right. No evidence. No proof. No point.

"Chom. Don't you have an urge to see justice done?"

"It's not nearly as strong as my urge to reach forty with a complete set of limbs."

"Then do it for me."

"Valor, you mean? Chivalry?"

"Don't tell me it's dead."

"You know in your heart it is."

"Fine. Never mind. I'll die without a hero by my side. Without ever knowing what it's like to have a man stand up for me, put his life on the line out of love."

"So I'm excused then?"

"I suppose."

"Good. Oh, and there was a message from the post office."

"What? Are you moonlighting for the Royal Thai Post now?"

"They have my number because I receive a lot of FedEx packages in plain brown envelopes full of evidence, if you know what I mean. And they know that you and I are seeing each other."

"In the romantic sense?"

"Naturally. In a place like Pak Nam they always hold out hope that people like me can see the folly of our ways."

"So?"

"So, Nat the manager said he'd had a suspicious visitor. A woman. She wanted to get in touch with her sister who'd given the Pak Nam Lang Suan post office as her return address. He'd told her that the sender sounded like the girl and her mother who were staying at your resort."

"Oh great."

"After she'd gone, it occurred to him that they'd only typed that information into the system at eight this morning and the parcel wouldn't be arriving till tomorrow. So he couldn't see how anyone would know. He tried to phone your mother. As he was calling, a cell tone rang out from his pile of outgoing mail. He hung up and tried again. And it rang again. He found a letter from your mother with a phone inside. He wondered whether she'd put it there by mistake."

"When was the woman there?"

"Just before I called you."

"About ten minutes?"

"About."

"Damn. We need help."

How on earth could they have traced it that soon, and how could they get down here so quickly? It was fifteen minutes from Pak Nam to our resort, if you didn't get lost. Most people got lost. But I couldn't count on that. I ran to the Noys' veranda and interrupted the mah-jong tournament.

"OK, I don't want anyone to panic," I said.

My hands were shaking and my legs were wobbling. The mah-jong players stared at me curiously. I was the only one panicking. But my mind was clear.

"Noy and Noy," I said. "We might have had a security breach at the post office."

The clock in Mair's cabin chimed midday. Our calm was over. The afternoon of the big chaos had arrived.

"They've found us," said Mamanoy.

"We have about five minutes," I said. "This is what I want everyone to do . . ."

Once they'd heard me out, they set to work. The Noys apologized to the old men for interrupting the game and calmly collected the tiles. I jogged over to the shop, selected two members of the cooperative, and dragged them and Mair back to the cabins. I'd barely made it wheezing back up to the shop when a metallic gray BMW pulled into the car park. "Mamma Mia" rang out from my back pocket. I took out the phone. *Sender — Aung.* Not now. Please don't let it be the message from Shwe. I turned off my phone and went to greet the new arrivals. The four doors opened simultaneously, and three middle-aged men in gray safari suits and a young woman in a skirt and blouse leaped out. It felt like a raid.

"Can I hel—" I began, but the visitors weren't in the mood for my reception niceties. Mair walked across to intercept them.

"Where do you think you're going?" she asked, stepping in front of the meatiest of the men. He grabbed the wrist of the hand she laid on him and attempted to fling her to one side. He obviously hadn't figured Mair's jungle training into that rash decision. With some innate sense of direction, her knee found the nest of his testicles. He sank slowly to the ground and issued a sound like a slow puncture in a whoopee cushion. But his colleagues were unconcerned. They hurried on to the cabins. Two of them held short metal bars, they used to jimmy open first door number one, then number two. We stood back, amazed. At room three they dragged two screaming women out to the veranda. They were in a state of undress, but nobody listened to their pleas.

The raiders moved on to the back tier of bungalows, using their bars to prise open each door of our family cabins, even though none of them was locked. In one of these rooms they found two frail old men, and they too were dragged to the veranda of cabin three. All this was completed in less than two minutes. We'd been rounded up like cattle, and every room had been searched. All businesslike and silent. Not even the gang of local women at the water's edge, dragging their cockle trays through the sand, had noticed anything untoward.

I'd been hoping the young woman was the head of this invading army. I like to see my gender assume dominant roles even in illegal activity. But I didn't hear her speak at all, so I had to assume she was the terror-pretty of the group. "Pretty" had become a noun in Thai to describe women who use their sex appeal to show men how pathetic they are. The meaty man whose family jewels had been devalued by my mother walked uneasily up to the veranda. He was about fifty, short-haired, and I could smell military about him, about all of them. He glared at Mair, who gave him a glimpse of her *Titanic* smile.

"There's more where that came from," she said.

"Mair!" I shouted through gritted teeth. "Let's not antagonize our guests."

"All right," said Meaty. "Where are they?"

"Excuse me," I said. "But who are you, exactly?"

"The two women staying here. Where are they?"

"Well, they're right here," I said, pointing to Ning and Somjit, neither of whom seemed the least embarrassed to be standing there in their underwear.

"And the least you can do is allow them to protect their dignity," said Mair.

She pushed past one of the other gray safaris into the room and came out with sheets, which she draped around the grinning co-op ladies. Another safari came back from the carport and whispered into Meaty's ear.

"Enough of this," said the boss. He was obviously used to striking terror into the hearts of people. Arny was off lifting weights at the gym; otherwise I knew he'd be quivering now at all this aggression. The rest of us weren't particularly impressed, but we felt obliged to assume the submissive role of ignorant country folk.

"I want the owner of that Honda, and I want her now," yelled Meaty.

He kicked the fence post in front of the cabin for effect. It shattered into a hundred shards. It was riddled with termites, so that wasn't as impressive as it looked. But the sound woke the dogs, and seeing their pack leader in danger, they came chasing at Meaty from the rear. Theirs, too, was a silent attack. He knew nothing until they were on him. He looked down as these three little dogs ran circles around him barking laughably. They weren't a fearsome pack, and he quite rightly ignored them. Sensing their failure, they lay down on the sand and scratched.

"Well, if you know them, you stay right where you are, mister," said Grandad. "If you're a friend of theirs, you can just pay their bill for them."

"That's right," said Mair with an impressive southern lilt.

"What?" said Meaty.

"Those two stuck-up bitches drive in here with their posh accents and their snobbish

280

airs, stay here for four nights, eat all our food and sleep in our luxury cabins, and the next thing you know, they've gone. Didn't pay a damned *baht* and wrecked the TV to boot."

Way to go, Grandad.

"When was this?" he asked.

"Sunday morning," I said. "We woke up and they'd gone."

"Why didn't they take the car?"

I hadn't thought that far.

"The heads had seized up in the cylinders," said Grandad. "Happens a lot down here from the salt water. Japanese. What can I say? No idea how to make a decent car."

"And you are?" asked Meaty.

"Retired mechanic," said Grandad. "Stockholder in this establishment."

"I bet they got a bus out to the airport in Surat," I said. "Probably long gone by now."

"Then explain to me why they were still in Pak Nam yesterday?" Meaty asked.

"Those bastards," said Mair. "I bet they're ripping off one of the other resorts now. If only I could get my hands on . . ."

At that moment, one of the safari suits tapped his boss on the shoulder and pointed toward the road. My hero in brown turned into the car park on his police motorbike and headed in our direction. Chompu should have stopped in front of the shop because the sand was soft out by the cabins, so his arrival wasn't as impressive as it might have been. He got bogged down in the sand and fell over sideways. The safari suits exchanged glances while he got himself up.

"They're vandals, officer," said Mair. "Look what they've done with our doors. Arrest them."

"What's going on here?" asked Chompu in a particularly manly voice.

Meaty sized him up, probably deciding whether to shoot him.

"Come with me, Lieutenant," he said and started to walk toward the kitchen block. Chompu stood his ground.

"Tell me why I should be taking orders from you," said Chompu.

"Because you'd be very sorry if you didn't."

Wisely, I thought, Chompu walked a few meters away and stood beside Meaty, who seemed to be getting something out of his pocket. They faced away from us, heads bowed while Meaty spoke in hushed tones. Chompu nodded, then *wai*'d. When Meaty returned to us, Chompu stayed back as an observer.

"What cabin were the women in?" Meaty asked.

"Two," I said. And one of the safaris went immediately into that room without being told.

"Did they leave anything behind?" asked Meaty.

"A busted TV," said Mair.

The safari came out of the room shaking his head.

"We'll be back," said Meaty. "You're to do nothing. Tell no one about this visit. If the women come back for their car, you'll call this number immediately."

He handed me a card with nothing but a cell phone number on it.

"Mr. . . . ?" I said.

The unwanted visitors turned and hurried back toward the car.

"Who's going to pay for all this damage?" Mair shouted.

I squeezed her arm. The car doors slammed, the tires kicked up gravel, and they were gone. The engine sound soon blended into the growl of the surf. I smiled and walked around to each of the members of our cast and squeezed their hands. It had been a creditable ensemble performance. Chompu came over to join us.

"My knight," I said. "Thanks for coming,

Chom."

"I'm not sure I helped at all."

"I don't know. They were a scary bunch. Who were they?"

"I've been ordered not to tell you that they were from Special Branch. But some elite faction that deals with — what he referred to as — higher matters."

"You'd better not tell us then."

"Sounds like the gray squad," said Grandad. "They only come out when there's something heavy-duty happening. And if they've been running checks on the banks and the post offices, that's a lot of manpower. Exactly what have your two ladies got themselves tied up in?"

"Exactly what two ladies are we talking about?" asked Chompu.

I'd had very little time to explain the details of our resort resident problem.

"I assume this has nothing to do with the Burmese?" he said.

I remembered Aung.

"The Burmese. Right," I said and I turned my phone back on. "I tell you what, Captain Waew, why don't you brief the lieutenant? We can't have any secrets here now. I reckon we'll have a couple of hours at the most before they've scoured all the resorts and come back here for a second round. We have to get the Noys to a safe house."

"We've got a little house out back," said Somjit of the co-op. "It used to be our grandmother's till the cow fell on her. It's comfortable though. Not much of a hike to the outside toilet."

"They can wear disguises," said Ning.

The girls had no idea what was going on, but they were quick to get into the spirit of things. Even when we'd first dragged them over from the shop and told them the Noys were in danger, they'd been quick to strip off.

"Call them up," said Grandad.

Waew let out an impressive whistle without the use of his fingers, and two of the cockle collectors looked up from beneath their broad cowboy hats. He gestured them over. The Noys walked up the sand wearing the sarongs and T-shirts the co-op ladies had been wearing earlier. Their cockle dredgers were cardboard election placards. Their shell harvest was unimpressive, but they had survived. All that remained was for them to collect their things from cabin three and prepare their escape. Mair kept watch in case the safaris returned. I dialed Aung.

"Aung. What's up?"

"Where have you been?" he asked. "I've been —"

"You're not my only emergency. Is it Shwe?"

"He called. His battery's very low. They were being herded into a small boat," he said. "I'm not sure, but I think he said the name of the boat had the word AMOR written on one side. He couldn't read the Thai on the other."

"Did he say how many they were?"

"Seventeen. Four women. They'd brought over another bunch from a different holding center."

So, they'd got their new crew. I wondered what had happened to the previous one.

"Can you help?" he asked.

"I hope so," I said. "Keep your phone on." And I clicked off.

I wasn't ready. I needed another day at least. I needed more people. I needed . . . I needed a miracle. I called Captain Kow.

"What is it?" he said. His voice sounded like rust deep in the back of the phone.

"Where are you?" I shouted.

"Nam Jeud," he said.

"It's started. I know it's short notice, but did you get in touch with anyone?"

"Ha! Started, has it? I haven't got through to everyone yet. I focused on boats around Sawee, like we agreed. My brother's up there."

"Are there any boats out at the moment?"

"This time of day? Not many. Only the squid trapmen checking their traps."

"Are they on walkie-talkie?"

"Normally they wouldn't need to be. They only use the wireless at night to tell each other where the shoals are. The trappers have permanent spots, but the transient boats have to follow the squid."

"But?"

"But, well, there's the karaoke."

"The karaoke?"

"The nights can be a bit long and boring, waiting for squid. And a lot of fisherfolk like to sing. So about a year back we started entertaining each other by crooning over the short wave. And someone came up with the idea of bringing along tape players and singing along with the music. So they —"

"Kow! We've got seventeen people about to be beheaded. Is there a short version of this?"

"Sorry. Almost done. So, every night you'd take your turn to sing. And the M-150 energy-drink people heard about it, and they launched a CB transceiver karaoke competition with cash prizes. The competition's next week and everyone's rehearsing. Night or day we have our channels open. Sing a bit. Get feedback from your mates."

"So what you're telling me is that the trap setters are on air."

"You could say. Them and the night boats."

"Can you contact them?"

"My brother Daengmo can."

Daengmo? Now, why did that name ring a bell?

"All right," I said. "Ask them if anyone saw a small boat leave Sawee before midday. It might be called *Amor.* At least that's what's written in English . . . or French. There were seventeen Burmese on board. You can't hide seventeen people in a small boat, so someone must have noticed it. We need to know what direction it was headed. And someone has to get after it."

"I'm on my way," he said.

"Where to?"

"If I can get the headings from Daengmo and the karaoke crowd, I can set a heading to intersect with it. It's all in the angles."

"Are you alone?"

"Yes."

"You have to be careful with these people. How far out before you lose this cell-phone signal?"

"About thirty kilometers unless I'm heading toward the islands."

"Then how do we keep in touch?"

"I'll give you Daengmo's number. I'll use the wireless transmitter. You'll be able to get the bearings from him."

"Kow?"

"Yeah?"

"I'll never forget this."

"I really can't tell you how much of a pleasure it is."

"We'll have reinforcements out there soon. Don't do anything stupid."

"Aye aye."

They really said "aye aye"?

When I went to join Mair in the shop, Captain Waew was just pulling out, with the Noys lying down in the bed of the truck. The co-op ladies were up front. Elain was on a rope on the flatbed. Mair was alone, waving to the monkey.

"Where are all the other ladies?" I asked.

"I sent them home," she said. "I sense danger. Your policeman said he'd call you later. I phoned Arny and told him to come home."

"Arny? Great! Who else would you phone in times of danger?"

"Don't make fun of your brother. He'll be there for you when you need him."

"And where's Grandad?"

"Last time I saw him he was rearranging

the flotsam on the beach."

"Why . . . ?"

An engine was gunned; I imagined wheels spinning. We ran down and looked along the beach. The tide was low but still only six meters from the cabins. Grandad Jah had laid out a long bridge of bamboo down the sand to the water's edge. It seemed rather pointless, considering the incoming tide would wash it all away before . . .

A roaring Honda City leaped from the carport, gained traction from the bamboo, and sped off over the bridge and into the water. I saw the grinning flash of Grandad's face as it vanished behind the splash. It had traveled fifteen meters at speed before the wheels began to spin in the sand and the Honda came to a standstill. Only the roof was visible above the waves. I raced into the surf, dismissing my water phobia as trivial compared to the love of my grandfather. But as the water began to crash against my waist, the fear waxed and the love waned. By the time I reached the Honda and the current was forcing me back it, occurred to me that I'd never really been that fond of him. Even so, some insanity saw me pinching my nose with my fingers and ducking my head beneath the surface. I opened my eyes and a stinging wash of salt filled them with pain. Everything was blurry. I pushed my head in through the open window. The cab was empty.

I burst, spluttering, into the atmosphere and looked around me for the floating corpse of my beloved relative. He was standing beside Mair on the beach, the bastard. I was furious. I wanted to stomp back to him, but the water was buffeting me around like laundry. By the time I washed up on the beach, I was out of breath and out of ire.

"What," I huffed, "was that all about?"

He came over to my supine body and crouched down in one of those impossible country squats.

"I've had an idea," he said.

"Please share it."

"Well, in an hour or so the tide will be fully up and the car will be invisible from the beach. We have the phone number of the Special Branch fellow. So, we give him a call and tell him the car's gone. We hint that the Noys came back and drove it off. And they'll spend the rest of the day, perhaps even the rest of the week, scouring the country for this car. We'll be out of the loop."

"And what happens if they come back at low tide when the car's visible?"

"We can drape it with weed and make it

look like something being washed up."

"And what about you — an ex-mechanic — telling them the pistons are seized up?"

"A miracle. The floodwater from the river rinsed out all the salt and the thing started working."

It didn't sound at all plausible, but Grandad Jah had that senile look so they'd probably put it down to dementia. And it was good to get one emergency off the front burner for a while.

"OK," I said. "Crazy but acceptable."

While I was telling them about the Burmese in Sawee, Arny and Gaew pulled up on her Harley, so I had to start all over again. When Ex-Police Captain Waew returned from concealing the Noys, I had to tell him too. After three times of telling it didn't sound any more hopeful.

"So what are we supposed to do?" asked Grandad.

"I have a plan," I said, and told him about Captain Kow and the small-boat squid men.

"That good-for-nothing wastrel couldn't organize fluff in a belly button," said Grandad. "I'm not putting my life in his hands."

"All right, stop it. Stop it now," said Mair. "I've just about had enough of you insulting Kow. Either you button your lip or I'll

292

punch it."

She looked furious, and I'd never seen my grandfather back down to her like he did at that moment, but I could sense some friction between father and daughter. There was too much going on around us to follow up on it, but I put a mental yellow Post-it sticker against that moment.

Gaew it was who brought us all back to practicalities.

"We need a boat," she said.

"That's right," said Mair, still glaring at Grandad. "We do."

A boat. Right. It was the one aspect of this mission that I'd tried to drown in my subconscious. As the leader, I could hardly send them all out into the deep ocean and wave my handkerchief from the quay. But I was petrified by the very thought of having nothing but a wooden plank between me and Davy Jones.

"We've got to get out there as soon as we can and help those poor people," said Arny, pushing his big chest ahead of him.

Actually, Arny was every bit as scared of the water as me. We'd both had life-threatening experiences in water that I won't go into now. But Arny had an image to project here, and if it involved wrestling sharks, I felt there was no turning back for him.

"Now, who do we know with a boat?" said Mair.

Actually, we lived in a fishing village. Everyone we knew owned or had access to a boat. What she was really asking was who would be dumb enough to lend us one so we could go and get it riddled with machine-gun bullets.

"Ed," said Arny.

"No," said I.

"Why not?" asked Grandad. "He's got a fine new boat. Just finished it a week ago."

"Look, just not Ed, all right?" I said.

"Then give us an alternative," said Grandad.

The effects of the antidepressant had abated some. I still felt a tickle when I thought of the male musculature, but I was no longer in heat. I was left with only the shame of the erotic thoughts that had forced me onto our grass cutter. I understood all those addicts who woke up in the bodies of complete strangers and lived those strangers' lives badly. If we didn't all die at the hands of slavers or government agents, I vowed I would volunteer at the local drug clinic. I acknowledged my addiction. I am Jimm and I'm a recovering sex addict.

Mair was talking on Arny's cell phone. When she finished, I asked,

"Who was that?"

"Ed," she said.

"Mair, we're a team," I said. "Teams consult. Teams don't ignore the opinion of their daughters. What did he say?"

"He's on his way."

"Chom, thanks for this afternoon. Can you speak?"

"Do you mean, have I learned the fundamentals, or am I in a position to discuss the illiterate ape I share my office with?"

"OK. Question answered. Where are you?"

"I'm sitting in a children's playground with a cigarette."

"You don't smoke."

"I didn't say I was smoking it. I'm just holding it near my lips so that from the police station opposite it looks like I'm smoking, and therefore I have an excuse to be out of my office."

"You're hiding."

"I've reached my limit. I'm imagining all the things I'd do to him if I were four times the man I am."

"You want revenge?"

"Absolutely."

"Good. You remember his address?"

"I've driven past it several times and thrown imaginary Molotov cocktails."

"Do you feel like going inside?"

"That would be what we policemen refer to as breaking and entering?"

"That's the one. I bet you're good at it."

"And what, apart from the stimulating rush of adrenaline, would be my motivation?"

"We're going after the slavers. Even if we get them, we still wouldn't have any evidence that Egg was involved. There's nothing incriminating in his files. We need something that ties him to this whole slavery thing. And we need to know what other police are involved."

"Other police?"

"The Burmese they've taken today were picked up by uniformed police."

"Do you have an actual witness this time?"

"We have seventeen of them. But they're on their way to the deep ocean. We're going to bring them back."

"Do you have a plan?"

"It's complicated."

"You don't have a plan."

"I do. It's coming. And your breaking and entering is a part of that plan."

He was quiet.

"Are you thinking?" I asked.

"I'm posing elegantly with my cigarette between two fingers as I consider the humiliation of being discharged from the police force."

"It can't be any worse than the humiliation you've suffered by being in it."

Another silence.

"You're right."

"So, you'll do it?"

"Nobody bullies big Chom and gets away with it."

12.

I Was Feeling Kinda Seasick, but the Crowd Called Arthur Moor

(from "Whiter Shade of Pale" —
PROCOL HARUM)

The small vessels generally set out for sea from Jamook Prong harbor, but this day Ed's new seven-meter squid boat was parked directly beside the Honda. The tide was full and the sea was once again nudging the cabins. I'd avoided eye contact with Ed, even while briefing him on piracy matters. I was impressed at how readily he'd volunteered himself and his boat. He'd brought along a friend, plastic awnings salesman and part-time private investigator Meng, to act as crew. I knew that with every new recruit there was one added chance of a double agent sneaking in. There was a lot of piracy bribe money going around. But I'd had dealings with Meng, and he appeared to be the type who found it hard to tell a lie. At 150 centimeters and 40 kilos, however, I didn't see him wrestling many armed guards to the ground.

"So, exactly what is the plan?" Ed asked.

I almost looked at him.

"I can't really tell you just yet," I said. "I'm waiting for the last piece to slot into place."

"So, you haven't, as yet, got one."

"I've got one," I began. "I just can't —"

"Ho, ho, what do we have here then?" came a booming voice.

Across the littered sand marched Bigman Beung in what could only be described as an admiral's uniform. It had more ribbons and twirls than a rhythmic gym club. It was lousy timing. The last thing I needed was drama with our sleazy headman.

"Beung," I said, "what are you doing here?"

"What are *you* doing here is a more likely question," he said. "And I must say I am very fond of the way your wet T-shirt adheres to your little brassiere, by the way."

I was still damp from my attempt to rescue Grandad Jah. That and sweating, and I'd probably end up with pneumonia. I fluffed out my T-shirt, but his gaze remained on my chest.

"We're having a launch party for Ed's new boat," I lied. "Grandad's gone to fetch the firecrackers. The monk's just left."

I looked over my shoulder, expecting to see Ed and PI Meng backing me up, but they were off along the beach having a stroll.

"Is that so?"

"Yes."

"Odd, that, considering we already had a launch ceremony for him three weeks ago."

"Yeah, right. But this is a private, family celebration. To thank him for all the good grass cutting he's done for us over the past year."

"Is that so?"

"Yes."

My breasts were heavy from his gaze, so it was a relief when he finally looked me in the eye.

"You shouldn't lie to a village headman, little Jimm."

"I'm not exactly —"

"Why do you suppose I'm here?"

"I don't know. To inspect the latrines?"

"Now, does this look like a sanitation uniform to you?"

He was right. It certainly didn't. It looked like a Gilbert and Sullivan costume.

"I'm here for the voyage," he said.

"Where are you going?"

"Where are *we* going?"

I shook my head.

"Captain Kow phoned me," he said.

A chunk of meteorite fell from space and landed in my stomach.

"W-why?"

"Don't look so surprised, honey. Me and the captain are like this."

He wound his fingers around each other like a nautical knot. I suddenly hated Captain Kow. In one foul phone call he'd doomed our project to failure. I was ready to call it off there and then. To make matters worse, Beung took my hand in his. His fingers were greasy.

"I'm the main man in these parts. Don't forget that. Me and the captain have been keeping our eyes on those deep-sea vessels."

"You have?"

"We may look like a disorganized rabble, but the Maprao Coastal Watch has its finger on the pulse."

His thumb caressed my palm.

"And?"

"We've long suspected foul play out there. Your findings have proven us correct. But we knew that we would be up against influential figures. We weren't certain how to progress. We lacked a solid plan."

I knew what was coming next.

"What's our plan?" he asked.

"I don't exactly —"

301

There was a scream from up the beach. Mair came running toward us, waving both arms at the same time, as if scaring off imaginary birds. All the crew members gathered around her, waiting for her to catch her breath. When her voice arrived, it did so in a conspiratorial whisper. We couldn't hear a word.

"Mair, speak up," said Arny.

She looked back toward the shop.

"I can't speak too loud. He might hear me."

"Who?"

"Him. One of the body snatchers. The bombers. The rats. He's back. He parked up on the road, and he's sneaking down the pathway. But I saw him. Father, get your gun. Let's show this motherf—"

"Mair," I shouted. "Calm down. Are you sure it's him?"

"I'd recognize him anywhere."

There was no time for the gun. We all ran up the beach, grabbing whatever weapons we could find among the debris: bamboo, shoes, used hypodermics. We took up positions behind walls and huts and waited. And waited. I was just about to step out and take a look when a stocky man in an airport baggage-handler's uniform walked brazenly across the car park.

"Get him," shouted Grandad Jah.

We charged, mindlessly, and the man put up his hands and dropped onto his back with his legs in the air like a submissive dog. Recognizing the signs, Sticky reached the intruder first and, without a second of thought, ripped the mustache clean off the man's face. There should have been blood, but I saw none. The victim did, however, give out a high-pitched scream that I recognized immediately.

"Hold back, everyone," I shouted. "It's a relative."

"Sissi?" said Arny, and rushed over to help his ex-brother to his feet. They hugged. I joined the maul. Mair was a little slow on the uptake.

"Who is that in there?"

"Hello, Mair," said Sissi.

It was obvious why we hadn't recognized my sister. Apart from the large baggage-handler overalls, she wore a peaked cap and, until recently, an orange mustache. To anyone who didn't know her as Miss Pattaya World 1992, she was all man, complete with a John Wayne walk and a mascaraed five-o-clock shadow.

"Somkiet?" yelled Mair and rushed to her first-born. She ripped her daughter away from me and Arny and cried all over her.

"Somkiet. You've come back to us."

The plan was complete.

"So, where should I set up?" Sissi asked me. "And are you planning to wipe that silly smile off your face anytime soon?"

"I'm sorry," I said. "I just think it's frogging hilarious."

"You'd prefer I'd turned up in redneck central, wearing high-heels and a bust-revealing halter neck?"

"Hmm, perhaps you're right. Where did you put them, by the way?"

"Strapped down, reluctantly."

"I hope they don't burst. You're a sight for sore eyes. Mair's so happy you're here."

"She looks healthy. All this sea and simplicity's good for her."

"Good for her body, anyway."

We were on my veranda, having a very hurried reunion before my boat sailed. Sticky sat at our feet, gnawing on the mustache. I'd told Sissi about the problem we had with the Noys and the Special Branch and that setting up her equipment at our resort might not be such a good idea. We didn't want them coming back to find a computer operation going on.

"Well," I said, "if you need other computers, the Internet shop in Pak Nam's the only place. If you're lucky, you might get there before all the high school gamers arrive."

"And why would the owner let me take over his shop?"

"We have a sort of . . . understanding. He thinks we're Internet police. You shouldn't have any trouble. Mair can show you where it is."

She reached into her gym bag and produced what looked like a slim slab of plastic slate.

"All right," she said. "Here's the beast. Treat it lovingly."

"That's it?"

"It's a heavy-duty XR2 double —"

"All right. Enough with the specs. I like it."

"You should. The Navy SEALs use it on missions. It's bulletproof."

"Really? I don't suppose you've got one about my height and width?"

"I didn't have time to get you external cameras or mikes, so you'll have to do your commentary directly into this little hole here. You'll get fourteen hours on the battery, but here's a back-up just in case you're shipwrecked or cast adrift."

That thought appalled me more than catching a bullet.

"And that's all I need?"

305

"No. What do you think I was doing on your boat just now? I've attached one other slice of magic. It's a lightweight Explorer 700 with —"

"Just tell me what it does, all right?"

"It connects to satellites. That's not so easy on a boat because the receiver usually has to be stable. Close to shore you might have got away with using a cell-phone signal. I didn't know how far you'll be going out to sea. But that beauty should give you an unbroken signal from wherever you are."

"Great, Sis. Thanks. I see you got along really well with the baggage handler?"

"What do you mean?"

"You got him out of his uniform."

"No. Not my type, as it turned out. He had a spare uniform. But talking about getting along . . ."

"What?"

"Ed?"

"What about him?"

"He could shiver my timbers anytime. I can see why you've got a thing for that lean machine."

"I do not have a thing for him."

"Oh, good. I'll have him then."

"Good luck. I've heard he's really turned on by mustachioed airport workers."

"You wait till he sees me out of drag."

"I'll do my best to keep him alive for you. Time to go."

We hugged but didn't say goodbye.

"Are you sure all this is going to work?" I asked.

"The technical side I can guarantee. All that other stuff — the boating and the shooting and the rescuing and the drowning — that's up to you lot."

I walked along the beach. Everyone was on the boat waiting for me. Seven long faces. I was the team leader, and I didn't want them to see how hopeless I thought this all was. I waded out to them with a hopeful expression. I'd remembered to bring a change of clothes in a plastic bag, even though the standard squid boat didn't come complete with a changing room. Captain Ed the grass cutter leaped from his little boat into the chest-high water. The waves didn't appear to buffet him.

"We ready?" he shouted.

The water was already up to my neck. I had the computer and the plastic bag on my head. Ed waded toward me. I knew his intention.

"I'm perfectly capable of getting into a boat without being manhandled," I said.

I thought there might have been a little ladder somewhere, perhaps a crane. But there was merely a sheer wall of timber. I couldn't even reach the top of it with my hand.

"Sorry," he said. "But you aren't."

He ducked beneath the water, put his arms around my upper thighs and lifted me as if I weighed no more than a large herring. Apparently the effects of the antidepressant hadn't quite worn off. Grandad Jah and PI Meng took my belongings, then grabbed my wrists and hoisted me up. In one effortless move, Ed was on the deck at the same time as me. He primed the motor, weighed anchor, and we were off with only a slight bump of the Honda. I wondered how that would look on the insurance claim. Mair stood on the beach waving a discarded plastic bag.

DEAR CLINT. THE FOLLOWING ACCOUNT OF THE SEABORNE QUEST AND THE SIMULTANEOUS LAND INVESTIGATIONS HAVE BEEN TRANSCRIBED FROM LIVE INTERNET FOOTAGE AND INTERVIEWS. IN THE MAPRAO CRIMINAL JUSTICE SYSTEM, THE PEOPLE ARE REPRESENTED BY TWO SEPARATE YET EQUALLY IMPORTANT GROUPS — THE

STAFF OF THE LOVELY RESORT, WHO
INVESTIGATE CRIME, AND THE FEW
STRAIGHT COPS OF THE PAK NAM STA-
TION, WHO MAKE ARRESTS AND OC-
CASIONALLY PROSECUTE THE OFFEND-
ERS. THESE ARE THEIR STORIES.

Sissi and Mair left the dogs to guard the
Lovely Resort and headed off to Pak Nam
in the Mighty X. They stopped off at the
post office and collected Mair's cell phone
and an apology from Nat the manager for
giving away her personal address so reck-
lessly.

Back in the truck, Mair used her phone to
call Meaty of the DSI.

"What?"

"My name is Mrs. Jitmanat Gesuwan. I
am the proprietor of the Gulf Bay Lovely
Resort and Restaurant in Maprao."

There was nothing but silence from the
other end.

"It was me who kneed you in the bollocks
this morning. I'm —"

"I remember. What do you want?"

"Shortly after you left, a man arrived to
look at the Honda. He didn't say anything.
He was short-haired and sour-looking, so I
thought he was one of your men. He played
around with the engine and somehow got it

309

going. My father was impressed. Next thing you know, it was gone."

"Someone took the car?"

"It wasn't you?"

"No."

"Then my neighbor might have been right after all. She said she'd seen two women driving away from our resort in a silver car. That must have been the women you were looking for. I bet you they hired a mechanic. And that would also explain why I found a plastic bag hanging in the carport with a large sum of money in it. It more than covered what they owed. I should think they're —"

"What time was this?"

"Ooh, I don't know. About two?"

"And what direction were they headed?"

"South. Although they could easily have —"

He hung up.

"Job done," said Mair, and took her son's hand. "It's nice to have you home."

"You're really something," said Sissi.

"Thank you, child. At last my family's all together. My dream has come true."

Live Internet feed. 5 P.M. Gulf of Thailand

(CAMERA — CLOSE-UP OF JIMM

JUREE)

JIMM: I am reporting live to you from an unstable squid boat rocking perilously in the Gulf of Thailand. This is a live feed. English is not my native language, so please forgive my accent. We are heading out to deep water where at least seventeen Burmese are being held captive as slaves on three forty-meter fishing boats. The slaves are most likely being held at gunpoint. We have no idea how many guards there are or what weapons they're using. We are one small boat against three large ones. We are a crew of eight with only one handgun between us. Among our number are old men, an engaged couple, and a woman with a fear of water. None of us knows if we will make it back alive. We have no plan other than to find the ships and rescue the Burmese. And, yes, as I speak a fine rain has started to fall. (CAMERA-NOTEBOOK TIPS UP TOWARD THE GRAY SKY. A BLOB OF RAIN HITS THE LENS.) Are we in for another blustery storm to make our venture even more difficult?

I am your reporter Jimm Juree and I intend to stay here talking to you online until the matter is resolved — one way or another. Will we save the lives of our abused neighbors, or will we be cut down in a hail of machine-gun fire? Only time and the intervention of Mazu, the Chinese goddess of the sea, will tell.

"She looks fat on this thing," said Mair. She was leaning over Sissi's shoulder as they watched the live feed.

"She is a bit overweight," said Sissi.

"But not fat, son. There isn't an ounce of fat on her. She's solid, I'll give you that. A good solid Chiang Mai girl. Look at her. She's so pretty. Wouldn't it be wonderful if someone saw her on this and took a liking to her? Do you think anyone's watching?"

"So far . . . two thousand seven hundred."

"Two thousand seven hundred what?"

"People . . . watching."

"No."

"I swear. Look at the counter. This is the number of real-time viewers."

"That's people?"

"Sure is."

"But how did they know? We've only just started."

"I've been putting up links all over. Advertising on Web sites. Facebook. Twitter. Next thing you know, it goes viral."

"That sounds unpleasant. So you think there might be more?"

"I'm sure of it."

"Oh. Then there's certain to be someone out there who likes her, isn't there?"

"A lot of weirdos on the Internet, Mair."

"Don't be cruel. She's a very attractive girl with a lovely personality and a good sense of humor. Perhaps you could just make her look a little slimmer?"

"Without the benefits of plastic surgery?"

"Look at all those buttons and dials. Surely you can do something with special effects?"

"I'll see what I can do."

Live Internet feed. 5:42 P.M. Gulf of Thailand
(CAMERA — CLOSE-UP OF JIMM JUREE)
JIMM: This is very exciting. We've just heard over the boat's communication system that Captain Kow, our man in pursuit of the kidnapped Burmese, has sighted their ferry and is holding back so as not to alert the skipper. He has given us his location and headings, and we have changed our own direction and are going at full speed to meet up

with him. Our own captain estimates that we should intersect his path in just over an hour. This is an awfully long time in a boat with no roof or restrooms. But we are warmed by the knowledge that the chase is on.

As I have already introduced you to our brave crew, and as nobody else speaks English, I am debating how I can best —"

GAEW: (OFF SCREEN) I can.

CAMERA PANS AROUND TO THE CREW AND ZOOMS IN ON GAEW, HAND ALOFT. SMILING.

JIMM: (OFF SCREEN) You can speak English?

GAEW: All those international bodybuilding tournaments.

JIMM: Well, you get yourself over here. Viewers, this is a golden opportunity for your reporter, Jimm Juree, to hand over to a woman from this very region who knows the sea and the plight of the Burmese as well as anyone.

GAEW: Actually, we had a rice shop. I only got to go the beach on holidays.

JIMM: Then let's hear about the . . . plight of international bodybuilding. I'm sure our viewers need a break from me.

Actually, I was dying for a pee. There are only so many things a live-feed audience can stomach. Even the *Big Brother* people balked at having closed-circuit cameras in the bathrooms.

"Where's the toilet?" I asked Ed.

I knew there wasn't actually a room, but I suspected there had to be a protocol. A lot of wives came out to sea with their husbands. They'd seen it all before, of course, but they didn't have an audience of seven — one of whom was admiral pervert Bigman Beung himself. Ed explained. Here again, the wonders of the sarong came into play. I won't give you a blow by blow. It wasn't a pretty sight, but my modesty was intact and I had learned one more skill for my résumé.

While Gaew spouted on about steroids and the cost of good body oil, I sat beside PI Meng the private eye, glad for a break from my live feed.

"Been busy?" I asked, ever keen to keep up with the local crime scene.

"Nah," he said.

I was hardly surprised.

"Nothing ongoing?"

"Well . . ."

"Come on. You can tell me. We'll all be dead by morning."

"That's true. Well, Ari hired me."

"The monkey-handler Ari?"

"When I say he hired me, what I mean is that he offered to give me a finder's fee if I could locate his macaque. But it's been gone since Tuesday, so I doubt we'll ever see that critter again."

"Right," I said. "Long gone, I expect. Across the border to Malaysia, I wouldn't doubt. It's like the southeast Asian version of Canada. They have a commune of escaped macaques down there, dodging the coconut draft, singing freedom from slavery folk tunes."

"Really?"

He didn't have any idea what I was talking about. Few did. I was just about to mingle some more when something occurred to me. I sat back down.

"When did you say the monkey went missing?" I asked.

"Tuesday," he said. "Someone just untied it from his truck and walked off with it."

"And you're sure it was Tuesday?"

"Certain."

I was confused, but it wasn't a priority matter. I skipped Bigman Beung and sat beside my brother.

"You all right, mate?"

"I'm starting to feel seasick," he said greenly.

"Focus on the horizon and imagine you live in that lighthouse over there."

"There isn't a lighthouse over there."

"I said imagine it."

"I thought you meant imagine living there."

"I did. See? You feel better now, don't you?"

"Yeah, a bit."

"You just needed your mind taken off the sea. Focus on cloud shapes. Focus on a distant light. Focus on Gaew. She's a lot prettier than the Gulf. You do know she's impressed with you? You planned this all very nicely."

"It was going all right. Sissi didn't help. Turning up like that."

"Why not?"

"Gaew's seen the genes now."

"Oh, don't."

"Now she knows what stock I'm from."

"It's a scientific fact that transsexualism isn't hereditary. You don't see me dressing up as . . . OK. Bad example. The fact is, you're all man, Arny. She knows that. And when the opportunity comes, you'll know it too. Look at you. You're on a boat in the middle of the sea. Miles from land. Who'd have thought that?"

His eyes rose in search of a cloud.

"I feel seasick again."

"Sorry."

I stood up clumsily and punched Grandad and Waew on their upper arms because I'd seen sports coaches do it on TV. It was for morale. They both complained. Said it hurt. I apologized. I returned to my computer and, I hoped, a small but faithful contingent of strangers on the Internet.

13.
SOME SHY BRUISED EYES
PLEASE GO AWAY

(from "I Wish It Would Rain" —
TEMPTATIONS)

Even after Lieutenant Chompu's third passing of the Egg house, all seemed quiet and peaceful. The properties on either side were unoccupied and overgrown. Egg's house had a concrete front yard, which no doubt made gardening that much easier, and a low brick wall. One short driveway led to an open carport, and one other curved around and headed beside the house toward the rear of the property. The building itself was a two-story show house with all those extras that looked fine in ancient Greece but were over the top for Pak Nam. Despite its opulence, it wasn't a loved house.

Chompu hopped over the side wall and landed on empties: bottles and cans and supermarket bags of garbage. The cockroaches objected to this surprise arrival and scattered around the yard.

"Barbarians," he said, aloud.

He walked to the rear door and tried the handle. It was locked. Behind him, where the concrete ended and the jungle began, there was a dirt trail that extended from the driveway. He walked it to a sharp turn and a second carport. This one was mostly corrugated tin with a cloth front flap. He pulled back the corner of the cloth to see a brown and cream police truck in the dark interior. It looked familiar. He checked the plate. Chumphon 44619. It was one of the three trucks registered to the Pak Nam police unit. One was off getting a new carburetor. When he was leaving his office just twenty minutes earlier, he'd heard the second truck crew on the intercom explaining how they'd just stopped a pick-up truck with an elephant in the back. They wanted to know what the safe weight limit was for a Toyota Hilux. Nobody knew. But wait! Wasn't the third truck parked in front of the station when he left? Surely he couldn't have imagined that. And did that mean that in the time it took Chompu to complete his reconnaissance and hop over the wall, Lieutenant Egg had driven it home? Was he inside now watching this trespass through a back window?

Chompu walked up to the truck and put his hand on the hood. It wasn't hot. There was no engine ticking. It hadn't been driven for some time. So perhaps the third truck had been fixed and returned and . . . he'd just confused the plates? But Chompu wasn't the type to confuse three numbers he'd signed off for numerous times. Something particularly odd was going on.

He walked back toward the house and paused at the door before trying the handle again. It was still locked. He looked under the flowerpots that now contained the skeletons of plants, but there was no key. So he had no choice. Breaking and entering. He'd even thought to bring the mini-crowbar from his bike. The door popped open, and not for the first time, he considered how much easier his life would have been if he'd pursued a career of crime. There was no discrimination in the underworld. The mafia didn't hold you back because you liked Kylie Minogue.

The reconnoitre of the ground floor took all of two minutes. Apart from a tacky table/chair set in the kitchen and a sink full of plates and utensils, and smells emanating from a mountain of black plastic garbage bags in one corner, there was nothing else. The other downstairs rooms were unfurnished and empty.

Halfway up the stairs, he heard the scratchy reception of a short-wave radio. The volume was down, but it was clearly the same local band used by the rescue foundations. It was currently tuned in to the police channel. Chompu took out his pistol. It had only ever been fired at the range. It was an old Glock, and it made such a horrid bang. But he was scared. The gun was more to hide behind than to use. He wasn't the brave hero type. He was a thinker. He would have made a great detective but for this defect.

He walked past the first open bedroom door. A pig sty. Clothes piled everywhere. Dirty magazines beside the unmade bed. Empties. But the radio sound was coming from the next room. He edged along the tiled landing and stopped to steady his heart before peeking in through the half-open door. The blind was closed. There were two single beds. On one slept a young man in undershorts. He had cropped hair and was a wiry mass of muscles and scars. His mouth seemed to cave in on one side. The radio played him a non-stop lullaby of traffic reports and static, and he snored through it. Between the beds were two chairs, and draped over each was a full police uniform.

Two . . .

. . . chairs.

He felt the knife tip in the small of his back. It pricked his skin and probably drew blood. He yelped. He was sure he'd never get bloodstains out of that shirt.

"This is what they call a knife," said a husky voice not far from his ear. "It's sharp. The slightest shove and it'll carve your kidneys in half. So how about you drop that gun?"

The weapon clanged onto the tiles and woke the sleeping youth. This was Ben of the rat brothers. Half awake, he was an ugly and angry boy.

"What? What's happened?" he asked, jumping up from the mattress.

"We got a guest," said Socrates, the ear voice. "Didn't even have the politeness to ring the doorbell. And you know? I think when he saw you lying there all naked and sweaty — I think he had a mind to do you."

"What? Whadya mean?" asked the youth.

"Well, you know who this is, don't you?" said ear voice. "This is the queer one. Egg's office mate."

"What's he doing here?"

"I told you. He's come looking for your bum."

Ben was incensed. He paced the few feet

between the beds as if he were trying to fathom it all. Chompu could see he was obviously experiencing some mental turmoil. Some inner yearning. He knew what to expect next. Ben, realizing he was barely dressed, grabbed a Thai manga comic from the foot of his bed and held it against his crotch. His modesty preserved, he fronted up to Chompu and poked a finger in his face.

"Is that it?" he shouted. "Is that what you've come for? You're a pervert. You're dead."

The second poke was directly in Chompu's left eye. The eye watered, but he was too numb to really appreciate the pain. The whole scene was as surreal as Janet Jackson's boob popping out at halftime in the Superbowl but perhaps a little more life-threatening. He was alert and aware but not as a participant exactly. There was a meditation-like clarity. Some mixture of Buddhism and shock. It was as if he were hanging on the wall with the lizards, observing his own impending humiliation.

Young Ben reached down to pick up Chompu's gun. He was shaking now. In a frenzy. Uncontrollable. Chompu felt the barrel bump into his temple, but there was still no here-and-now reality to it. No fear.

In fact, he might have even smiled. The finger squeezing the trigger was seven centimeters from his eyes. It had a long dirty fingernail.

"Not yet" came the ear voice of Socrates.

"Why not?"

"Because I'm standing behind him, you thickhead."

Ben was in a red funk that Chompu doubted the calm voice of logic could ever penetrate. But after a shudder, the gun was lowered and the youth sent a gob of spit against the policeman's cheek. Chompu looked down at the uniforms. This was why there was a fake truck in the yard. Why Egg was on the radio all the time. He needed to know where the real police were so he could send out his fake ones to pick up Burmese. Impersonating police officers was a serious matter, and he knew, once they were found out, there was no way they could let him go.

Live Internet feed. 6:30 P.M. Gulf of Thailand

(CAMERA — CLOSE-UP OF JIMM JUREE)

JIMM: We've been at sea now for an hour and a half. The constant drizzle has finally let up, but the waves continue to bat us back and forth like a Ping-Pong ball. The conditions are taking their toll.

(CAMERA SCANS TO THE RIGHT TO THE REAR ENDS OF ARNY, WAEW, AND BIGMAN BEUNG, WHO ARE LEANING OVER THE SIDE OF THE BOAT. THE SHOT BECOMES UNSTEADY AND WE HEAR THE SOUND OF A FEMALE RETCHING OFF-CAMERA)

ED: (OFF-CAMERA) You all right there, Jimm?

JIMM: What? Why wouldn't I be? I'm fine.

ED: You just —

JIMM: Shut up, Ed.

(CAMERA RETURNS TO THE PASTY FACE OF JIMM)

JIMM: It's the elements. That's what puts woman in her place. Out here we are insects. We are termites compared to the power of the universe. But even in our little ant farm, we can demand justice and fair play for —

(CAMERA DROPS TO SHOW CLOSE UP OF JIMM'S FEET AND WE HEAR MORE OFF-CAMERA RETCHING)

"Do you think they'll be all right?" Mair asked. She was at the Internet shop, sharing a seat with Sissi, watching the screen.

"They're on a boat in a monsoon sea," Sissi reminded her. "They might even capsize before they reach the slavers. But that's why it's so great."

"It is?"

"Of course it is. You couldn't write a better script. Who's going to move away from their computer with this all going on? It's so tense."

"But what if they . . . I don't know . . . die?"

"Exactly. That's the spirit. It's the ultimate thrill trip. There's no Hollywood-ending clause. The tension's real because the actors are expendable. And look at that, Mair. We've got fourteen thousand real-time viewers online. That's more than Susan Boyle's first day on YouTube."

"But I'm serious. What if they don't make it?"

"None of us makes it, Mair. We all die. But how many of us get to die live on the Internet?"

"I suppose you're right."

"Excuse me."

They looked up, surprised to be disturbed by the spotty Internet shop owner who'd been sitting at his desk watching customers turn away from the locked glass door. The five-thousand *baht* Sissi had handed him for the use of his establishment seemed to give him no pleasure at all. But now he was enthralled by what was happening in front of him.

"What?" Sissi asked.

"This is all real, isn't it?"

"It's taken you two hours to work that out?"

"I've been sulking. I can't focus when I sulk. Can I Tweet about this?"

"The more the merrier," said Sissi.

Live Internet feed. 7:30 P.M. Gulf of Thailand
(CAMERA — CLOSE-UP OF JIMM JUREE)
JIMM: We've been at sea now for almost as long as our last prime minister was in office. But we're just hearing some exciting news from Captain Kow in our lead boat. He's there at the handover spot. You'll hear the dialogue between the two captains over the radio. I'll translate as best I can.
(CAMERA ZOOMS IN ON ED)
KOW: I've held back as far as possible. The three squid boats are lit up like

Bangkok. I'm dark here. I'm using my binoculars, and I can see that the three big boats have come together in a huddle around the ferry. They're . . . they seem to be sharing out the Burmese between the three boats. I can't make out how many guards there are. It's far, and the conditions are shitty. But . . . wait. There's some kind of conflict. I can hear the guards shouting. It might . . . I don't know. It might be someone refusing to get out of —
(SOUND OF AUTOMATIC WEAPON CARRIES OVER RADIO)
ED: Kow! You all right? Kow?
KOW: Yeah. They just . . . they just shot one of the Burmese. Threw his body overboard. I guess it was a reminder of who's in charge. I . . . yeah. (SILENCE) The ferry'll be coming back this way soon. What do you suggest I do?
ED: Stay out of sight, but stay with her.
JIMM: (OFF-CAMERA) I'm sorry. I was . . . I was a little behind on the translation there. I'm just . . . yeah. Oh, man. These people are serious. Ed, are you sure Kow should follow the boat?
ED: Yeah. I've got a plan.

14.

THE COLORS OF THE RAMBO, SO PRETTY IN DISGUISE

(from "What A Wonderful World" — BOB THIELE, GEORGE DAVID WEISS)

Live Internet feed. 7:55 P.M. Gulf of Thailand
(CLOSE-UP OF JIMM JUREE SWINGS ROUND SLOWLY TO THE DARK SEA)
JIMM:(WHISPERED) We're sitting here with our lights off because the ferry, on its way back to the port after dropping off its slaves, is passing only fifty meters in front of us. We can see the red signal light of Captain Kow in pursuit. We're hoping to catch the skipper by sur—
(SOUND OF THE LOUD CLICK OF THE SPOTLIGHT BEING SWITCHED ON.)
JIMM: Our boat and Captain Kow's have both switched on their full beams.

You can now see the little boat quite clearly. My grandad is standing up in the front of our boat beside Bigman Beung in his impressive uniform. I'll translate.

GRANDAD JAH: (OFF-CAMERA) Cut your engine.

(SOUND OF GUNFIRE)

JIMM: That was the sound of Grandad firing his gun over the head of the ferry skipper. At least, I don't think he was trying to hit him. I imagine with the lights and the uniform, this must look like a navy raid of some kind. He's . . . he's cut his engine sure enough, and he's got his hands in the air. Our own engine kicks up, and we head toward him. Will he reach for a gun when he works out we're nobody official?

BIGMAN BEUNG: (OFF-CAMERA) Keep your hands where we can see them.

JIMM: As we get close, it's obvious that the skipper isn't in any fit state to reach for anything. He's either drunk or drugged. That's Captain Kow you see pulling alongside him. He's tying up his boat and jumping aboard. Well done, Captain. (CLOSE-UP OF CAP-TAIN KOW OPENS UP TO TAKE

IN THE CAPTURED BOAT) And here it is. The open boat that carried seventeen slaves to the fleet, one of whom was killed right in front of the captain's eyes. I will take you aboard so you can see the cramped conditions under which the Burmese were forced to endure the journey out to the deep ocean. Here. Two narrow wooden benches. Leg irons. The smell of vomit. No food or drink. My grandad is interrogating the prisoner of war. Like many fishermen, he's probably spaced out on amphetamines.

(ZOOM IN ON THE INTERROGATION)

GRANDAD JAH: What's your name, old man?

FERRY SKIPPER: Yeah. Whatever.

GRANDAD JAH: Do you realize that what you've just done is an infringement of international law?

FERRY SKIPPER: You finished? I got a night job to get to.

GRANDAD JAH: You aren't going anywhere, son. You're under arrest.

FERRY SKIPPER: Is that so? I don't see any police. Just old farts and tarts.

GRANDAD JAH: Then you aren't looking hard enough.

(POLICE CAPTAIN WAEW GOES ROUND BEHIND THE SKIPPER AND SNAPS ON HANDCUFFS WHILE GRANDAD MANHANDLES THE PRISONER DOWN ONTO ONE OF THE BENCHES)

FERRY SKIPPER: You can't do this. I've got contacts. I've got a number to call. I'm protected.

GRANDAD JAH: Yeah? Where is it? I'll call it for you.

FERRY SKIPPER: In my shirt pocket.

GRANDAD JAH: Thank you. That'll come in very useful. In court.

(CAMERA ROTATES BACK TO JIMM)

JIMM: So, there you have it. The first victory. We are now three boats. But how do we use this windfall to our advantage? Stay tuned.

"Oh, this is just it, Mair. Just it."

"It is?"

"Absolutely it. Look at the counter."

"That's certainly a lot of numbers."

"We just jumped like some mad thing. We're fifty thousand short of half a million. And they're everywhere. Look at this."

Sissi dragged her mother to a far computer.

"See this, Mair? This is a stat-counter. It tells you where people are logging in from. Look at this: London, Rio, Cape Town. Look at the figures. We're global."

"That's nice. But I don't think I'd want her with a bushman. A nice Englishman would be fine."

"Mair, this isn't a dating service."

"I know, but you did promise to make her look thinner."

"She'll have every man in the world drooling over her. She'll be a celebrity. It doesn't matter what you look like if you're a celebrity."

Mair looked at her daughter and touched the screen.

"Being a celebrity isn't like being a person," she said. "It's just another two-dimensional brick in the entertainment empire. It's temporary. I want her to find someone because she has a good heart."

"They'll see her heart, don't you worry. Look what she's doing. Heart's about all they're running on out there."

"Why's he naked?"

"Lady boys don't like being, you know, exposed. They're lost without their queer clothes, and . . ."

"What psychology book did you get that

out of?"

"Everyone knows."

"Right."

Lieutenant Egg was standing in the doorway looking down at Chompu, who was handcuffed to the headboard by one wrist. It was a Home Art two-thousand *baht* bed, so if Chompu had been of a certain mind and musculature he could have destroyed the whole thing in seconds. As it was, he lay on the mattress with one manacled hand above him and the other on his genitals.

"And the bruises?" Egg asked.

"He resisted arrest," said Ben. Socrates sat on his own bed, watching. Both were now dressed in their fake police uniforms.

"You know, normally I'd say that was excessive violence," said Egg. "I'd say, 'You have a foe. You have a need to dispense with him. You do it cleanly and without personal animosity. It's a job.' But there are times when the would-be victim rubs you so far up the wrong way, you just want to make it last as long as you can."

Egg sat on the bed beside Chompu.

"Why didn't you gag him?"

"He hasn't said nothing," said Ben.

"Probably got a sore throat from all that man juice," said Socrates.

Egg grabbed Chompu's modesty hand

335

and yanked it away from his organ.

"Well. You're well equipped for a lady boy, aren't you?" said Egg. "What a waste. And I bet your reporter girlfriend hasn't even seen it. Am I right? But as she's got the balls in this relationship, I wouldn't be surprised if you coming here was her idea. Yeah, you haven't got the sense to put all this together by yourself. This and all that filing-cabinet bullshit. You think I'd leave anything in-criminating in a police station? Do you?"

Egg clicked his fingers, and Ben handed over his stiletto blade.

"And his cell phone," said Egg.

The rats went through the crumpled clothing on the floor and came up with the mobile. Egg scrolled through the numbers.

"OK. Here she is," he said.

He pressed the number and handed the phone to Chompu. At the same time he slowly slid the razor-sharp knife under the policeman's pride and joy.

"You get her here any way you can," said Egg. "But you make it sound innocent. You've got something to show her. I don't care how you do it. But one stupid com-ment and you'll be half the man you never were. You know what I mean?"

Chompu pressed the phone to his ear and coughed.

"Hello, Jimm? It's me. Can you hear me? . . . Yes, of course I got that *Blue Streak* DVD you asked for. But that's not why I'm calling. I've got good news. I broke into rughead's house like we planned."

The knife lifted a few centimeters, as did Chompu's pitch.

"I mean, Lieutenant Egg's place . . . That's right. You remember where it is? . . . Third building after the hospital turn-off. Set back from the road. I've been looking around, and I found something you'd really want to see . . . Yes . . . Yes . . . That's correct. Can you get here soon? It's really urgent . . . Where are you? . . . OK. It should take you thirty minutes to get here then. Ring the doorbell. I'll come down and let you in . . . Right. I love you too."

He handed Egg the phone.

"You know?" said Egg. "You really are a little girly. You're a coward. I don't know who you twiddled with to get into our man's police force, or how the hell you got to the rank you are, but I'm ashamed to be wearing the same uniform as you."

"May I speak?" Chompu asked.

They all laughed.

"She's so polite," said Socrates.

"What?" asked Egg, drawing the knife face across Chompu's skin.

"You might have to put off killing me. She's going to call again when she arrives on the street. If she doesn't hear me, she won't come in."

"Don't worry," said Egg. "There are so many better ways to kill time than just doing away with you. That's far too quick."

He leaned over and punched Chompu in the face three times with all his might. The third blow broke the lieutenant's nose. Chompu didn't make a sound and didn't take his eyes off his attacker.

Sissi and Mair were interrupted by the wind-chime version of "Mamma Mia."

"What's that?" Sissi asked.

"It's Jimm's cell phone."

Sissi burrowed into her bag.

"Why's it in there?" Mair asked.

"Jimm thought she'd be out of cell-phone range soon so she left it with me to coordinate the ground troops. Do you know someone called Lieu?"

The name on the screen didn't mean anything to either of them. Sissi set the phone to speaker.

"Jimm's phone," she said.

"Hello, Jimm? It's me."

"Who's me?"

"Can you hear me?"

"Yes, but you don't seem to be hearing me. I'm not Jimm. I'm —"

"Yes, of course I got that *Blue Streak* DVD you asked for. But that's not why I'm calling. I've got good news. I broke into rughead's house like we planned."

"It sounds like Chompu," whispered Mair.

"The gay cop?" asked Sissi. "Jimm said he'd be checking out that other lieutenant's house."

"I mean, Lieutenant Egg's place," Chompu continued.

"Are you in some kind of trouble?" Sissi asked.

"That's right. You remember where it is?"

"No."

"Third building after the hospital turn-off. Set back from the road. I've been looking around, and I found something you'd really want to see."

"Is somebody there with you?"

"Yes."

"OK. That's why you can't talk. Is the DVD relevant?"

"Yes."

"How many of them are there? One . . . two . . . three?"

"That's correct. Can you get here soon? It's really urgent."

"I'll try."

"Where are you?"

"At the Internet shop in Pak Nam."

"OK. It should take you thirty minutes to get here then. Ring the doorbell. I'll come down and let you in."

"Listen. Tell them I'm going to phone you again in twenty-five minutes just to make sure it's safe. That should keep you alive a little while longer."

"Right. I love you too."

"You should be so lucky."

Sissi turned off the phone and stared at her mother.

"It sounds serious."

"He's in trouble," Mair agreed. "Does the DVD mean anything to you?"

"*Blue Streak.* It was a Martin Lawrence movie. He impersonates a police officer."

"So, we should call the real police?"

"Except we don't know who it is who's impersonating a police officer, Mair. He might be at the police station. It might be a warning to stay away from the police. I'll have to do this myself."

"You certainly will not."

"Not what?"

"Do this by yourself. I'm not about to lose all my children and my father in one evening."

"It'll be dangerous."

"Have I not told you about the time I used a chair to beat off a knife-wielding drug addict?"

"You were younger then."

"It was last October."

"Even so."

"You are not going alone."

"All right. All right. But let's think about this. There are three of them. They're probably armed."

"Chompu's in an upstairs room."

"How do you know?"

"He said he'd come down to let us in."

"Well spotted. How long would it take us to get to the house from here?"

"No more than five minutes."

"Then why did he say . . . ? OK. We need to come up with something soon. They'll be expecting Jimm in half an hour. If we can get there earlier, it should catch them by surprise."

"This is fun, isn't it?"

The spotty shop owner was staring openmouthed at the discussion before him.

"You," said Sissi.

"Me?" said Spotty.

"You're in charge here."

"I am?"

He seemed delighted. Sissi explained the set-up and the ongoing maintenance. There was an external block he needed to keep an eye on to see if anyone was trying to hack into the system to shut down the site. There was also a back-up site if anything went wrong. Everything was explained in some alien nerd language and understood. Mair looked on, impressed at how wonderful her eldest son had turned out.

Piper Porterfield was sitting in her office at Hope for Myanmar, playing spider solitaire on her laptop. Hers was a hardship posting, and she missed decent wine bars and civilized Western culture. Mae Hon Song was a bustling northern town, but it was so rural. It didn't even have an English-language cinema or a deli worth its salt. She invariably delayed going home to sit in her uncomfortable living room beneath a ceiling dotted with lizards and the eerie sounds of God-knew-what insects buzzing in the trees outside. Only seven months to go before a return to civilization.

A chat box flashed in the corner of her screen. It was Pao. Pao had gone home at six but was still online doing her office management work.

Have you seen this? was the message, together with a Web address: www.gulf slaverhunt.co.org

Pao was into computer games. Piper was just about to dump the site, along with all the other annoying spam the girl sent her. But boredom made her cut and paste and click.

A scene appeared on the screen. The picture wasn't that clear. There were little pixel accidents here and there. But it was obviously a seascape looking out to the horizon. The dots of boats far away. And there was a voice-over that seemed somehow familiar.

JIMM: (OFF-CAMERA) We should be within eyesight of the three slaver ships in under half an hour. Under cover of darkness, our chances of sneaking up undetected are increased. The large boats will have their bright lights trained downward to attract the squid, and they shouldn't be expecting visitors. We've been trying to gather reinforcements. Captain Kow has been on the radio for an hour. But the karaoke finals are coming up soon, and it seems like the lives of Burmese take a back seat to those luxury consumer goods prizes.

Piper looked first at the counter on the

top of the screen. If it was to be believed, almost half a million people had entered this site at some time during the evening. A logo indicated that what she was watching was concurrently live on YouTube. There was a button, bottom left, that apparently led to Slaver Hunt Home. She clicked it. She was taken to an unspectacular homepage, which explained that Jimm Juree and her small band of heroes had set out at four this afternoon to rescue seventeen kidnapped Burmese from three slave ships. The Burmese were under armed guard. Jimm and her crew had just the one weapon. They were alone in the Gulf, a lawless no-man's-land. The odds were considerably against them. Et cetera.

To one side was a column of times. By clicking any time, you could see a replay of what had happened then. Important moments were tagged with a skull and crossbones. The whole thing looked as if it had been put together in a hurry. The artwork was shoddy. But it all did the job. The girl, Jimm, leaned a little too heavily on clichés and drama, and her English accent needed work, but there was no doubting her determination. The amateur nature of it all made it just that much more credible. This was powerful stuff.

Piper reached for her telephone.

Live internet feed. 20:24 P.M. Gulf of
Thailand

(COMPUTER ON NIGHT SCOPE
EFFECT)

JIMM: I've just worked out how to
switch on the night vision. Sorry about
that. In our wake you can see two small
boats. One belongs to our hero of the
night, Captain Kow, who bravely followed the ferry to meet the slaver
ships. Behind him is the captured
ferry, driven now by PI Meng, the
private detective, who has asked me to
point out that he's prepared to cut his
rates twenty percent to customers who
have been watching this live feed. He
also produces excellent plastic awnings. And there are probably those of
you out there wondering why I'm
resorting to advertising at such a tense
moment. It's partly because nothing
has happened for half an hour, and I'm
also feeling under pressure to —

GRANDAD JAH: (OFF-CAMERA)
Jimm!

(CAMERA SWINGS CLUMSILY TO
THE FRONT OF ED'S BOAT,

WHERE WE SEE WAEW, BEUNG, AND GRANDAD LOOKING AHEAD THROUGH BINOCULARS.)

GRANDAD JAH: That's them.

(CAMERA SCANS THE HORIZON. ZOOMS IN ON THREE SMALL DIA- MONDS OF LIGHT.)

JIMM: It's true. That must be them.

ED: All right. I'm turning side on. The other two boats can stay behind me. If the slavers do look this way, they'll see just the one squid boat out of its depth. They won't think too much about us.

JIMM: Why not?

ED: Because this is spawning ground. We're twenty kilometers out of the legal fishing zone. We're all criminals out here.

(CLOSE-UP ON JIMM)

JIMM: And so, our target has been spot- ted. The clouds have blocked the moon, so it's like sitting in a velvet glove out here. Soon we will advance on our prey. May the force be with us.

In a half-empty house you can feel the vibrations of a loud front doorbell.

"It's her," said Ben rat.

"It's not her," said Egg. He was standing

at the upstairs window in the front room with the lights off. He had a clear view of the concrete front yard. It was lit by the porch lamp. "It's a couple of hookers."

Ben and Socrates rushed in from their room and joined Egg at the window.

"Did you two . . . ?" Egg asked.

"Nah," said Socrates. He glared at Ben. "You?"

"No way," said Ben indignantly. "I don't need to pay for it."

The bell rang again. There was nothing to see in the yard below until one of the hookers took a few steps back out of the shelter of the porch roof. She looked up at the window, and all three men instinctively took half a pace back. Short skirt. Heels. Low-cut top. Peek-a-boo hairstyle. Beautiful smile framed in crimson.

"I'd give that one," said Socrates.

"Me too," said Ben. "If it was free, of course."

Egg turned to look at them.

"You two do realize this probably isn't the best time to be thinking about recreation?" he said. "We're just about to kill a couple of people."

"I swear," said Socrates. "We've got a number, but we didn't call it. Not tonight."

A second woman stepped back and waved

at the window. If it was possible, she was even sexier than the first. They were both shouting, but the window was double-glazed to keep the air-conditioning in and the traffic sounds out.

"Maybe one of them's her," said Ben. "The Jimm girl."

"Come on," said Egg. "You've both seen her. Does she look like either of those two?"

"Be nice if she did," said Socrates.

"Doesn't look like they are going away," said Ben. "Lieutenant Egg, that one's pointing to your bike. She knows you're a cop."

"I'll have to go talk to them," said Egg. "We don't want them hanging around when the girl arrives. You two stay here."

Egg scrambled down to the front door. The two hookers were leaning against his bike. They were a lot older than they'd let on. They *wai*'d sincerely.

"Get off my bike," said Egg. "What do you want?"

Sissi turned to Mair.

"See, Deang? I told you this was a police bike. I could tell by the number plate."

"That's typical of you, Noy. You love to gloat about being right."

"Who's gloating? I'm just telling you I know a police motorcycle when I see one."

" 'Cause you been on the back of one

often enough."

"That's right. Overreact. Make everything dirty. I can't make a simple comment anymore without you turning it into a TV drama."

"Me? What about you?"

"Just leave me —"

"Oi!" shouted Egg. "Shut up. What are you doing here? This is private property."

"Oh, really?" said Sissi. "And there we were thinking it was the provincial sports stadium."

"Don't get smart with me, you old whore," said Egg.

"Oooo," said both women.

"Now aren't you jumping to conclusions," said Mair. "What, may I ask, leads you to believe my colleague here is a lady of the night?"

"Respectable women don't dress up like you two with skirts up around their arses, and you know it," said Egg.

He'd had enough. He took his gun from his holster.

"Oooo," said both women.

"So, not satisfied with insulting us, you're now going to shoot us," said Sissi. "That's police brutality in its extreme."

She waved and blew a kiss to the two uniformed men in the upstairs window. The younger waved back.

"And how would you explain that to the Lions Club?" Mair asked.

Egg laughed.

"What connection would two old slags like you have with the Lions Club?"

"We're members," said Mair.

"The cabaret, more like," said Egg.

"Ooo," said both women.

"That's it," said Sissi, "I'm phoning your superiors." And she walked to the open door in a huff.

"Stop right there," shouted Egg and ran after her. "You're not going in there."

When he reached her, she was directly underneath the porch roof. He grabbed her arm and pointed his pistol at her ear. She spun suddenly and Tasered him on the neck. He dropped like an actual egg from a chicken's rear end. Mair smiled and walked gaily toward the porch, blowing another kiss to the boys upstairs. Once out of sight from above, she helped Sissi drag the dead weight of Lieutenant Egg into the house.

"He'll be out for five minutes," Sissi whispered and shut the front door. She pulled the plastic flexi cuffs from her handbag and snapped his wrists together behind him. Then she produced a large foam ball, which she inserted into his mouth.

"I shall have to rethink my own handbag contents," whispered Mair.

"Now comes the hard part," said Sissi. "You up for it?"

"Let me at 'em."

The rat brothers had lost sight of Egg and the hookers. Everything was quiet downstairs.

"What are they doing down there?" asked Ben.

"Forgot to bring me X-ray glasses, didn't I?" said Socrates.

"No need for —"

"You boys!" came a woman's voice from the lower floor.

"They're in the house," said Ben.

"What's he doing letting them in?"

"Perhaps he made . . . an arrangement."

"We've got the girl coming in ten minutes. He's the one who said we didn't have time for any arrangements."

"Boys? Can you hear me?" came the voice again. "I'm a bit lonely down here. Your lieutenant's entertaining my friend in the front room, and I haven't got anyone to play with. I don't suppose one of you could help me out?"

"I'll go," said Ben.

"No, wait."

"I said it first."

"No, I mean. This doesn't make sense."

"I'm younger. I can —"

"Listen, stupid. I mean it really doesn't make sense. Egg's not going to get frisky when we got hits to take care of. Doesn't matter how sexy those two are."

He walked to the bedroom door.

"Egg? Egg?" he shouted.

"He's on the job," said Ben.

"I don't think so. Listen. You go down first. See if these hookers are really, you know, legit. I'll creep down after you with the gun. Got it?"

They walked to the upstairs balcony, and Socrates shouted, "That's all right, young man. You go. I'll stay up here and watch . . . television."

Lucky. He'd almost said, "watch the hostage." It was reassuring when your intellect kicked in at the last minute. Ben took the stairs three at a time. Socrates counted to five, checked that the lady boy was still chained to his bed, and started slowly down the staircase. He paused halfway down. The door to the front room was shut. There were familiar female porn sound-effects coming from beyond it. He went down two more steps and heard "But you're such a handsome boy" coming from the direction of the kitchen. "Come closer."

Socrates grimaced. He was always the damned bridesmaid. Why was it that good fortune always landed on everyone else? Hookers arrive from heaven on a door-to-door relief mission and he misses out. Typical. Well, at least he could perv. He took the last ten stairs on tiptoe and shuffled silently over to the kitchen door. He looked around the jamb expecting to find some form of laying on the kitchen table. But it was empty but for empties. He took in the fridge, the oven, then stretched his neck all the way to the sink unit. He had barely enough time to notice the legs of his partner akimbo on the kitchen floor before some big-arsed electronic python zapped him from behind and the world was soot.

15.
OLD PIRATES, YES, THEY'RE RABBI

(from "Redemption Song" — BOB MARLEY)

"So, what do we do with them?" asked Mair. "It's been such a long time since my last S&M experience. And that was with the clergy."

Sissi and Chompu turned their heads, raised their eyebrows, and stared at her. Mair's day clothes were in the back of Sissi's rental, but she'd insisted on staying in character. She had a good figure for a fifty-eight-year-old and didn't have too many opportunities to show it off. Sissi had changed into a sensible Japanese cardigan twin set and a long skirt. Chompu was back in his uniform, but his face was a mess.

"I'm rather enjoying this Taser," he said, leaning over the three manacled villains supine on the living room floor.

"You'll tire of it," said Sissi. "We all do, eventually."

"New toy syndrome," said the policeman.

"You know?" said Mair. "It's rather a pity my father can't be here. He would have so enjoyed electrocuting these bullies. In fact, you make it look like so much fun I'm tempted to have a little zap myself."

"You've had enough excitement for one day," Sissi reminded her.

"You're probably right. Too much of a good thing. But seriously, what do we do with them? Concrete boots five kilometers out to sea?"

Chompu found it hard to smile through swollen lips.

"We have the two morons here for impersonating police officers," he said. "We have the fake police truck out the back. There's probably some law against cloning police vehicles. We might find witnesses to say they saw these two driving it the day your shop blew up. And even if nobody did, I'm sure we can manufacture some. Our problem is . . . this one."

He nodded at Egg. There was a button on the Taser that gave a brief shock. Chompu had been trying out its effects on his office mate. He knew how irresponsible and childish it was, but it was so much fun. He edged the muzzle up Egg's thigh one yelp at a time. The three men were gagged with Sissi's foam balls, and Chompu was trying to dissociate himself from any sado-erotic undertones he might have been enjoying. He didn't want to become — heaven forbid — a pervert. He kept his voice steady.

"We still don't have anything solid against our lieutenant here. We might be able to convince the other two goons to give evidence against him. We have a trunk-load of circumstantials, but we don't have . . . the piece."

His hand gesture was such that the Taser flipped to one side and accidently shocked Egg.

"Oops, sorry," he said. "I really didn't mean to . . . Never mind. Do we need to recharge this super little piece of equipment at all?"

"You have two more hours," said Sissi.

"Remarkable. You and I will certainly have to exchange notes some time. But Mair, to answer your question, I certainly have enough to contact my police station and have this rabble collected. My only fear is that little fluffy head here wasn't acting alone. I mean, if it transpires he has an influential sponsor, he could be back on the streets by tomorrow. These things happen all the time. So if that turns out to be the case . . ."

He smiled at the lieutenant.

"I'll kill him here and bury him in the bushes."

"Oh, yes. By all means, let's do that," said Mair. "We can't possibly rely on the system."

Sissi looked back and forth between the two, wondering where the bad cop/bad cop routine might end. Or indeed, if it was a routine at all. Chompu was eyeing the lieutenant hungrily.

"Mair," said Chompu, "I think you'd better avert your eyes. I'm about to do something quite obscene with this prisoner." He put down the Taser and picked up one of the sharp knives they'd confiscated from the rat brothers.

"Son, I've been around," she said.

"So be it."

Chompu strode around the three prisoners and knelt at their heads. With the knife in his left hand, he reached forward with his right and grabbed the thatch that sat atop Lieutenant Egg's skull. He yanked with all his might. There was a faint ripping sound but little resistance. Chompu held his scalp aloft and looked down at the sorry state of Egg's head. It was a sight of rampant deforestation. Of butchery and disease. It was a hopeless head.

"How's everything going?" Sissi asked. He and Mair had been about to use the provided key to reenter the Internet shop, but the door was unlocked. There were a dozen people sitting on stools at the computers. All were viewing the slavery site.

"Who . . . who are you?" asked the spotty owner, rising from the comfortable swivel chair.

"Such a short memory," said Sissi in his baggage-handler voice. "How's the block holding up?"

"It's you," said Spotty, sitting back down.

"Right. I'm in disguise. Get out of my seat. And what are all these people doing here?"

The lad fled to his desk.

"This is my Twitter network," he said. "I couldn't keep them away."

"All twelve of them? You're a popular man."

Sissi checked the counter and smiled at Mair.

"Eight hundred and ninety thousand," she said. "Almost the population of Swaziland have spent some of the last four hours watching our slaver drama unfold. Not bad.

Not bad at all. Even if you assume that seventy percent of them will be too spaced out or high or sleepy to notice it's reality, or to care, there'll still be a happy band of activists and journalists and bloggers in search of a point. There'll be some big names voicing outrage that we haven't come a long way since the thirteenth century."

"Who's your friend?" the shop owner asked quietly, grinning at Mair, who flirted demurely back at him.

"Don't even think about it," said Sissi. "What's happening on the site?"

The owner reluctantly left Mair's gaze and returned to the computer.

"It's dark," said the man.

"I can see that," said Sissi. "The XR2's got night vision. Why isn't she using it?"

"Ah, but Jimm and Ed have turned all their lights off," said a soft man with a feathery mustache.

"That doesn't make any . . ." Sissi started.

"Those lights up ahead," said a young woman with bluish skin, "they're the slaver boats. Ed's using the tide to drift nearer to them. Everyone on Ed's boat has taken a vow of silence except for Jimm, and she's whispering her commentary. Even so they're afraid the sound might carry in the night air. It's like . . . incredibly intense."

"It makes *The Blair Witch Project* look like it wasn't real," said the mustache man.

"It wasn't real," said Sissi.

"You say," said the owner and winked at Mair.

"Yeah, OK." Sissi got the feeling she was losing control. "Mair, are you sure you don't want to go and get changed?"

"Yes."

"OK, so let's turn up the volume and see what our sibling is talking about," said Sissi.

"About time," said blue skin.

Live Internet feed. 9:44 P.M. Gulf of Thailand

(CLOSE-UP JIMM)

JIMM: . . . and so we've come up with a plan. It's dicey, but we have few options. Grandad Jah and Waew have been plying the ferry skipper with rum. Combined with whatever made him high earlier, he's now completely out of his mind.

(PAN AROUND TO SHOW THE OLD MEN ENCOURAGING THE SKIPPER TO DRINK FROM THE BOTTLE. CAMERA CONTINUES AROUND TO SHOW ARNY AND GAEW HALF UNDRESSED.)

JIMM: Our brave volunteers, my brother Arny and his fiancée, Gaew, are disguising themselves to look like Burmese peasants. That's Arny ripping his T-shirt. And there's Bigman Beung attempting to rip the T-shirt of Gaew. And that's Gaew punching him in the solar plexus — a lot quieter than slapping his face. You can see the tension's mounting here. Arny and Gaew will travel on the slave ferry with the inebriated skipper and PI Meng as captain, and me, hidden under a plastic tarpaulin. Ed and Bigman Beung will head off east and circle round. Captain Kow and Waew and Grandad Jah will do the same to the west. As we won't be able to outshoot them, we'll have to try the same tactic that got us access to the ferry. If we can convince them we're there in some official capacity, it might buy us time to get aboard and disarm them. That, at least, is the theory.

(CAMERA TAKEN DOWN INTO THE SMALL BOAT, AND WE SEE THE SKIPPER PROPPED UP AGAINST THE LITTLE CABIN AND PI MENG AT THE RUDDER.)

JIMM: And off we go. It's a fine evening for a raid. The rain has stopped now, but let's hope that the cloud cover remains. There's a full moon up there somewhere, and on a bright night you can see for miles by moonlight. At some point, when this boat is close to the three slavers, they'll turn their lights in our direction. I'll continue this broadcast from beneath the tarpaulin. (ZOOM IN ON THE PASSENGERS) But for now I'm on the open boat with my brave brother and his lady friend. How are you feeling, Gaew?

GAEW: It's like before a big bodybuilding tournament, you know? The butterflies. Not knowing what's going to happen. No access to steroids. But I feel proud tonight.

JIMM: Proud about what?

GAEW: Proud of my man here. He was the first one to volunteer. No hesitation. That's what I like. A brave, decisive man. In situations like this, you find out who a person really is.

(CLOSE-UP ON A VERY PALE-LOOKING ARNY)

JIMM: And what about you, little brother?

ARNY: OK.

JIMM: That's all?

ARNY: Yeah.

JIMM: There you have it. A strong man of action but few words. Good luck to both of you. We will see —

PI MENG: Jimm, get down.

(CAMERA LENS IS BLINDED BY A STRONG ARC OF LIGHT. WE SEE A MASH OF ANGLES AND SKY AND A BLUR OF ACTIVITY. SHOUTED VOICES IN THE BACK-GROUND. A ROUND OF GUNFIRE. THE SCREEN GOES BLACK. ALL WE HEAR IS THE SOUND OF HEAVY BREATHING, AS IF IT'S COMING FROM THE COMPUTER ITSELF. THIS IS ALL WE HAVE FOR ALMOST A MINUTE. AT LAST THERE IS AN EXTREME CLOSE-UP OF JIMM UNDER THE PLASTIC. NOSE RUNNING. NIGHT VISION. A FACE WRUNG WITH PANIC.)

JIMM: (WHISPERED) They . . . they've spotted us. That came (BREATHS) came much faster than we expected. Their spotlights are on us. I don't know if they've seen me. I was directly in their beam . . . I don't . . . just don't know. One of the guards fired at us. PI Meng stopped our engine and put up his hands. They shouted for us to state our business. They . . . wait, it's hard to hear everything from . . . OK, PI Meng is telling them the story we worked out. He's the skipper's nephew. The skipper's so stoned he radioed for his nephew to come and help him get home. But in the boat the nephew found two more Burmese hidden under the tarpaulin. Wait. I can hear one of the boats start up its engine. PI Meng's doing a good job in the telling of this lie, but I don't know if the slavers are buying it. I can't see anything. I hope they don't hear the engines of our other two boats.

It sounds like one of their slaver ships is alongside us now. The voices seem to be right over me. I'll have to be . . . to be careful. Praise Clint they don't come on board.

(INDISTINCT SHOUTING)

JIMM: The slaver boss seems to be angry. He's shouting at the ferry skipper, but he's not getting any answer. Not surprising, considering the amount of rum we poured into him. I'll translate.

BOSS: You were supposed to bring us seventeen. Isn't that right? That's what they . . . He's not listening. Someone throw him overboard.

SKIPPER: Brahhhl'tppaabbrrr.

PI Meng: He gets like this often, sir. I'll take care of him.

BOSS: I don't give a damn about him. I want to know about the numbers. Seventeen, they said. One stepped out of line and in front of a few bullets. Now that, to my tiny mind, leaves sixteen. Is that wrong? Anybody here think that's not right? And that's what we got. And I don't like this. Who are you? How did you just happen to be bobbing about in the sea at the right time?

PI Meng: I wasn't bobbing, sir. I've got me own boat. Me and me brother. We wasn't far away, so when he radioed, we went and met him. That's when I found the stowaways.

BOSS: Who was riding shotgun on the ferry? Su, get over here.

CREW 2: Yes, boss?

BOSS: You know anything about this?

CREW 2: About what, boss?

BOSS: This unknown person's claiming there were two extra Burmese in this shipment.

CREW 2: Really?

BOSS: Really? What do you mean,

really? You were supposed to count 'em onto the boat. Were there seventeen or nineteen?

CREW 2: When I counted 'em, there was seventeen, boss.

BOSS: And you counted 'em as they arrived on the boat?

CREW 2: Yeah. When they was sitting on the boat.

BOSS: Well, which? As they boarded, or after they were on board?

CREW 2: There was a lot of stuff going on all around. Boats coming in and out. People walking around. We had to get 'em on in a hurry. And there was a lot of 'em. So I had to help with the round-up. Hurry 'em up, you know? Then me and the police boys had to chain up their ankles. Then I counted 'em.

BOSS: Did the police boys tell you there were two extra?

CREW 2: We don't exactly talk. Not exactly best mates, you know? They're animals, those two.

BOSS: So it is possible that they brought two more Burmese?

CREW 2: Very possible, boss. Very possible.

BOSS: And what are the chances that

these two enormous people hid themselves under a tarpaulin, like that one over there, and you and the police boys didn't notice 'em?

CREW 2: I suspect we would'a been so stressed out just tying these ones down that we wouldn't of thought of looking.

BOSS: Jeez! This is the quality of staff we pay the big money for.

CREW 2: One armed guard for all them —

BOSS: Shut up. Just shut up. Moo, get down there.

(THE SOUND OF A THUD AND HEAVY FOOTSTEPS VERY CLOSE)

JIMM: One of them has boarded our boat. Please don't search. Please don't search. This is the only place anyone can hide on this little boat. No. OK. OK. He's at the front. He . . . he wants to know why the skipper's tied by the ankle to the bollard. PI Meng's explaining that when the skipper gets plastered, he likes to throw himself overboard. The family spends hours searching for him. This is the only way to save him from himself.

SKIPPER: Shmmooou tttepbluappat.

JIMM: The guard's laughing. That might

be a good sign. Oh . . . oh shit. He's speaking Burmese to Arny and Gaew. That's going to mess everything up. I have to lift this sheet a little to see what's . . . Oh, no.

(CAMERA FACES FORWARD TO CATCH A SCUFFLE BETWEEN ARNY AND THE GUARD. A SHOT IS FIRED FROM SOMEWHERE.)

JIMM: (CLOSE-UP. OUT OF BREATH.) I can't believe it. Arny went for the guard. Wrestled him. Even got the gun off him. Then someone in the boat beside us fired his rifle. PI Meng ran over to Arny with a big machete in his hand. He pulled Arny off, and it looks like he hit him over the head with the handle. Arny went down like a sack of soggy mice.

(CAMERA RETURNS TO THE AC-TION. SLIGHTLY BLURRED SCENE OF GAEW RUNNING FROM HER SEAT AND THROWING HER-SELF AT PI MENG. THEN PI KICKS HER TO THE GROUND AND STANDS OVER HER AS IF TO FIN-ISH HER OFF WITH HIS MACHETE.)

BOSS: Hold it. Hold it.

(CAMERA RETURNS UNDER THE

TARPAULIN. CLOSE-UP OF JIMM)

JIMM: There are boats all around us now. I think the other two have come to watch the show. This is all too much. It's happening too fast. Where the hell are Kow and Ed? Whose idea was all this? Oh my Lord. The boss is pacing around saying they were only supposed to have seventeen warm bodies. Nobody mentioned nineteen. Nobody mentioned nineteen. He'd have to call headquarters. It sounds like he's talking to himself. The crew have other suggestions.

CREW 1: I say, kill 'em. They're trouble already.

CREW 2: They look strong, though. Look at them muscles. We could get a lot of work out of 'em.

BOSS: Nobody does nothing till I sort this out with them in Lang Suan. If I get a definite seventeen, we shoot these two.

JIMM: The boss is calling land. It sounds like an open channel. If we're lucky, the reply will be loud enough to hear who he's talking to and what's said. But I don't know. There's a lot of static.

BOSS: R2 to base. R2 to base. Come in.

(PERIOD OF SILENCE)

(STATIC)

RECEIVER: Can't you boys do anything by yourselves? Don't you know I've got better things to do than sit by the radio all night?

JIMM: I know that voice.

BOSS: This is urgent.

RECEIVER: It's always urgent.

BOSS: Let me talk to your father.

RECEIVER: He's at dinner. What do you want?

BOSS: Can't you get him away from dinner?

RECEIVER: No. Who do you think you're talking to? You get your own little boat, and suddenly you think you're —

JIMM: The channel's shut down. The boss is angry.

BOSS: All right. Split 'em up. Put Shrek on my boat and Mrs. Shrek on Dan's. You! You get out of here and take your uncle with you. When he sobers up, tell him he's fired and he's lucky he's not fired at. And you and him don't mouth off to anyone. We know where you and your relatives live.

PI Meng: What about me?

BOSS: What about you?

PI Meng: I can do his job. I hate Burmese.

BOSS: Get lost.

PI Meng: I've got me license and —

BOSS: Get lost or get dead.

PI Meng: Yes, sir.

JIMM: Meng's trying to kill time till our other two boats make their play. But it's not working. And we can't leave. I can hear other feet walking on our boat. They'll be teaming up to split Arny and Gaew. Of course, I can't let that happen. This is the moment. If this live telecast terminates in the next few minutes, and if anyone else in the world cares, we have been killed by Thai slavers operating off the coast of Chumphon. Don't let them get away with it. Don't rest until these people are found and punished. This whole, dispensable Burmese operation is being run out of the Southern Rescue Mission Foundation in Lang Suan. Voice-print checks on the woman we just heard over the radio will confirm that she is the receptionist there and is probably related to the founder. I'm going to expose myself now in the hope that I can briefly capture the faces of the leader of these villains and his crew on this camera. There are armed guards out there. Anything could go wrong. But let it be remembered that I . . . we all sacrificed our lives for our Burmese neighbors who are subjected to these terrors every day.

"Oh, come on, sibling," said Sissi. "Enough's enough. You're sounding like Miss World."

"Shh!" came a chorus from the Internet Tweeters.

"You said she can't see how many people are watching this," said Mair.

"She can't, not on her machine. But she must sense it. You can't have two million eyes on you and not feel the hairs stand up on the back of your neck."

"It's too much," said Mair. "We had a TV, you know."

"Will you two keep it down," said the mustache guy.

"You ever attempted to have a webcam removed from your nostril?" said Sissi. "Mair? What's this about the TV?"

"Just that we had one. Me and Jarooat."

"Who the . . . ? Who's Jarooat?"

"You don't remember your own father's name?"

"My . . . ? Why should I? I was only, what . . . four or five . . . when he left us? You never talked about him. I barely remember his face."

"We'd sit together, hand in hand, watching exciting programs like this."

"This isn't a program, Mair. It's —"

"And we'd try not to get upset by them. I'd try not to cry. Because we knew they were sponsored by the Suzuki motorcycle company and Tonaf anti-foot-rot cream and the like. And we knew everything would work out fine in the end because sponsors didn't want death. They wanted happy endings. That's what sells foot-rot cream. And we were never disappointed. Who did we finally get to sponsor our show, Margaret?"

"It's . . ." Sissi smiled at her mother. "You know? I do think we had somebody down from Coca-Cola in the end."

"Oh, well. There's nothing to worry about then."

"Where's the logo then?" asked blue skin. Sissi ignored her.

"We should be getting back, I suppose," said Mair. "There's nobody feeding the dogs."

"You asked someone from the co-op to do it," said Sissi.

"Are you sure? Good for me. At least I've

been good for something. I wasn't worth a shaved-ice sundae as a mother, if you ask me."

"Mair, you —"

"Will somebody shut the old woman up?" said some lanky chopstick of a teenager.

Sissi scraped back her chair, grabbed the youth by the neck, frog-marched him out the door and locked it. There was no more backchat from the Tweeters.

"I put my only two children up for adoption, you know?" said Mair.

"Mair, stop talking now."

"Yes, I should. The show's on."

JIMM: 3 . . . 2 . . . 1 . . . Here goes.

(THE CAMERA IS EXPOSED TO THE BRIGHT LIGHTS FROM THE SQUID BOATS, AND THE SCREEN IS TEMPORARILY BLINDING. WHEN WE REFOCUS, WE SEE THE SURPRISED FACES OF THE GUARDS. THE FOLLOWING SECTION HAS NO ENGLISH TRANSLATION.)

JIMM: Smile everyone. You're on the Internet — live. Shown worldwide in approximately a billion homes.

BOSS: Who the bloody hell's that?

(CAMERA PANS UP TO THE DECK OF THE LARGEST BOAT AND ZOOMS TO THE FACE OF A SEMI-HANDSOME SOUTHERN MAN WITH A SCAR DOWN ONE CHEEK. IT'S UNEVEN, AS IF THE TWO SIDES WEREN'T MATCHED UP BEFORE THEY WERE SEWN TO-GETHER. A NUMBER OF BUR-MESE HEADS ARE PEERING OVER THE EDGE OF THE BOAT.)

CREW 2: (OFF-CAMERA) She's got a gun.

(MISCELLANIOUS SCREAMS)

JIMM: It's not. It's not a gun. Don't shoot. It's a computer.

(JIMM DOES A SLOW PIROUETTE, TAKING IN ALL THREE BOATS AND THREE CREWS OF HALF-STARVED BURMESE. THE GUARDS ARE HOLDING RIFLES. ONLY THE BOSS HAS AN AUTO-MATIC WEAPON. EVERYONE SEEMS TO BE FROZEN TO THE SPOT AS THEY WATCH JIMM.)

BOSS: Don't just stand there. Grab the little bitch and get that thing off her.

JIMM: (OFF-CAMERA IN ENGLISH) That was perfect. A close-up of the gang leader. Get to work now, you

375

computer wizards and come up with a record for him.

(A CREW MEMBER MARCHES DIRECTLY TOWARD THE CAMERA)

JIMM: OK. OK. I'll put it down. Look. It's a very expensive com —

(BUT THE CAMERA ISN'T PUT DOWN. IT DROPS TO THE DECK ON ITS SIDE. A LOT OF PIXELS GET REARRANGED, BUT THE PICTURE RIGHTS ITSELF IN TIME TO SEE THE BOTTOM HALF OF JIMM BEING DRAGGED ALONG THE DECK TO A POINT BELOW THE BOSS.)

JIMM: (SHOUTED) Now would be a very good time for back-up. Hello!

BOSS: (OFF-CAMERA) What are you going on about? Who are you?

JIMM: I am Jimm Juree, a world-famous crime reporter. And this entire operation has been captured digitally and distributed to the World Wide Web — live.

BOSS: We're in the middle of the sea.

JIMM: So?

BOSS: There's no phone towers out here. How stupid do you think I am?

JIMM: Obviously not nearly as stupid as you actually are.

(THERE IS A PAUSE, THEN THE SOUND OF A THUD, AND JIMM FALLS INTO FRAME ON THE DECK. THERE'S THE SOUND OF A SCUFFLE OFF-CAMERA.)

ARNY: Jimm!

BOSS: Keep hold of them two.

(JIMM COMES AROUND SLOWLY AND TURNS TO FACE THE CAMERA — SPITS)

JIMM: (IN ENGLISH) I have just been hit with the barrel of an AK47. I might have lost a tooth. This is —

BOSS: Enough with the foreign crap. Someone bring me that computer.

(SKINNY LEGS IN SHORTS APPROACH THE CAMERA, AND WHEN THE PICURE IS RIGHTED, WE HAVE AN EXTREME CLOSE-UP OF A PARTICULARLY UGLY SEAMAN. HE'S FASCINATED TO SEE HIS OWN FACE ON THE SCREEN. WE CHANGE THE POINT OF VIEW TO THE HANDSOME BUT DISFIGURED BOSS. HE SMILES.)

JIMM: Wait! What do you think you're —

(THE CAMERA SAILS THROUGH THE AIR, AND THERE'S A MOMENT THAT WOULD LATER

LOOK SPECTACULAR IN A SLOW-MOTION REPLAY, WITH THE LAP-TOP BREAKING THE SURFACE OF THE WATER, FLIPPING AROUND IN THE SURF, THEN BREAKING BACK INTO THE AIR LIKE A RUB-BER RAFT. AS IT BOBS THERE, THE REAR END OF THE SLAVER BOAT IS IN CLEAR VIEW.)

"Now that is why the Navy SEALs use the XR2," said Sissi. "Waterproof. Shock proof. Missile proof. Sends out e-mails at the speed of light. I love that baby."

"It's away from the ship now," someone shouted. "Is there some way to make it louder?"

"Yes, genius," said Sissi. "It's a new invention called the volume control. You've all got one on your computers. *Voilà.*"

"He hit her," said Mair, shocked, stressed, distraught.

"Only with the barrel, Mair. It would have been a lot worse if he'd used the stock."

"So, where's her back-up?" asked the shop owner.

"Yeah," they all echoed. "Where's her back-up?"

Live Internet feed. 10:02 P.M. Gulf of

(CAMERA ROCKING AND ROLL-
ING ON THE WAVES. HARD TO
WATCH. BOATS PASSING IN AND
OUT OF SHOT. BUT THE SOUND
QUALITY IS GOOD. ALL OFF-
CAMERA)

BOSS: There goes your evidence. Now
all we gotta do is get rid of you and
your journo pals and maybe we'll
finally get a bit of work done around
here.

JIMM: We aren't alone out here, you
know?

BOSS: Oh, right. It's the "look behind
you" routine. Nice. Kill 'er.

(SOUNDS OF STRUGGLING)

ARNY: You leave her alone or there'll be
trouble.

BOSS: I see your Thai's not bad for a
Burmese. All right. They all go. This is
how we do it. We shoot 'em. All of 'em.
The uncle and the nephew too. Tie the
bodies to their boat and sink it. We'll
be long gone by the time they find it.
You know? You newspaper people
think you can stick your noses anywhere. Who do you think you are, darling? And look where you are. This is

my kingdom out here and I'm God. I give and I take away. But mostly I take away. Here, I'll do the girl.

(ON ONE OF ITS CIRCUITS THE CAMERA SHOWS THE SILHOU- ETTE OF THE BOSS WALKING THE LENGTH OF THE FERRY BOAT WITH HIS WEAPON RAISED.)

CREW 2: Boss, look.

BOSS: What?

CREW 2: It's a light.

CREW 1: There's another one over there.

(SILENCE)

BOSS: What? That's it? That's your back-up?

(HE LAUGHS UNTIL HE SPITS UP PHLEGM.) Two bitty little boats? Two little mackerels that we can outrun and outshoot and sink without even breaking a sweat? Don't make me laugh. You know? I hate women like you. Arrogant, the word is. I'm doing the world a favor here.

JIMM: I bet you couldn't do it without a gun.

BOSS: What?

JIMM: I bet you couldn't kill me with your bare hands, like a real man.

CREW 2: Listen. Can you hear that?

BOSS: Shut up.

JIMM: Little men like you are all talk.

CREW 1: It's music.

BOSS: Here. Take this gun. The lady wants a beating.

CREW 2: It is music.

BOSS: What the . . . ? Who gives a shit? One of those little boats has got its transistor on. They're trying to soften us up with music. Can I just get this over with?

CREW 1: No, boss. It ain't coming from them two boats. It's like it's . . . it's all round us.

BOSS: What is it about today? Has everyone gone nuts?

CREW 2: He's right, boss. It is coming from all round.

CREW 1: And it's getting louder.

SONG: Friday nigh and de ligh are low.

BOSS: Don't be stupid. It's just the radio waves bouncing off the sea. It's a trick of the water.

SONG: Lookin ow for a play to go.

CREW 2: No. It ain't a trick, boss.

CREW 1: And it ain't a radio. It's live.

CREW 2: And it's more than one voice.

SONG: Where dey play the righ music, gettin in de swing.

You cummin to loo for king.

BOSS: Who is it?

CREW 2: It's Abba, boss.

BOSS: No, I mean, where's it coming from?

CREW 2: Sweden.

BOSS: Look, idiot. I–

SONG: Anybody cou be dat guy Nigh is young and de music high

CREW 1: Look, boss. There's another light over there.

BOSS: So? Three boats. No big deal.

CREW 2: Make that four. Look.

SONG: Wiv a bidda rock music, ev-erytin is fai

You in de moo for dan

CREW 2: They're really terrible.

CREW 1: More lights, boss.

BOSS: My God. They're everywhere.

SONG: And when you get de chan

CREW 1: There must be twenty . . . thirty of 'em. We're surrounded.

BOSS: Stuff it. All right. Put down your weapons, boys. We'll sort this out tomorrow. Couple of phone calls and we'll be back out here on the next tide.

SONG: You are de dancin quee

Young an swee, only sewentee

Dancin quee, feel de bea

From de tambolee

BOSS: Nothing to worry about.
SONG: Oh yeah

16.
START SPREADING MANURES

(from "New York, New York" —
JOHN KANDER, FRED EBB)

"But they were arrested?"

"Every last one of them. The ministry police task force was there waiting for them at the dock in Pak Nam. TV crews. Interviews. Helicopter. Media frenzy. They were whisked off to Bangkok."

"And you think, in spite of all that, they'll get off?"

"I don't want them to, of course. But as hot news, it's relegated to page three by the airport takeover. And public memories are short. In a week it'll all be forgotten."

I was sitting with Noy and Mamanoy in their simple but comfortable granny flat at the back of Somjit's house. They'd been well looked after, and nobody had seen a sign of the Special Branch people since Mair sent them on a wild goose chase. Elain seemed to have taken a shine to the Noys. She was hiding shyly behind Noy's legs.

"Plus the fact they knew some important figures," said Mamanoy.

"Well, at this point it's looking like we might have got them too," I said.

"How?"

"We had the link to the Rescue Foundation, evidence, sound recordings. There was a raid, and they found documents that tied them to the slavery. Or, at least, to the slave ships. The foundation godfather is the older brother of the current shadow minister of education. A lifetime Democrat from an old southern family. He's registered as the owner of the slaver boats. Our present prime minister and his cabinet would be only too delighted to make all this public and put pressure on the police ministry to rush the case through the courts. That reduces the time our southern MP has to bribe witnesses and make the Burmese slaves go away. But you know how these things work. A change of government tomorrow and suddenly there was never a charge to answer. On the positive side, all the foreign attention might make a difference. There's pressure on the police to get convictions on this case. And as all the work was done for them . . . by us . . . the Royal Thai Police

385

force could look good on the world stage without having to do very much. At the very least they'll get convictions against the villains that don't have family connections: the slave boss and his crew, all the people involved on dry land."

"Your Lieutenant Egg?" asked Mamanoy.

"Facing charges. The rat brothers are prepared to give evidence against him. Say they were just hired help. Everything was his idea. And there was the cloned truck in his garage. His physical attack on Chompu. I think this might be one police case that doesn't get lost in the system."

"Did it really make any difference?" Noy asked.

"What?"

"The coverage. The Internet. Isn't it temporary entertainment? A fad? Then tomorrow the cyber world moves on to the next burst of excitement."

Our Noy was short on optimism. It was time to reveal my secret identity.

"The Internet isn't all Tweeters and mindless surfers and Facebookers," I said, even though it pretty much was. "What happened out there in the Gulf has been picked up by a lot of international press. I was the deputy head of the crime desk at the *Chiang Mai Mail* before I moved down here." All I picked

386

up was a look of disbelief. "I was online as often as I could be, looking for stories to follow up on. The newspapers get a lot of their content from the Web. You wouldn't know where to start if it was just you and the Internet. The newspapers are like your dinner ladies. They give you your lunchbox all packaged, apple and all. You can get through the content in your canteen break."

"And be as knowledgeable as the newspaper allows you to be," said Mamanoy.

"You can choose your newspaper," I said. "Find one you trust."

"I'm not sure I trust any of them," she said.

"Then you'll have an opportunity to discuss your fears with *The New York Times*," I told her.

"*The New York Times?*"

"They're coming for an interview this afternoon . . . with you. Just a Bangkok-based journalist and his photographer. I imagine they're getting bored with strolling around the airport asking people their feelings. As we still haven't completely rid the Lovely Resort of its Special Branch threat, Somjit has kindly agreed for us to conduct the interview in her garden gazebo."

The Noys exchanged a glance, then laughed. This was all some fantasy. Their lack of faith was starting to annoy me.

"Listen," I said, "I've lost half a tooth, which won't do my modeling career much good. I've thrown up a dozen times . . . which might. I haven't slept for forty-eight hours and my nervous system is ragged. I would have had a very successful day today if only I could find the energy to type up this whole trafficking drama and send it off to the newspapers. I've had every daily in Thailand contact me. I could be the flavor of the week. All I need to do is put in the time . . . type, type, type. My career is standing on the runway waiting for permission to take off. And where am I? I'm here with you. And why am I here? Because you aren't concluded."

"I don't understand," said Noy.

"I have to put your story to bed before I can get some rest myself. I could have had a few hours' sleep when I got back from the media circus at five this morning, but I lay on my lumpy mattress and all I could think about was you two."

"I'm sorry we gave you insomnia," said Noy. "But this is one story that won't be put to sleep."

"Yeah, I'm sorry too. But it's what I do. I can't stop until I get you two off the hook."

I'd been trying to keep the bed/sleeping

analogy going, but it was exhausting.

"You know, I think it might be a good idea for us to move out before the reporter gets here," said Noy.

"Well, that would be a terrible shame," I told her, "considering the guy didn't drive all this way just to photograph me. He's got an even better story. An exclusive, in fact. I've told him all about you and what happened in America."

Both Noys stood as if they'd heard a silent rendition of the national anthem.

"You've what?" said Mamanoy. Her face was flushed with anger.

"They think it's a great story," I went on. "You're going to tell your story to *The New York Times.*"

Noy's jaw dropped and almost banged the monkey on the head.

"You are out of your mind, you know?" said Noy.

"Some people tell me that. But why? What's wrong?"

"What's . . . ? I'll tell you what's wrong. Apart from the fact there's no way on the planet Earth I'd do it, you're mad if you think a newspaper with an office in Bangkok would even think about running it. There would be implications far beyond the political."

"I suppose that depends how you tell it," I said.

"There are options?"

"There's one I can think of."

"Tell me."

"Fiction!"

She laughed.

"You want me to lie?"

"Only if you have an aptitude for it. There's nothing more embarrassing than a poor liar."

"And how do you propose my daughter lies her way out of the mess we're in?" asked the mother.

I reached dramatically into my shoulder bag and produced three sheets of Times New Roman. I handed them to Noy.

"When we got back this morning I was a little too psyched-out to sleep. When the slaver story broke, all the wire services were on the phone. Justin from *The New York Times* contacted me for quotes. I know him from articles we'd worked on together. Nice fellow. Bit serious. But when I mentioned you, Noy, and told him about the predicament you were in, he was fascinated. He's good-looking and available, by the way. We came up with a solution. Neither of us believe they'll take up the story in the newspaper, but they have a long list of subsidiaries, magazines, Web sites. So I took the liberty of writing up your press statement. I'm pretty darned pleased with the way it turned out. But you read it. Talk about it with your mother. If you really don't think it would solve everybody's problems, then I'll give you our truck and some money, and you can live on the road one step ahead of the police. All that in spite of the fact you haven't actually broken any laws. Face-breaking isn't illegal, as far as I know. Read it."

Noy opted to read it aloud so her mother could hear.

"The Poor Student Who Said, 'I Can,' " she began, then looked up and glared at me.

"Just read it," I told her.

"My name is Thanawan and I was one of the lucky ones. Based on my results at a suburban school and a generous quota system, I won a scholarship to study in the U.S.A. It was a science program at George-town University in Washington D.C. It's one of the top learning establishments in the country. And from the day I arrived, just looking around at the brilliant students from all over the world, I felt really out of my depth. The knowledge I'd acquired at my school suddenly felt so inadequate. And to make matters worse, I shared many of my classes with ML Chaturaporn, a young lady of aristocratic blood from a family I had admired all my life. She let me call her by her nickname, Goong. I was surprised at how amenable she was, how friendly and helpful. Not only was she a beautiful person, she was also a brilliant student."

Noy put down the paper.

"Is this the point where I throw up?" she asked.

"Just keep reading," I told her.

She sighed.

". . . a brilliant student. While I was stumbling through the textbooks, scratching a C here, a D there, she was sailing along with As and distinctions. And yet, for reasons I have yet to understand, she continued to see me as a friend. She helped tutor me on difficult points. She talked to me as an equal. She even helped me through a bad relationship I fell into — through my own naiveté — with an American boy. She was there to hold my hand when I cried. She . . . OK, pass me the bucket."

To my surprise, Mamanoy told her to keep reading.

Noy's eyes passed from me to her mother, then back to me. She understood that this wasn't a game.

"I can't tell you how close we became,"

Noy read. "Me, the daughter of a school-teacher. She, of refined birth. I couldn't believe my luck. But then the final exams drew near and I fell into a panic. I considered how it would destroy my parents if I failed. How disappointed it would make my local community. How would I be able to go on living if I didn't graduate?

"My friend Goong felt my fears and set herself a challenge of tutoring me to excellence. She told me that I had a solid basic knowledge. All I lacked was confidence. During the break before the final semester, we worked every day and late into the night. Bottomless coffees. No sleep. All the theories that had baffled me became clear through her eyes. She was an amazing tutor. And so we were in the final semester and I was full of confidence. I hardly noticed how pale and wan my friend was becoming with every month that passed. She missed classes. Was late with some homework assignments. Yet still she continued to tutor me. It wasn't until just before the last assessments that she confessed to me about her poor health. She had low blood sugar and was taking medication. Our late-night blitz had taken its toll. On the night before one important exam, her body temperature was way down. Her doctor said she had severe hypoglycemia and recommended immediate hospitalization. But this was finals week. She too had obligations to her family. And so we sat those exams. Me with my new-found confidence. She, dull and sedated — barely able to read the words on the paper. It's incredible, given her circumstances, that she was able to pass anything at all that term."

Noy sighed, not for the first time.

"Well, there's some truth, at last."

"Final paragraph," I said. "Be patient."

"But I excelled, just as she had promised," Noy read. "I felt I had stolen her glory. I was so embarrassed. I knew she would never hold a grudge against me. She's such a kind person. She comes from a fine, upstanding family. All I ask and pray is that Georgetown University can find it in their hearts to give her a second chance. To allow her to resit her final courses and show the world what a brilliant scholar she is."

Noy laughed.

"Wow," she said. "What a bunch of lizard poop."

"Smelly though it may be," I said, "this way you keep your degree, the duchess maintains her dignity, and if we're lucky, you can go home and live your old lives."

"I think it's perfect," said Mamanoy.

"Mum, you can't be serious?"

"I am. This is exactly what Jimm says. It's a get-out clause. It's a face-saver. If *The New York Times* runs this in one of their magazines as a feel-good piece, all the media in Thailand will pick up on it. They'll have you and Goong hugging on national television. The bigger it is, the safer we are."

"Then she comes out of this as a heroine," said Noy.

"So what?"

"She's an asshole."

"It doesn't matter," I said. "It's a little late to start worrying about pride. At the end of the day, you end up with a degree from Georgetown. That's all that counts. Once your picture's out of the press, nobody will tie your name to this farce. You'll have employers queuing up to hire you."

"You expect me to sit through an interview and read all this . . . crap?"

"No. I want you to tell it as if it really happened. As if you're remembering it. I want you to add little personal details. How you exchanged Hello Kitty e-mails. Taking photos together in a passport photo booth. Late nights in pajamas eating marshmallows. The sloshier the better. I want it all to really have happened. And if it makes you feel better, just imagine how uncomfortable the duchess is going to be when her family forces her to join in with the charade. They'll come out of it smelling pretty sweet if the daughter plays along. I can see you having a grand old time at the TV interview."

Noy stared at her mother. Mamanoy smiled and shrugged.

17.
AND ALL THE
LETTUCE WAS ALONE

(from "Papa Was a Rolling Stone" —
NORMAN WHITFIELD and BARRETT STRONG)

It had been a very discreet return invitation. My own verbal invite to our party had been loud and glorious.

"Aung, this'll be great," I'd said, leaning over him at the metalwork shop, his Thai and Burmese co-workers looking at me from their lathes. The boss was seated at a desk at the rear, counting the minutes to dock from Aung's salary for this lack of production.

"It's a party," I went on. "I want you to bring Oh and the kids and all the Burmese you can muster. It'll be the defining moment when Thais and Burmese forget their differences and meet on neutral ground. All those invasions and historical massacres forgotten. We'll drink together and share rice and the world will be a lovelier place."

Aung looked up at me briefly. The boss docked another minute.

"Jimm, I'm sorry," he said. "We have a religious ceremony planned for that date."

I got the hint. I hadn't yet told him when the party would be. But I understood. Hundreds of drunk Thais? The Burmese were more likely to take their chances against the military junta in Yangon.

The return invitation arrived in the hand of a beautiful, long-haired, powdered-cheek girl on a bicycle. When she was asking for me, she pronounced Jimm like a Western man's name. No rising intonation. She looked away when I took the note from her. It said: *6:30 tonight. Burmese party. Don't bring anyone.*

It was written in Thai by a child's hand. I didn't know what to expect of a Burmese party. It was on the eve of our own shindig. I thought I might convince a few to come along. I wanted to know what had become of Shwe and the other sixteen slaves — fifteen, if you didn't count the dead man. I checked the beach every morning, expecting him to turn up. Despite the warning, I had Arny along as my after-dark back-up. We lefted and righted our way through the Pak Nam back lanes until Aung's door cast a yellow glow across the alleyway in front of us. Nobody lifted my skirt as I stood in the doorway, and to my surprise, the little living room was crowded. There had been no indications of a throng from outside. The shoes had been placed elsewhere. There was no music and everyone spoke in a whisper. The Burmese had learned not to make a spectacle of themselves.

Aung welcomed us and cleared us a place on one of the small mats in a circle of shy Burmese. Oh brought us each a glass of warm beer, whose chill factor had been entrusted to a single ice cube. Me and Arny appeared to be the only beer drinkers. All the other guests were sipping tea or had water glasses on the ground in front of them. I looked around and was surprised to see Shwe and his wife two circles away. I waved at him, and he nodded in recognition.

"I thought they'd sent everyone to the immigration holding center," I told Aung. "What's Shwe doing here?"

"He came to collect his family," said Aung. "He's going back to Myanmar tomorrow."

"How did he get out?"

Aung smiled.

"It isn't a prison," he said. "There are no locks. We sent him money, and he hiked to the bus stop and came back south."

"But what about . . . ?"

"The trial?" His eyes sparkled. "Jimm, it's your country, so I'm sure you understand the system better than we do. Court procedures take time. Especially bringing a conviction against policemen. The witnesses would have to be there in the center for another four months before the case against the MP and his brother made it to court. One reason the center isn't secure is that they'd prefer it if we left. With no witnesses, the perpetrators can't be charged. And, honestly, what Burmese is going to sit in a holding cell for four months? Not earning. No money going back to his family. To the world community, it looks like the witnesses aren't reliable. The Thais can say they did all they could to bring a conviction, but those damned Maungs . . ."

I wasn't really surprised.

"You're right. No point."

"Oh, there was a point, Jimm." He sipped his tea and looked around the room. "The point is that from a group of seventeen, sixteen survived. Shwe will have stories to tell his grandchildren. The others will have another life to do better with."

"Did they all go back to Burma?" I asked.

"The survivors?"

"Yeah."

Aung smiled for the first time.

"Look around you," he said. "You don't recognize them?"

"You're kidding me."

I did look around. Of course I didn't recognize anyone other than Shwe. It had been dark that night and I was exhausted. I hadn't had time to study faces. And the Burmese? Well, they do kind of look alike.

"They're all here?" I asked.

"Every one of them. They all left the holding center and came back here to collect up this failed part of their lives and move on to the next misery."

Arny leaned into my ear and voiced a thought that already nestled in my mind.

"You'd think they'd be happier to see you," he said.

We stayed there for an hour. There were nods. Shwe practiced some English on me. But, largely, it was Burmese in conversation with Burmese. If we didn't leave soon, Arny and I were in danger of vanishing completely. But when I made a point of studying my watch and telling Aung we had to go, I noticed one or two stares in my direction. That was as excited as anyone got.

As Arny and I walked back to the Mighty

X parked on the main street, it occurred to me that nobody had said thank you. There had been no leis, no cheek kisses, no gushy promises of eternal friendship. No Thai *wai*s or name-card exchanges. Not even a greetings card with sixteen signatures. But as we climbed into the truck, I noticed that the party had broken up behind us. The guests were skulking their ways home in the shadows. Some would have to walk for an hour. And that's when I understood their gift to me. They had come. The first thought in every one of their minds was to get the hell out of this nutty country, but they'd stayed. They'd attended this non-party to pay respect to me. They didn't express their gratitude in words because it must be hard to show gratitude for something everyone else takes for granted. Freedom. Human rights. But they'd come . . . for me. Arny drove home and wisely made no comment about me bawling my eyes out beside him. He had a little bit of a sniffle going too.

It's common at the Lovely Resort and Restaurant to have parties to celebrate good fortune. In the past year we'd had exactly . . . one party to celebrate the engagement of Arny and Gaew. That was it. But our second party was something special.

With everyone rushing off either for police interviews or to avoid police interviews, Sissi conducting live conference calls to Korea from a Bangkok studio, and Mair down in Pak Nam painting the walls of her forthcoming Burmese school, we'd had to wait five days before we could have a party to celebrate our victory on the high seas.

Because we were fundamentally broke, we couldn't afford to provide free booze for everyone. That, ironically, would have liquidated us. So we announced it was to be a traditional Aussie BYO party. The "bring your own" was one of the few impressive cultural norms I'd picked up during my stay in Aus. You announce you're having a party, open your front door, and guests arrive with all the drink you need. That's the theory. I was doubtful it would work in Maprao. Thais expected to be catered for at parties. But because this was to be a cultural theme night, they dipped into their stills and their bottle cellars and turned up with a vast array of dangerous liquor. Luckily, I still had my stash of Chilean red. I was starting to wonder whether the stock I'd brought with me from Chiang Mai would ever run out.

Fortunately, the effects of the lady Viagra had worn off, so I wasn't likely to find any men in our district attractive. Certainly not engaged-Ed, who had left his new fiancée at home. There were plenty of other single men to choose from, were taste not an issue. The whole village was there, and it felt splendid for our little resort to have a blast of atmosphere. I decided we should have BYO nights more often. The monsoon was set at "off" that night, so we could light garbage bonfires on the sand without filling up the cabins with smoke. The back stream was all but dry. The tide was low. There were even stars in the sky.

The Noys weren't there. The *New York Times* reporter had tried to rush the story through. There was never much hope of getting it into the actual newspaper, but we'd hoped for a subsidiary magazine piece. In the meantime the finished article with photographs did make it onto their Web site. Spotted early by Tweeters in Thailand, the story was already big on various radio stations, and Noy had repeated her statement to half a dozen newspapers. There was a quote from the duchess, saying that she bore no ill-will toward the poor student and would be happy to meet up with her — "to renew their friendship." Channel Five was arranging that reunion on-air. A spokesman from Georgetown University was quoted as saying that they would be delighted to examine the medical records of the student who was too ill to pass her exams. More good news was that the Noys and the father were back in their house and were minor celebrities in their suburb. All the current attention made them safe. Only time would tell how deep the venom ran through the veins of the nobles. But that wasn't really good enough. As a sort of back-up, Sissi and I sent an anonymous e-mail from a U.S. account to the father of the duchess under the heading, *Blackmail*. It went on to say, *We have photographs of your daughter at a drug party in D.C. Accept this version of the truth or we release them to the press and tell the real story of what happened in the States.* We didn't have any evidence that the daughter attended a drug party, but given her lifestyle, it was fair to assume that she had. The fact that Sissi had hacked into the father's private e-mail account should have been enough to let him know we weren't just talk.

We were a couple of hours into the party. Everyone had brought seafood, so there was plenty to eat. Neither Bigman Beung nor Captain Kow had arrived, and my darling Lieutenant Chompu would be turning up late as he was coming directly from Phuket, where he'd been undergoing cosmetic surgery on his nose. The surgeon decided, as it was broken anyway, now would be a good time to set it to order. Evidently, misshapen noses were only fashionable in those who took the male role in gay relationships. If anything, Chompu would be going for the Audrey Hepburn look.

But the rest of Maprao had turned out in full. There were still news and radio reporters mingling and getting quotes from people who'd slept through the entire slaver night. Last count, there was one computer in Maprao. PI Meng was there, as well as a bunch of other people I'd never seen in my life. And the spotty guy from the Internet shop. And Ari, the monkey handler, who we had to keep away from Mair's cabin. The dogs were there — four-legged vultures, doing the "I don't get fed by my owners' routine and stuffing their faces with barbecued seafood.

I was chaperoning Mair, keeping her away from the booze. One sniff and she was the Marchioness de Sade. The cheapest date on the planet. I knew I couldn't keep an eye on her the whole night. She'd sneak a shot of whiskey and be doing her *Coyote Ugly* on the bamboo table. So I wanted to get her alone and sober before all that happened.

"Mair," I said.

"Yes, Sissi darling?"

See? She really didn't need booze. We were in the kitchen deep-frying mini squid and swaying to one of her old Boney M. tapes. Yes, she still had tapes. She kept them in a box with her stone clubs and flint axe-heads.

"I'm Jimm."

"Of course you are. Don't be ridiculous."

"Mair? We've all been a bit preoccupied these past few days. But there's something I've been meaning to ask."

"Fire away."

"The monkey."

"Well, that was hardly a question, was it? And her name's Elain. Show some respect."

Marvelous that she could remember the monkey's name but forget mine.

"Elain, sorry. She disappeared on Tuesday."

"Yes. If you say so."

"That was a day after . . ."

"After what?"

"After the headboard of your bed first started banging against the wall of your cabin. The night me and Grandad went to your room to see what had happened. The night you screamed the resort down."

"You've probably got the dates mixed up."

"No."

"Then it must have been the wind."

"You do realize that mothers who lie to their own children get warts on their tongues and grow claws."

She laughed.

"That was just a story, child. You're all grown up now."

"But that doesn't stop it being true. Show me your tongue."

"Don't be ridiculous."

"Show me."

She glared at me. I glared back. She poked out her tongue.

"My God. Mair!"

"What?"

"How can you eat with all those warts? Your tongue looks like dinosaur skin."

"I was afraid that might happen."

"Who was it, Mair?"

"I can't tell you."

"But it was human, right?"

"What type of a pervert do you think I am?"

"Oh, Mair. It's true. You were having sex."

"Shout it for all the world to hear, why don't you?"

"Why not? I think it's great."

"You do?"

"Of course I do. You're almost a hundred years old and you're still active."

She laughed.

"Remind me again who it was," I asked, hoping to tap in to her senility.

"Nobody you really know."

"Give me a clue."

"I'm not playing."

"All right. I'll work it out myself. It must have been someone we're used to seeing because a stranger would never be able to sneak in and out of our snoopy little community without being spotted. Oh, my gosh."

"What?"

"It's Bert. The kid who collects the palm berries."

"Child, he's only twelve years old."

"He's nineteen and randy."

"He only has one eyebrow."

"But it's long enough for both eyes. And I doubt you'd notice in the dark."

"Your mother does still have her pride, you know?"

"Well, your pride woke us up at two o'clock that morning, so he's fit. Agile, by the sounds of him. And it didn't sound to me like you were faking it."

"All right. That's more than enough. It was a dream. I was calling out to Indra to stop the damned rain. Let's leave it at that."

She looked out the window.

"Your policeman's here," she said.

I stood beside her and saw Chompu parking his motorcycle in the car park. He had a bandage on his nose that made him look like a parrot. I had to give him credit for agreeing to be seen in public like that. I was just out the door with a tray of squid when I remembered.

"Mair, if I see you drinking . . ."

"I wouldn't think of doing such a thing."

I handed my tray to one of our co-op ladies and went over to hug Chompu. His reaction told me he still hadn't fully recovered from his beating.

"I didn't get a chance to tell you how great you were," I said.

"I confess I do have certain skills when it comes to being punched. I tend to roll rather well."

"Come on. You did it. You solved the case."

"If it hadn't been for your mother and sister, I'd be receiving this accolade posthumously."

"Smile," I said, and I took his photo with my cell phone.

"Oh, really. Not my best angle."

"But so colorful. The purples, browns, and greens of Benetton bruising. And that darling little beak. And if I didn't, you'd always regret not having a photo of your first serious beating to show your grandchildren. I wish I had one of mine."

We walked into the cauldron of the party, where we both found ourselves with unidentified drinks in our hands.

"Any news on Egg?" I asked.

"He's in a lock-up in Lang Suan."

"You think he'll get out?"

"Probably. Arrests like this are usually for show. I'm scheduled to give evidence against him, but it's bad form for the police to be locking each other up. I doubt he'll find it in his heart to forgive me when he's sprung."

"Do you think anyone will be punished?"

"They'll put the poor ones away. The armed guards. The rat brothers. Maybe even the slave boss. The rest will buy their way out. Without witnesses or evidence, there'll be no murder charges. Captain Kow witnessed one of the Burmese being shot, but he wasn't in a position to say who pulled the trigger. And as yet, there's no body. It rather reads like a fairy story."

"So, why did we bother?"

"I think I asked you that same question when I still had a functioning nose."

"I think you look lovely battered."

I gave him an air kiss on the cheek.

"What was that for?"

"Being an honest cop."

"I'll be lucky if I still have a rank tomorrow."

"They don't dare fire you. You're a hero. The world loves you. My sister thinks you're adorable."

"She's quite special too."

"I don't suppose . . . ?"

"We do both have posters of Antonio Banderas on our walls. I've known relationships to start with a lot less."

"You would make a lovely couple."

"You and I would stand more chance."

"That hopeless? I'll break the news to her gently. Let's go and see her. They're all waiting for you."

I took him along the beach. We'd rented a large plastic awning on legs from PI Meng just in case it rained. We'd set it up near the forty-five-degree latrine. There were ropes anchored on the beach running down into the bowels of the toilet block. We called it extreme peeing. Of course, at night, few people bothered to use the facilities.

There was a standing ovation for Chom when we joined the group. Our almost complete band of heroes was there sitting around one large table: Sissi, Arny, Gaew, Grandad Jah, Ex-Police Captain Waew, Ed, and PI Meng. Sissi was in her countryside casual, baggy chinos, tight spaghetti-strap top, hair in a ponytail. Lots of make-up. It was remarkable — after her Howard Hughes year of solitude — that she would allow herself to be here on show. Yet she was relaxed, making fun of the local dialect, hitting shamelessly on Ed. Apart from that last part, I loved having her here. Before he sat down, Chompu leaned over and gave her a real kiss on the cheek. She feigned a faint. There was a silent pause followed by a loud "Oooo" from the crowd. I wondered how many sitting there understood that my sister and the lieutenant had just officially become girlfriends.

"What's in the box?" Chompu asked me.

At the center of the table — actually a lot of small tables joined together and covered in plastic — was a small wooden chest. I'd considered leaving it open but decided that wasn't such a tasteful idea. The chest was just big enough to fit a foam box, which in turn contained ice, which in turn . . .

"I went to the Rescue Foundation yesterday," I told him. "It was under lock and key, but another foundation had won the bidding war to take over its stock. One item of that stock was the head we found on the beach, which started all this. Nobody had claimed him and I thought it would be fitting . . ."

"He's in the box?"

"I've arranged a ceremony for tomorrow. I thought he should have one more night out before his trip."

"You're a most peculiar child."

"I know."

Once drinks were replenished, the debriefing began.

"Shouldn't we wait for Bigman Beung and Captain Kow?" Ed asked.

"No," said Grandad. "Get on with it."

We discussed the things we might have done better and gloated over the parts that had gone well. I was a little concerned that I had edged so close to being killed merely for the sake of a musical end to the evening.

"OK, Ed," I said. "When was it exactly that you knew you had thirty little boats joining us?"

He looked sensational. His hair greased back. A white cotton shirt with no collar contrasting with his tan. He and my sister were getting along a little too well for my liking. It was time to put him in his place.

"I think it was all Captain Kow's doing," said Ed. "He was in touch with the little boats all the time. I think what sold them was the idea it was all being broadcast to the world on the Internet. They gave up fishing for the night. Nothing like an audience to bring out the showman in a man. So once they caught up with us, Kow and I directed them into a circle, and the rest you know."

"I know I almost died," I told him.

"No, you didn't. I was watching through the binoculars. You were safe."

"And you didn't think 'Dancing Queen' might be inappropriate for the situation?"

"It's the only one in English they've got on the checklist. They've got it written down phonetically."

"They didn't have any idea what it meant," said PI Meng.

I had more complaints to level at Ed, but Mair arrived just then with a tray of squid and a red glow. I knew she'd been tippling. She too received a standing ovation, to which she curtseyed, and half the squid dropped onto the table.

"Is he still in there?" she asked, referring to our head in the box.

"I didn't see him leave," said Grandad Jah, which was as near to a joke as we'd heard from him for a long time. He got a laugh from the heroes.

"How about a toast to head," I said. "If it wasn't for him, a lot more of his brothers and sisters would probably be dead by now."

"To head," said Sissi.

"To head," said everyone else.

We downed our drinks and refilled our glasses just in time for the next standing ovation.

"You all just go ahead and start without me" came a voice.

We turned to see Bigman Beung dressed in a pure white naval dress uniform. We turned away from the glare.

"Where's your wife?" I asked.

"Which one?" he replied. "I have so many of them, major and minor."

"What are you tonight, brother?" asked Ed.

"British navy," he boasted. "Gunner. First class. Found it in a locker when they gave tours around the *Queen Elizabeth II* before they turned her into a hotel. It's a bit big, but it really gets the girls damp."

"Let's give him a welcome before he says anything else inappropriate," I said.

We all stood and saluted the headman.

"I have experience with British sailors," said Mair.

"Not now, girl," said Grandad.

"I'd like to hear it," said Gaew, who hadn't left my brother's arm all evening.

Again we were rescued by an arrival, this time of Captain Kow who'd been parking the headman's truck for him. He looked dashing in a button-collar shirt and jeans with a leather belt.

"Ah, a real hero," said Waew.

Grandad muttered something under his breath.

We all stood.

"Captain Kow," I said. "I thank you. The head thanks you. We all thank you."

"*Chaiyo,*" we all said, which was much more rousing than "cheers." We drank to the captain and retained our seats. All, that is, apart from Sissi, who remained standing. It occurred to me she hadn't yet met our brave fisherman.

"This is Captain Kow," I told her. "He's the one who followed the ferry out to the slavers and organized the karaoke attack. This is my brother, Somkiet," I said. "Although most of us call him Sissi."

There was an odd, uncomfortable moment when Sissi just stood there, staring at the captain with an astounded expression on her face. The captain smiled, almost apologetically.

"How are you, Dad?" Sissi said at last.

"Fine, son. You?"

AUTHOR'S NOTE

Correct Lyrics for Chapter Headings

1. Sleeping on the job
2. Because a vision softly creeping, left its seeds while I was sleeping
3. It's amazing how you can speak right to my heart
4. I'm gonna shoot you right down, right off of your feet
5. All my dreams fulfilled
6. It's been a hard day's night, I should be sleeping like a log
7. I thought love was more or less a given thing
8. Our love is like a ship on the ocean
9. We rely on each other
10. Something in the way she moves
11. Give me my profits when you get home (Aretha Franklin version)
12. I was feelin' kinda seasick, but the crowd called out for more

13. Sunshine, blue skies, please go away
14. The colors of the rainbow, so pretty in the sky
15. Old pirates, yes, they rob I
16. Start spreading the news
17. And all he left us was alone

I'd like to claim I'd made up that whole story about the Burmese, but sadly, in a less bizarre form, it's true. If you want to see what indignities our Burmese brothers and sisters face, take a look at this BBC article from 2011: www.bbc.co.uk/news/world-asia-pacific-13189103. And things aren't any better today.

The employees of Thorndike Press hope you have enjoyed this Large Print book. All our Thorndike, Wheeler, and Kennebec Large Print titles are designed for easy reading, and all our books are made to last. Other Thorndike Press Large Print books are available at your library, through selected bookstores, or directly from us.

For information about titles, please call:
(800) 223-1244

or visit our Web site at:
http://gale.cengage.com/thorndike

To share your comments, please write:
Publisher
Thorndike Press
10 Water St., Suite 310
Waterville, ME 04901